SOE in Denmark

SOE in Denmark

Special Operations Executive's Danish Section in WW2

An Official History

FRONTLINE BOOKS

SOE IN DENMARK
The Special Operations Executive's Danish Section in WW2

This edition published in 2021 by Frontline Books,
an imprint of Pen & Sword Books Ltd,
47 Church Street, Barnsley, S. Yorkshire, S70 2AS.

Up to and including Appendix X, this book is based on file reference HS
7/109, from a series of SOE records held at The National Archives, Kew,
and is licensed under the Open Government Licence v3.0. Appendices
XI, XII and XIII are based on file reference HS 7/110, which is also
which is held at The National Archives, Kew, and which is also licensed
under the Open Government Licence v3.0.

Text alterations and additions © Frontline Books

ISBN: 978-13-9901-504-2

Pen & Sword Books Ltd incorporates the imprints of Air World Books,
Pen & Sword Archaeology, Atlas, Aviation, Battleground, Discovery,
Family History, History, Maritime, Military, Naval, Politics, Social
History, Transport, True Crime, Claymore Press, Frontline Books,
Praetorian Press, Seaforth Publishing and White Owl.

For a complete list of Pen & Sword titles please contact:

PEN & SWORD BOOKS LTD
47 Church Street, Barnsley, South Yorkshire, S70 2AS, UK.
E-mail: enquiries@pen-and-sword.co.uk
Website: www.pen-and-sword.co.uk

Or

PEN AND SWORD BOOKS,
1950 Lawrence Road, Havertown, PA 19083, USA
E-mail: Uspen-and-sword@casematepublishers.com
Website: www.penandswordbooks.com

CONTENTS

PUBLISHER'S NOTE

This 'official history' and its various appendices are reproduced in the form that they were originally written. Aside from correcting obvious spelling mistakes or typographical errors, we have strived to keep the edits and alterations to the absolute minimum.

Chapter 1

INTRODUCTION

In order to gain a true perspective in appreciating the operations carried out by S.O.E. in Denmark, a brief study of Danish conditions is necessary. Experience has shown that the direction of S.O.E. work in Denmark calls not only for an intimate knowledge of the country and its people, but also the ability to appreciate these factors in terms of subversive and para-military warfare. The succeeding chapters will mention where mistakes occurred due to both lack of experience and failure to appreciate these elementary principles.

Denmark is composed of a mainland, Jutland, and some five hundred islands of which one hundred are inhabited. The larger of these, Fyn and Zealand, are separated from Jutland by the Belts – stretches of water half a mile and fifteen miles wide respectively. The country is, for the most part, undulating, well-cultivated agricultural land, somewhat similar to East Anglia and, where the ground is more broken in Jutland, similar to East Fife. Of the population of 3,800,000, 890,000 live in Greater Copenhagen, some 2,000,000 form the agricultural population and the remainder are distributed among the provincial towns. With the exception of the border districts of South Jutland, where the German Government did everything possible to encourage the expansion of Pan-Germanism among the small German minority, the Danes are quite racially distinct from their southern neighbours.

It will, therefore, be readily appreciated that in undertaking subversive operations in Denmark, there are a large number of inherent difficulties which must be overcome before successful results can be achieved. The existence of the Belts makes internal communication in the face of enemy controls a hazardous business, and the highly populated countryside together with the absence of any inaccessible or mountainous region which might act as a base for guerilla operations presents a similar problem to conditions which exist in Holland. In addition to these difficulties the long sea passage across the North Sea, and the unsuitable nature of the

West Jutland coast, make clandestine communications by sea between the United Kingdom and Denmark virtually impossible.

The Danes had not been involved in war between 1864 and April, 1940. During this period their energies had been devoted to an intensive development of agriculture and industrial production, of which the most important are ship-building, the production of cement and engineering. A steadily increasing national prosperity resulted in an improvement of social conditions, so that at the outbreak of war Denmark was among the most advanced nations in Europe in the field of social development.

The concentration of all their energies on social and industrial improvements, coupled with the belief that they would be able to preserve their neutrality through a new world war as successfully as they had done during 1914-1918, plus the contention that whatever preparation Denmark might make to defend herself against an act of treachery from her southern neighbour would in any case be hopelessly inadequate and might be construed as provocative, led the Danes sadly to neglect all defence measures.

History has shown that the respective Ministries were incredulous of reports which they received in March 1940, that Germany was concentrating troops with the obvious intention of undertaking operations in Scandinavia. On the fateful day of 9th April 1940, when German troops crossed the frontier into Denmark, it was not surprising that, after a brief and ineffective opposition, the Danes bowed before this display of overwhelming force and were obliged to accept the German occupation.

Government reaction to these events was to maintain as correct an attitude as possible towards the Occupying Power and to persuade the population to avoid any provocation of the Germans. M. Christmas Møller alone took an independent line, which was later to lead to his enforced resignation as Minister of Commerce. He was the first member of the Government to call the Germans "the enemy". Among members of the armed forces there was, somewhat naturally, a feeling of extreme mortification at their inability to act at the decisive moment, and it was at this period that the seed was sown in the minds of senior officers in the services that they should prepare for the day when they might justify themselves in the eyes of the population. As far as the general political position was concerned the Cabinet, Rigsdag [the name of the national legislature of Denmark from 1849 to 1953] and the

Administration continued to function, while the Army was obliged to withdraw its garrisons from Jutland and to affect a considerable reduction in its peacetime strength of two divisions. It is worthy of note that the strength of the initial forces of occupation amounted to little more than two divisions.

At this juncture it is well to review briefly the position of Danes abroad. In Sweden, the outstanding personality was Ebbe Munck, the well-known journalist and explorer. Munck had accurately foreseen events in good time and had moved to Sweden with the object of providing a link with the outside world in the event of Denmark being occupied. The British reaction to this event was the immediate occupation of Iceland and the Faroe Islands, and the speedy application to the Danes of all regulations affecting the nationals of Enemy Occupied Territory.

The Danes were, in the British Commonwealth, in fact classified as enemy aliens. Meanwhile, the Danish Minister in London, Count Reventlow, was permitted to continue his functions as representative of King Christian, although he was, of course, denied any direct communication with the Danish Government. His failure to adopt a more positive attitude was a disappointment, not only to the Danish colony in the United Kingdom, but to many influential friends of Denmark in British Government circles.

Accordingly, a small "Danish Committee", including representatives of S.O.E., was set up under the chairmanship of Christopher Warner, Head of the Northern Department of the Foreign Office, with the object of stimulating a Danish contribution to the Allied war effort. Subsequently the Danish colony in the U.K. formed an Association of Free Danes and set up a Danish Council which was formally recognised by the Foreign Office as representing the Danes in Great Britain. The object of the Danish Council was to assist the Allies by every means in its power. The Council was under the chairmanship of Mr. Kroyer Kielberg, one of the leading members of the Danish colony in London, and it set to work without delay in raising substantial funds which it presented to the British Government, while it also encouraged young Danes to enlist in H.M. Forces.

Under the auspices of the Danish Council, a Recruiting Office was opened and an active interest was taken in the welfare of Danes in the British armed forces. The initiative to this was taken by S.O.E. with the object of providing a cover for recruiting and training Danish nationals to organise resistance. With no general recruiting of Danes in process at the time, it would have been difficult to conceal the reasons for which one War Office Department was so interested in training these "enemy nationals".

The Danish Council was selected as the best cover and rallying point, and W.M. Iversen was granted a commission and selected to run the Recruiting Office. The Danish Council was, however, devoid of any political significance, and it was remarkable that the Danish Minister, Count Reventlow, was careful to avoid publicly committing himself to supporting either the Council or the Association of Free Danes. In this attitude Count Reventlow was surpassed by the Danish Minister in Stockholm, Mr. Kruse, whose over-cautious and neutral policy during the whole period of occupation did much to hamper S.O.E. efforts in Denmark.

Finally, a word should be said about the comparatively large number of Danish-American citizens in the U.S.A. Their interest in Denmark was largely sentimental and very little material support was forthcoming from those Americans of Danish extraction. The Danish Council's recruiting delegation, which had been sent out to the U.S.A. on the initiative of S.O.E., failed completely, for the above reasons, to produce any recruits. Denmark, however, had the good fortune to possess in Minister Kauffmann, the Danish Minister in Washington, a strong and vigorous representative whose firmly pro-Allied attitude did much to help the Danes to regain the political ground which they lost in 1940. It was perhaps unfortunate that Minister Kauffmann was geographically handicapped in bringing his influence to bear to assist S.O.E. in their initial efforts.

Chapter 2

THE EARLY DAYS

From the preceding chapter it will be seen that the problem of conducting subversive operations against the Germans in Denmark was indeed formidable. From the enemy point of view Denmark was of importance, firstly as laying on their line of communications with Norway and thus enabling them to control the exit to the Baltic, and secondly for the contribution which Danish industry and agriculture could make to the German war machine. Before the German declaration of war against Russia, it was the object of S.O.E. to impair the economic advantages which the Germans derived from the occupation of Denmark. Concurrently, therefore, with the recruiting and training of agents, S.O.E. had also to find some means of reconciling the latent pro-Allied sympathy of the Danes with their aversion to the destruction of their factories by sabotage.

The Danish Section at the time was composed of Pay Lieutenant Commander R.C. Hollingworth, R.N.V.R., Mr. Reginald Spink, Mr. Ronald B. Turnbull and Mr. Albert E. Christensen (British), all of whom had resided for many years in Copenhagen. The lack of operational intelligence and any means of communication with Denmark made it essential that some form of communication be established without delay. To this end it was decided to train W/T operators concurrently with sabotage instructors for despatch to the field, and the first task of the Danish Section was to recruit suitable personnel for these missions.

The resources were slender indeed, and the Section was obliged to depend very largely on the Danish merchant seamen, who were exiled by the German occupation of their country. The other sources which could be tapped were the small number of Danes already in the armed forces, and a large number of civilians spread throughout the world.

Liaison was quickly established between the Danish Seamen's Pool in Newcastle and the Danish Recruiting Office, and a number of men were selected to undergo training as agents. By an arrangement S.O.E. had made with the Foreign Office, Captain W.M. Iversen also made a broadcast on the B.B.C. to Free Danes wherever they might be to volunteer for service with the local British Council, who would arrange for a medical examination and despatch to the U.K. Partly as a cover for S.O.E.'s own recruiting and partly to enhance the prestige of the Danish fighting men in their homeland and abroad, S.O.E. were successful in persuading the East Kent Regiment (Buffs), whose Colonel-in-Chief was King Christian of Denmark, to open its ranks to all suitable Danish volunteers.

It can, however, be admitted that, without inferring any slight on the recruits, the material was not of the finest quality for S.O.E. agents. While it was undoubtedly important that S.O.E. should be able to enlist the influence and support of leading personalities from Danish press, political and industrial circles at the earliest possible moment, it could not be expected that the type of recruit available would be able to mobilise the influential support which S.O.E. required.

At this time S.O.E. was represented in Stockholm by Mr. Peter Tennant, who was officially on the books of the Ministry of Information as Press Attaché. It was now decided to strengthen this representation with a small body of Danish experts, who would have the opportunity of making contacts among the large number of travellers between Denmark and Sweden, on whose movements the enemy had so far imposed few restrictions.

Mr. Ronald Turnbull, who had been Press Attaché in the British Legation in Copenhagen until 9th April, 1940, was selected to lead the Danish Section in Stockholm. Travelling via South Africa, Abyssinia, Turkey and Russia with his wife and Miss Pamela Tower as secretary, being in all three months on the way, he took up his duties under cover of being Assistant Press Attaché (later becoming honorary Attaché to H.M. Minister as special adviser on Danish affairs). It was this long journey which enabled Dr. Hugh Dalton, the Minister of Economic Warfare at that time, to point out to the War Cabinet the necessity for resuming an air service to Stockholm. This air service being re-established in February 1941, Mr. A.E. Christensen was then flown out, being only four hours on the way and arriving only one day after Turnbull, and took up his duties as S.O.E.'s representative in Gothenburg under cover of being British Vice Consul.

In the beginning Turnbull had to devote his energy to securing contacts and establishing communications across the Sound [between Denmark and Sweden]. In addition, he had to establish his position inside the British Legation and produce some sort of organisation for the S.O.E. staff. Quick results were not expected and it was some three months before S.O.E. managed to persuade the skipper of a small boat plying across the Sound to agree to carry messages and cargo.

In the meantime, contact was established in Stockholm, through the good offices of Ebbe Munck, with the Intelligence Section of the Danish General Staff. This section was known as the "Princes" and consisted of Lieutenant Colonel Nordentoft, Ritmester Lunding, Major Gyth and Major Winkel. The "Princes" rendered invaluable assistance in providing one of the first direct links with the country, and it was this association which placed in S.O.E. hands a large and steady flow of intelligence reports on conditions inside Denmark, both from a military and an economic point of view. Lt. General Ebbe Gørtz fully supported this collaboration, but, for security reasons, kept personally well in the background.

At this time the Danish Section of S.O.E. was considerably occupied with rendering all possible assistance to its sister organisation, the Political Warfare Executive (P.W.E. – then known respectively as S.O.2. and S.O.1.). Regular weekly visits were paid to "the country" for discussions as to propaganda policy, both overt on the B.B.C. and in the printing of air leaflets, etc., and covert in the preparation of programmes for the so-called Danish Freedom Station, known as Research Unit, or R.U., and in the production of printed matter to be infiltrated through underground channels. This important aspect of the work created many problems for Mr. Turnbull and his staff who had to arrange the infiltration of bulky printed matter from Sweden. For security and other reasons, however, this material was never allowed to take precedence over operational material which the Danes needed.

In the meantime, at H.Q. progress was being made with the training and weeding out of various agents who had been recruited and two men, Bruhn and Hammer, were selected for despatch to Denmark in the winter of 1941. Bruhn was to be the chief representative with Hammer as his W/T operator. It was hoped that a start could at last be made with operations in the Field.

A dropping point near Haslev in Zealand was selected as being suitable, but no reception was arranged for the two agents; nor indeed was this possible, owing to the very indifferent communications which existed at this time. The agents were, however, given the names and addresses of two men in Copenhagen believed to be reliable. One of these was Erik Seidenfaden, a journalist, who later became a close collaborator of S.O.E. Mission in Stockholm. For emergency use the men were provided with a simple newspaper code which would enable them to notify their safe arrival in case Hammer should have any difficulty in establishing W/T communications with H.Q.

The party was dropped on the night of 27/28th December 1941, and it was a bitter disappointment for the Danish Section in London to know, by means of the newspaper code, that Bruhn had been killed on landing. Subsequently it was learned that his parachute had failed to open and that the wireless set in which so much store had been set, was smashed on reaching the ground.

After various delays and setbacks in which the lack of any direct communications with Hammer in Denmark was a contributing factor, the second party was despatched to Denmark on 16th April 1942, and their safe arrival was reported the following day in the first wireless message received from the Field. One of the first essentials for subversive operations in Denmark was thus achieved after eighteen months of work.

In the meantime, developments of political interest had been taking place. By the early autumn of 1941 it was apparent that the work which was carried out by the Danish Council was prejudiced by the fact that the Council's members were little known in Denmark, and need was felt for securing the presence of a well-known Danish politician who could add prestige to the council. Messages were sent to M. Hedtoft Hansen, leader of the Social Democrat Party, and to M. J. Christmas Møller, inviting them to come to the U.K. It was felt that a representative of the left wing as well as the right wing would contribute to maintaining the political neutrality of the Danish Council.

For various reasons M. Hedtoft Hansen declined the invitation and, after lengthy negotiations, the Chairman of the Danish Conservative Party, M.J. Christmas Møller, consented to come to the U.K. The detailed plan for exfiltrating Christmas Møller and his family was undertaken by Turnbull's staff, Mr. A.E. Christensen in Gothenburg playing the leading part, and, on the Danish side, by one of Turnbull's contacts named Borch Johansen.

After a lengthy period of waiting, favourable conditions arose to put the plans into effect. M. Christmas Møller and his family sailed to Gothenburg hidden under a cargo of chalk and were smuggled ashore by Mr. Christensen, eventually arriving secretly in the U.K. in May 1942. They were handed over for temporary concealment in the keeping of P.W.E. in the country pending news as to the fate of those who had been involved in their escape on the Danish side. Unfortunately, as a result of an indiscretion on the part of the Dane who had driven the family to its point of embarkation, both Borch Johansen and the Skipper who had helped them over to Sweden were arrested.

In Denmark, Hammer had by this time succeeded in establishing contact with the "Princes", who were maintaining steady progress in the volume and standard of intelligence reports. At this point, however, another problem began to arise. In addition to their intelligence activities, the "Princes" had conceived an ambitious plan for establishing an organisation of resistance groups, led by senior army officers, by which, at the right moment, notably when the Allies had weakened the enemy sufficiently to prevent drastic reprisals, they hoped to seize power by a military coup d'état. At the same time, supposedly for reasons of security, they placed great stress on the fact that the organisation was primarily intended to resist communist elements which might gain the upper hand in the event of the country being liberated. These ambitions caused grave disquiet at S.O.E. H.Q. who had no intention of encouraging local factions and where it was believed that at the first hint of trouble the Germans would arrest every Danish Army officer from the rank of Captain upwards. London's views in this matter were vehemently shared by Borch Johansen, who had escaped from arrest, and by M. Christmas Møller, who had knowledge of the plan.

Another factor which contributed to the attitude of the Danish Section in London was that the standing orders were to wear down the German war machine in Denmark, to detain as many German troops there as possible and, by a series of carefully planned and successful acts of sabotage, to educate the Danish population to the standard of resistance which would be required of them when the Allies switched over to the offensive. The "Princes" Plan, or "P" Plan as it was called, depended for its achievement on Denmark remaining in German eyes a "Model Protectorate". If the patriots were stirred to too great an activity the Germans would be forced to take over the Administration and the "P" Plan would be doomed. In this, therefore, the policy of the "Princes" towards sabotage was diametrically opposed to that of S.O.E. H.Q.

An achievement worthy of record at this time was that the first financial transaction took place in the middle of May. This resulted in the sum of Kr. 126,500 being made available for financing the work of S.O.E. agents in the Field against an equivalent credit in sterling being made in London.

As a result of further dropping operations, S.O.E. had in Denmark by the end of July 1942, 2 W/T operators in regular communication with H.Q., and 5 agents, one of whom was Captain Rottbøll, who had been selected to take over the leadership of the Organisation from Hammer who had become compromised. Having handed over to Rottbøll, Hammer escaped to Sweden and eventually arrived in the U.K. on 27 September 1942. In the meantime, Borch Johansen had also arrived in the U.K. and was engaged by the Section on planning. The work of Rotbøll and his staff was confined to the building up of a sabotage organisation. This, however, was abruptly terminated by enemy counter action. One operator, P.H.D. Johannessen, was surprised in the act of transmitting and committed suicide. Rotbøll himself was shot dead while resisting arrest, while two further sabotage instructors and a W/T operator were captured by the enemy when trying to escape to Sweden.

Hammer's return to London enabled him to report at length to H.Q. on conditions then existing in Denmark. The nucleus of S.O.E. agent instructors, which were known under the name of the "Table" Organisation, had made contact with a group of Communists under the leadership of Professor Mogens Fog, who was sufficiently aggressive and determined to be relied upon to undertake sabotage operations. In addition to these Communists, contact still existed with the "Princes", who were of considerable assistance, not only in maintaining lines of communication with Stockholm, but also in assisting the "Table" Organisation in the Field with the selection of dropping points. It was also due to the "Princes" that Hammer was successfully evacuated to Sweden.

Contact had also been made with the Danish Police, which from time to time was able to give the "Table" Organisation advance information of enemy counter-espionage plans. Special mention should be made of Roland Olsen, a leading member of the special department of the Copenhagen Police which was charged by the Germans with investigating all cases of underground activity. Two further local recruits are worthy of mention. Flemming Juncker, a Jutland landowner, turned out to be a keen and active member of the organisation and was extremely useful in organising reception committees and dropping points in Jutland. The second was L.A. Duus Hansen, who later became well-known under the code name of "Napkin", by which name he will be referred to throughout this narrative. "Napkin" was a fine radio technician and being employed in the Danish Radio Security Control, he was able to render useful assistance by informing the "Table" Organisation of the extent to which the enemy were able to locate S.O.E. W/T operators.

Fortunately, in spite of the liquidation of the "Table" Organisation at the time of Hammer's return to London, these local contacts had not become compromised. It was essential to replace Rotbøll by a leader who could hold the remaining elements of the organisation together for the time being. Unfortunately, as it had not been foreseen that Rotbøll's term of service would have been quite so short, no suitable replacement could be found with the necessary training. It was therefore decided, and bearing in mind the security risks involved, to return Hammer to Denmark so that he might pick up the threads of the old organisation and keep things going until a new leader could be got ready.

On the night of 18/19 October, Hammer returned to Denmark. Owing to his exceptionally heavy build, it had been decided that he should be dropped in water. He landed in the sea one hundred and fifty yards from the shore in the north of Zealand and got ashore safely. Liaison with H.Q. was again hampered by lack of communications, as at this time there was only one W/T operator working in the Field and Hammer had considerable trouble contacting him. Consequently, the planning of dropping operations was a slow and protracted affair.

Outside Denmark work was proceeding apace. Although he was under constant criticism both from at home and from abroad, M. Christmas Møller had rallied the Free Danes and, although he caused S.O.E. many difficulties in regard to security, the Danes had in him one very great asset in that he kept Denmark's name constantly to the fore.

The work of the Mission in Sweden was steadily increasing due to the larger number of S.O.E.'s collaborators who were travelling backwards and forwards as couriers. The work of organising infiltration and exfiltration of goods, messages and personnel had also grown. Tasks in connection with P.W.E. were growing and S.O.E. gradually became the major channel for political information from Denmark. Meanwhile, Mr. Turnbull was rapidly establishing himself as an expert on Danish political affairs and, in addition to his other work, was responsible for drafting H.M. Minister's political despatches to the Foreign Office concerning Denmark.

During these months, progress in the Field was slow and, due to the circumstances which originally forced him to leave the country, it was evident that Hammer was working under great limitations. It must also be remembered that as Hammer had originally been selected as a W/T operator he had not had the benefit of an organiser's training. At this time, however, Flemming Bruun Muus, who had shown great qualities as a leader, had completed his training and it was decided to despatch him to the field at the first opportunity to take over the leadership of the "Table" Organisation from Hammer. Muus had been a business man in West Africa and had come to the U.K. at S.O.E.'s expense in response to Iversen's broadcast.

Determined efforts were materially aided by a visit to Stockholm on the part of Flemming Juncker, who was able to return to Denmark with precise instructions regarding the dropping programme, and during the three weeks previous to 14th March 1943, no less than two W/T sets, four containers, four bicycles and eight men, among whom were Muus, Gunnar Christiansen, a new W/T operator, and Ole Geisler, a sabotage instructor, were safely dropped into Denmark. The W/T section was further strengthened by the despatch to the Field via Stockholm of plans and crystals for the use of "Napkin".

It seemed reasonable to suppose, therefore, that 1943 would produce a considerably bigger dividend for S.O.E. in Denmark than the receding year had done.

Chapter 3

THE FIRST OPERATIONS

Before continuing further with the adventures of the new nucleus of the "Table" Organisation, a word should be said about the general conditions existing in Denmark and the political developments which had taken place since 1940. Two events in the outside world were largely responsible for infusing resolution and courage into the would-be resisters in Denmark. The uninterrupted series of victories with which the German armies were favoured from the beginning of the war was brought to an abrupt and bloody end at Stalingrad and El Alamein, and the German myth of invincibility was exposed once and for all by their headlong retreat after these two battles.

It was, therefore, interesting to note that the Germans had given the Danes permission to hold a General Election in March 1943, with the hope, no doubt, that German interests and prestige would be furthered by increased representation in the Rigsdag of the Danish Nazi and Peasant parties. The result, in fact, was a demonstration in favour of Danish democracy and the old parties were returned with a comfortable majority led by the Social Democrats and Conservatives. The Danish Nazis failed to increase their representation, while the Peasant Party lost two of its four seats; in addition, an extremist anti-collaborationist party called Dansk Samling won three seats. It may be said that at this election, in which a record number of votes were cast, the results could not be interpreted as a vote of confidence in the collaborationist tendency of the Scavenius Cabinet, but rather as a demonstration against the two political parties which were actively sponsored by the Germans.

The work of Muus and his collaborators, therefore, can be assessed against this background of national self-confidence and there is no doubt that conditions were more favourable than they had ever been since the initial occupation by the Germans. It now required a vigorous leadership to set "Table" firmly on its legs, and Muus, in fact, filled the bill very neatly at this particular juncture. A ruthless and clever man, he made full use of his persuasive manner, a liking for bluff, and a shrewd assessment of the Section in London H.Q. to flatter, bribe, cajole and drive the Danes to greater activity.

The Danish Section in London had, in the meantime, a new recruit in the person of Second Lieutenant R.L. Taylor, who had for many years been resident in Copenhagen as a teacher of English, and between the outbreak of war and the German invasion of Denmark had been closely associated with Lieutenant Commander. Hollingworth and Mr. R. Spink as a member of the British Consul's staff in Copenhagen. He started his career with S.O.E. as a Conducting Officer.

Muus now had two telegraphists at his disposal and he was quick to realise that by a strict personal control of W/T communications he could strengthen the position of S.O.E. in Denmark enormously. His next step was to make a drive to secure increased deliveries by air in order to enable the Communist and Holger Danske groups to undertake sabotage operations. The Communists, it will be realised, were under the leadership of Professor Mogens Fog, while Holger Danske was a non-political group which had been formed on Danish initiative and was led by Jens Lillelund, known as "Finsen", about whom more appears later.

In this work most valuable assistance was rendered by Flemming Juncker, who was now closely connected with the leadership of the "Table" Organisation. During April and May 1943, 5 sabotage instructors, one telegraphist and eight containers arrived safely in Denmark by air. Although these results may seem small compared with what was achieved later, the good work of the earlier sabotage instructors began to bear fruit.

In each of these two months no less than ten successful sabotage operations took place, including a successful attack on the Lyngby Accumulator Factory, which was engaged in producing accumulators for U-boats, and the destruction of the transformer of the Dansk Industri Syndikat. The latter was Denmark's only armament works and somewhat naturally the Germans were making full use of its productive capacity. Another notable operation was an attack on the Power Station in Svendborg Harbour, where a number of German merchant navy vessels were undergoing repairs. These operations were followed up during June by successful attacks on eight more targets.

In July dropping operations were able to proceed satisfactorily, thanks to the efforts of Flemming Juncker in reconnoitring a large number of dropping points and in training reception committees to man them. Three sabotage instructors and fourteen containers arrived safely during the period May-July 1943. This was followed up by eight further air operations in August, comprising a total of forty-eight containers. At the same time, sabotage operations were carried out on an increasing scale and no less than four ships were sunk, including one enemy auxiliary cruiser.

The outbreak of sabotage which swept the country during these three summer months led to the Germans demanding, during the first week of August, that Danish saboteurs should be tried by German courts according to German Law, and that any sentences imposed should be served in Germany. The Scavenius Cabinet unanimously rejected this demand and Scavenius threatened that, if it were pressed further, he would resign. The Germans accordingly dropped the question.

It is interesting to note that at the end of the first week in August Muus sent a telegram to London informing S.O.E. H.Q. that if the present rate of sabotage continued the Germans would be forced within three weeks to take over the Danish administration; he duly requested a directive. The situation was discussed at a high level, and it was considered that the time had now come to force the Germans to take just that action which they could so ill afford. Sabotage was, therefore, speeded up still further.

It should be understood that according to Danish constitutional practice the King invites the leader of the majority party in the Rigsdag to form a cabinet. It is constitutionally impossible for a new Government to be formed unless the King accepts the resignation of the retiring Government. Towards the end of the month public unrest, sporadic strikes and increased sabotage obliged the Germans to renew their demands. Scavenius placed the resignation of his Government in the hands of the King, which, however, the latter did not accept, and from then on until the day of its liberation Denmark was thus without a functioning Government.

Muus's prophecy proved accurate almost to the day, and on 29th August, 1943, the Germans seized complete control. Martial law was declared, the Rigsdag was prohibited from meeting and a curfew was imposed. The fears of S.O.E. H.Q. in regard to the "P" Plan were justified when the Danish Army was disbanded and its officers interned. Similar treatment was meted out to the Danish Navy which, however, succeeded in scuttling the greater part of its ships before they could be seized by the enemy.

These measures had, of course, a considerable effect on the conduct of subversive operations in Denmark. The Danish Police who, up to this juncture, had been extremely helpful, now came under closer German control and certain people in the Police Force were obliged to flee the country owing to being deeply compromised in their efforts to protect the "Table" Organisation.

The internment of the Danish forces had far reaching consequences. It had always been the boast of the "Princes" that their secret organisation inside the Army would form the basis of all para-military resistance groups and, as mentioned above, they had on several occasions shown themselves apprehensive of the pace at which subversive activity was being carried on at the instigation of S.O.E. The "Princes" themselves were successful, with the exception of Ritmester Lunding, in escaping to Sweden where they immediately set about organising an Intelligence Office and a half-way house for communications, under the name of the Hamilcar Office, which later proved of such value.

The Hamilcar Office consisted of Lieutenant Colonel Nordentoft, Comdr. Mørch, Major Gyth, Major Winkel and Miss Jutta Graae, who had acted in Denmark as a courier. Ritmester Lunding was captured by the Germans and deported to Germany for interrogation. The events of 29 August 1943, led to the breakdown of the "Princes" Intelligence Organisation inside Denmark, although before departure the task of re-organising the service was entrusted to a reserve officer, Lieutenant Svend Truelsen, who had been earmarked for this eventuality.

The repressive measures of the Germans, who were now obliged to reinforce their garrisons, brought a serious realisation to the Danish population that any form of further collaboration was now impossible, and there was now no doubt that the Danes would respond by underground warfare. Sabotage operations continued during September although on a slightly diminished scale owing to the introduction of martial law and to the fact that the enemy's new forms of control which were instituted throughout the country made it increasingly difficult for illegal couriers to travel between Jutland and the islands.

Early in October the Germans committed a political blunder of the first magnitude in attempting to deport all Danish Jews to concentration camps in Germany. The result was astonishing and it would be hard to describe the extreme indignation felt by the Danes. The practical form in which this indignation was expressed was to give every possible aid to their unfortunate fellow citizens to escape to Sweden. From an S.O.E. point of view two definite benefits resulted. Danish anti-German feeling was roused to a new height and illegal traffic across the Sound received a tremendous impetus, which resulted in a great many more lines of communication for S.O.E. cargoes across the Sound being opened.

The presence in Sweden of many thousands of refugees, including many Army and Police officers, presented the Mission in Stockholm, the Hamilcar Office and Ebbe Munck and other leading Danes, with many new problems. The Danes formed a refugee office in Stockholm with the object of attending to refugee welfare, and much of the contacting of Turnbull by couriers arriving at the British Legation was done under the cover of the refugee department established on the initiative of S.O.E. in the Legation. At the same time, police camps were formed with the apparent object of training personnel on military lines to police the country after its liberation. In actual fact, however, under the leadership of Major General Knutson, recruits were being trained with the object of providing a task force which could assist in the final stages of the liberation. This task force eventually became known as Danforce or the Danish Brigade.

In London it was felt that the "Table" Organisation was sufficiently firmly established for the whole of S.O.E. plans for Denmark to be reviewed, and Muus was accordingly instructed to travel to Sweden and thence to London where he was to take part in important conferences. He made his way over to Sweden on 7th October 1943, and was in London a week later. Turnbull followed him over at a later date in the month in order to take part in the conference at H.Q. Two other arrivals of note in the U.K. were Captain Gyth, one of the "Princes", and Roland Olsen, S.O.E.'s collaborator in the Special Department of the Copenhagen Police, who has been mentioned previously.

In the meantime, in Denmark further air operations were undertaken during October leading to the safe delivery of twenty-one containers comprising a total of 1,722 lbs of explosives, 70 Sten guns and ammunition, 42 pistols and ammunition and 208 hand grenades.

The conferences which took place in London could be viewed against a very different background to that of 6 months previously. S.O.E. now possessed a secure and compact organisation which controlled sabotage groups all over the country. The H.Q. in Copenhagen had been selected with cool impudence in a building next door to a Gestapo office. In Jutland, Juncker was the acknowledged leader, while in Copenhagen, Geisler was responsible for co-ordinating sabotage activities. A valuable political contact had been found in Herman Dedichen, who had a wide acquaintance in political and commercial circles in the capital, and who provided lengthy weekly reports on the political situation, primarily for the benefit of M. Christmas Møller but with copies for the Foreign Office and P.W.E. A special section of the "Table" Organisation, under the leadership of editor Aage Schock, was solely concerned with propaganda and assisting the flourishing illegal press.

Thanks to the good work of the telegraphists and the patient efforts of Turnbull and his staff, communications with London, both direct and via Sweden, were reasonably secure and efficient. The Danish Section made extensive use in both directions of micro-photography on undeveloped film which would be instantly destroyed on exposure by an unauthorised person. Lengthy written messages were being passed daily via Sweden disguised in tubes of toothpaste, tablets of soap etc., and latterly in specially constructed rectum containers.

Danish public opinion was slowly moving towards a healthier outlook. In illegal circles after the crisis of 29th August, the need was felt for somebody who would provide political leadership and co-ordination to the efforts which were being made by the whole Resistance Movement, and this tendency, which received the closest support from S.O.E., gave birth to a committee which operated anonymously under the name of the Freedom Council. The members were as follows: Professor Mogens Fog, Chairman, Frode Jakobsen ("Ringen"), Arne Sorensen ("Dansk Samling"), Muus ("Table") and Houmann and Alfred Jensen – Communists. The Council was represented in Stockholm by the Danish engineer Erling Foss, who had escaped after 29th August and who worked in close conjunction with Turnbull, the Hamilcar Office and Ebbe Munck. Although lacking in political experience, the Freedom Council, which wisely remained anonymous, appealed to the Danish imagination and speedily established its leadership of the Resistance Movement.

In general, it must be said that S.O.E. was now in a position to undertake more ambitious plans in which the build-up of para-military resistance groups was a key objective. Muus was awarded the D.S.O. for his work in the Field and returned by air to Denmark on 7th December 1943. His return trip was not without incident, for the plane in which he flew was shot down in flames by an enemy fighter which appeared on the scene just as Muus was about to do his jump. It was due to the pilot's efficiency that the plane crash landed with all of its occupants unhurt. Once more Muus showed extreme coolness and courage. He divided the crew into two parties, advising one as to the direction they should take to avoid being spotted by the enemy and to give them the maximum chance of being picked up by his organisation. This party was, unfortunately, captured. The other party he led personally to Copenhagen, where his first action was to secure their safe evacuation to Sweden.

In the meantime, certain changes took place in the Danish Section in London. Captain J. Gellard, East Yorkshire Regiment, was employed as operations officer in charge of air operations and W/T communications. Mr. Spink left the Danish Section in October to take charge of the Danish R.U. under P.W.E., while Captain J.A. Ray, Intelligence Corps, was transferred from P.W.E. to the Danish Section in July. Owing to the increased volume of work which had to be undertaken in Stockholm, Captain Ray was sent there in December as an assistant to Turnbull who was now Head of the S.O.E. Mission with a supervisory control over the Norwegian and Swedish Sections. The Section at H.Q. had been further strengthened by the arrival in November of Captain A.T. Garrett, Black Watch, who took Ray's place as Intelligence Officer.

During December two sabotage instructors and one ton of stores were delivered to the Field and the tempo of sabotage operations was sharply accelerated. The Gestapo, however, was equally active, and in the last quarter of the year a larger number of Danes were arrested than ever before, including three S.O.E. agents. Fortunately, the swift evacuation of persons likely to be compromised by these arrests was arranged without difficulty thanks to the improved communications with Sweden.

Chapter 4

THE EVENTS OF 1944

It was the policy of S.O.E. that the first quarter of 1944 should be devoted to the organisation of para-military resistance groups throughout the country and orders were accordingly given to the "Table" Organisation to restrict its activities. Sabotage operations were, therefore, on a very reduced scale, although it is worthy of mention that during January and February, six enemy ships were successfully attacked.

Owing to the unfavourable weather no stores were dropped in January, but in February two sabotage instructors and twenty-four containers comprising a load of 500 lbs of explosives and 228 Sten guns and ammunition reached the Field safely. In the beginning of February two further recruits were added to the strength of the Section. Mr. A. Blanner, a civilian engineer who had escaped from Denmark in September 1943, and Lieutenant G.C. Bowden, Intelligence Corps. The former was to work at investigating the possibility of undertaking sea operations and at exploring a rather ambitious project of blocking the Kiel Canal, while the latter was employed as Conducting Officer to assist Captain R.L. Taylor. Owing to the integration of S.O.E. with O.S.S. a further change took place – Captain Kai Winkelhorn, a Danish-born American officer, came to the Section as Planning Officer.

In Denmark, although major sabotage operations were on a restricted scale, the German initiated a terror campaign murdering peaceful Danish citizens, which included the brutal murder of Pastor Kai Munck, a leading Danish dramatist and poet and a member of the Danish Church, who was uncompromising in his attitude towards the Occupying Power. This terror campaign only resulted in arousing the Danes to a still grimmer determination to fight the enemy by every means at their disposal.

The build-up of Resistance Groups was not an easy task owing to the suspicion that existed over the attitude of the Army. This suspicion was in the main due to two reasons. The illegal organisation of the Army, which had been formed at the express orders of General Gørtz, was carried out, as mentioned above, under the cover that groups were to be formed for maintaining law and order after German evacuation and with the special task of preserving the Danish populace and property from a possible Communist coup d'etat. The fact that this was in effect a cover story was known neither in London nor Stockholm, nor was it known in Denmark except to a very small number of high-ranking Army officers.

The arrival of Captain Gyth in London in October 1943 did nothing to mitigate the misgivings of S.O.E. In fact, it only served to make the Danish Section more suspicious than before. There were, furthermore, very good grounds for believing that Army politics were determined by the desire to gain control of Resistance Groups, and to use this control to enable the Danish Army to regain its lost position in the eyes of the Danish public as the ultimate saviours of the country.

In order to clear up this anomalous position, it was considered in London that the only solution would be to invite General Gørtz to send to the U.K. a representative with full powers to negotiate on the position of the Army's illegal organisation. This desire, however, was anticipated by General Gørtz, who despatched Lieutenant Colonel H.L. Hvalkof for this purpose. Hvalkof arrived in the U.K. on 17th February 1944, and a series of conferences took place in London. It was, however, speedily apparent that Hvalkof lacked any intimate connection with or knowledge of the Army's illegal organisation, and all that he was able to accomplish as far as S.O.E. was concerned was to allay previous misgivings about the Army's anti-Communist tendencies. The explanation that these were in fact only a cover story was fully accepted. A major obstacle to collaboration with the Army officers was thus removed.

Whatever his qualities as a soldier might be, Hvalkof lacked a vigorous personality, and he was completely ignorant of the situation regarding underground activity in Denmark. Gyth, on the other hand, was impulsive and lacked maturity and judgement. In short, neither of them was suitable for inclusion in the Section, but it was considered that they might be of some value to S.H.A.E.F. in a planning capacity. A further reason for turning down their services lay in the recent dismissal of Captain Borch Johansen for security reasons, which had in turn made it necessary to dispose of the services of Lieutenant Broberg R.N.V.R., who had been employed with Borch Johansen as local adviser to the Danish Section.

During this period and throughout the month of March 1944, the work of the organisation proceeded satisfactorily in the Field. Good progress was made in the building-up of Resistance Groups in Jutland through the tireless energy of Flemming Juncker, while in Zealand a small committee, named the M-Committee, was set up under the auspices of the Freedom Council and the chairmanship of Stig Jensen, one of S.O.E.'s most useful local recruits. This committee was charged with the duty of building-up Resistance Groups in Copenhagen and Zealand and co-ordinating plans between the Army's illegal organisation and civilian groups.

Meanwhile the work of Turnbull and his collaborators was progressing favourably. The Hamilcar Office, benefitting by Truelsen's splendid genius for organisation in Denmark, were supplying S.O.E. and, through the latter, S.I.S. with an ever-increasing volume of high-grade intelligence. All naval information was being passed direct by Turnbull to the Naval Attaché in Stockholm for reporting to the Admiralty. Communications were improving and illegal routes were started between Gothenburg and Jutland. Mr. E.T. Grew, who was now representing S.O.E. under the cover of Vice Consul in Helsingborg was covering the ferry traffic to Elsinore, whilst in Malmö S.O.E.'s close collaborators Madsen and Dinesen were running a regular service to Copenhagen. In all this Captain Ray proved to be a very valuable asset to Turnbull in taking over practically the entire operational control.

At the request of M.I.9. a separate escape organisation had been established in Denmark and a large number of R.A.F. pilots had been looked after and successfully evacuated. It was due to the tactfulness and firm handling by S.O.E.'s representatives in Sweden and to the magnificent co-operation with their Danish collaborators, who were able to obtain concessions from the Swedish authorities, that all these evacuated airmen were saved internment and reached England without undue delay. In all cases where the local organisation had picked up an airman his evacuation in quick time to U.K. was 100% successful.

One further aspect of the work which is worthy of mention is the financial transactions which were carried out on an ever-increasing scale, by means of which Muus's organisation was financed. In addition to the raising of funds locally against sterling credits in London, Turnbull succeeded in smuggling diamonds into Denmark and finding a sale for them at a good profit. By these means not only were the needs of S.O.E.

itself covered, but S.O.E. was able to provide the Treasury with all the Danish funds needed for other Government departments as well as the R.A.F.

Simultaneously, efforts were being made to improve W/T communications. Of all the telegraphists sent out by S.O.E., only one, Gunnar Christiansen, had avoided capture. He was ably assisted in his work by "Napkin" and another local recruit called Tage Fischer Holst. These three telegraphists all worked in the neighbourhood of Copenhagen, although this often proved to be a disadvantage when it came to arranging air deliveries to Jutland and Fyn, owing to the difficulties which couriers had to face in crossing the Belts.

"Napkin's" brother was enlisted at the end of February as a telegraphist to work in Fyn. His exceptionally good security and high technical standard made him a most valuable member of the organisation. Efforts were also made to get a telegraphist into Jutland and a local recruit called Jack was sent over escorted by Lieutenant P. Lok Lindblad, an S.O.E. agent. Unfortunately, they were both arrested shortly after arriving in Jutland, although Lok Lindblad had the good fortune to make a successful escape. It should be realised that all messages concerning sea operations, which had been planned to take place during March, had to pass through Copenhagen to Esbjerg, a slow and insecure procedure which eventually caused the Danish skipper to run straight into an English port instead of waiting to contact the S.O.E. boat at the agreed rendezvous.

The re-organisation which was taking place in the Field was greatly assisted by the contact which was established between Muus and the leader of the Intelligence Organisation, Lieutenant Truelsen. The two men rapidly established the most intimate collaboration and Truelsen used his influence to bring about a complete reconciliation between the "Table" Organisation and the Army officers. The effects of this step soon made themselves felt throughout the country. It also gave London a direct contact with the Intelligence Organisation which enabled S.O.E. to exercise a more effective control over intelligence activities than had hitherto been possible through the agency of Lieutenant Colonel Nordentoft's office in Stockholm.

It should be remembered that since the early days S.O.E. had been S.I.S.'s sole agency for high-grade intelligence from Denmark. All the urgent items were received by W/T and detailed typewritten foolscap reports were received via Stockholm, in sometimes as many as 50 foolscap sheets at a time, by "film message". The Hamilcar Office in Stockholm rendered a valuable service in the collation of these reports and the compiling of battle orders, whilst the network of intelligence built up by Truelsen throughout Denmark was giving S.O.E. very accurate advance information on troop movements which were immediately flashed to S.H.A.E.F. It was now clear that the stage had been reached when further conferences with Muus would be useful, and it was accordingly planned that Lieutenant Commander Hollingworth should pay a visit to Stockholm in order to meet Muus, Turnbull, Ray and representatives of the Freedom Council for discussion of future plans.

The Section in London had in the meantime produced a comprehensive plan for resistance operations in Denmark. This plan was based on the division of the country into six regions, and its chief object was to ensure an efficient de-centralisation of control from Copenhagen and a closer contact between each region and London. To assist this project, Muus was instructed to approach General Gørt with a view to obtaining the services of six specially selected Army officers. These officers were to undergo training in the U.K. and to return to the Field as liaison officers between S.O.E. and the resistance leaders in the Field. They were successfully exfiltrated via Sweden and arrived in the U.K. on 22nd March 1944.

The Danish Section was now organised as follows under the command of Pay Lieutenant Commander R.C. Hollingworth, R.N.V.R.:

Administration Officers	Major H.L. Lassen R.A., Intelligence Captain A.T. Garret Black Watch, and Lieutenant G.C. Bowden.
Operations	Captain J. Gellard and Mr. A. Blanner.
Training	Captain R.L. Taylor, and
Planning	Captain K. Winkelhorn, U.S. Army.

Towards the end of March sufficient progress had been made in organising Resistance Groups to resume major sabotage operations once more. This was necessary to enable S.O.E. to implement the deception plan of the Supreme Commander, known as "Plan Fortitude" in so far as it related to Denmark. At the same time, it provided a suitable opportunity for testing the efficiency of the system of controlling operations by means of code signals on the B.B.C. It was felt, however, that, before sending these signals out, the question should be discussed at the meetings which were to take place in Stockholm, whither Lieutenant Commander Hollingworth proceeded on 13 April 1944.

In building up the Resistance Groups, efforts had been made to achieve the greatest possible measure of de-centralisation, and the B.B.C. code signals enabled a greater degree of decentralisation to be obtained than hitherto, where orders for action had to pass through a limited number of W/T operators. The programme envisaged for the coming months entailed an intensification of activity against lines of communication as opposed to industrial sabotage, which had hitherto been given preference.

Unfortunately, however, Muus was unable to attend as he was laid up with an attack of malaria, but his second-in-command, Ole Geisler, took his place. Frode Jakobsen represented the Freedom Council. The ensuing discussions were also attended from time to time by Ebbe Munck, Lieutenant Colonel Nordentoft, Commander Mørch R.D.N., Major Ray and Erling Foss. From an S.O.E. point of view, these meetings proved to be most successful, as not only was the S.O.E. plan accepted in its entirety, but the most excellent personal relationships were established with Ebbe Munck, Lieutenant Colonel Nordentoft, Commander Mørch and Erling Foss.

For the sake of security, it was decided that Geisler should not himself carry the plans in the form of micro film on his return journey, but that they should be carried by Frode Jakobsen. This was mistakenly interpreted by Frode Jakobsen as meaning that it was his responsibility to inform the Freedom Council of the results obtained from the Stockholm meetings, which from an S.O.E. point of view was unfortunate as Jakobsen was not able to carry this plan through as quickly and tactfully as Muus himself might have done.

The Freedom Council did in due course accept the plan, but were at first under the misapprehension that they should be consulted as to whether local conditions were suitable before action signals were actually issued. Under battle conditions the time factor involved would, of course, have debarred such consultations. From the point of view of S.O.E. H.Q. the issuing of these action signals was, in fact, regarded as a battle exercise and it was, of course, impossible to explain to the Freedom Council, who thought it premature, that many of the actions S.O.E. called for were part of a wide-scale deception plan.

Chapter 5

BUILDING UP THE RESISTANCE

While the Danish Section was busy with planning and conferences in Stockholm, further developments took place in the Field. Successful sabotage operations included the destruction of the Nazi Labour Office and Scandinavisk Motor Company in Copenhagen. In addition, a successful attack was made on the shipyard at Helsinger, where various key installations were destroyed and damages estimated Kr. 1,000,000.

S.O.E. telegraphists were strengthened by the arrival of a new recruit, Steve, who was successfully installed in Aarhus. The improvement occasioned by this telegraphist was offset by the arrest of Christiansen by the Gestapo. It will be remembered that he was the only telegraphist operating in the Field who survived from those who had been trained and despatched by S.O.E. The W/T organisation was, therefore, as follows: "Napkin" and Holst operating in Copenhagen, "Napkin's" brother from Fyn, and Steve from Aarhus in Jutland.

During the month a total of six-and-a-half tons of stores and three agents were safely delivered to the Field. Of these agents, one was a sabotage instructor, one, Hecht Johansen, was to be in charge of reception work on the Island of Fyn, and Herschend was sent to work as a propaganda agent under the direction of Aage Schock, chief of the Freedom Council Illegal Press Committee. Herschend, after completing his training as a propaganda agent, had been sent on loan to P.W.E. for instructional purposes and was sent to Denmark in accordance with their express wish that S.O.E. should have a representative closely connected with the illegal press direction who was thoroughly versed in their work. It is worthy of note that the delivery of stores included a special S-Phone known as "Minestrone", which was to be used in establishing direct R/T communications across the Sound with Sweden, and also a Eureka Beacon which was to be installed in mid-Jutland. In May, thirty-six containers were successfully delivered to the Field and sabotage attacks numbered no less than seven major operations and twenty-two of lesser importance.

The development of the Resistance Organisation in Jutland, under the inspiring leadership of Flemming Juncker, resulted in the latter becoming a marked man and, rather than risk compromising a number of leaders by his possible arrest, he was evacuated to Sweden and immediately flown to the U.K. Juncker proved to be of the greatest value to the Danish Section in London into which he was integrated after some delay, which was caused by the security ruling which prevented foreigners from gaining access to the Section.

Juncker reported that he had handed over the leadership of Resistance in Jutland to two men, Anton Jensen, better known under the name of "Toldstrup" (by which he will be referred to hereafter), and Lieutenant Colonel O. Bennike, a regular officer in the Danish Army. "Toldstrup", an energetic Lieutenant in the Reserve of thirty years of age, was placed in charge of reception work, while Bennike, a staid and elderly Sapper officer, was in charge of the para-military groups. The difference in age and temperament of these two men did not make for smooth co-operation.

Later in the month Truelsen, chief of the Intelligence Organisation, unfortunately became compromised after a brilliant operation resulting in the successful penetration of the German Experimental Station at Høruphav. Having handed over the command of the Intelligence Organisation to a local Danish Army Intelligence Officer, Captain F.B. Larsen, he was obliged to evacuate to Sweden and arrived in the U.K. early in June where he was integrated into the Danish Section. It would be appropriate here to devote a little space to describing these two men, who were to exercise considerable influence, not only in the Danish Section, but in Danish political circles in London.

Juncker, who was approaching forty, had been a successful business man and became a large and wealthy landowner in Jutland. His political inclinations led him to be an ardent member of Dansk Samling, an extremist anti-German party which in domestic politics was animated by an idealism which looked to the younger generation of Danes to provide a new and vigorous leadership for the country. Juncker's personal convictions were stimulated by a strong strain of impetuosity, but his boundless energy, his imagination and his local knowledge proved of the utmost value to the Danish Section.

Truelsen, on the other hand, was a considerably younger man approaching his thirties, who had previously been employed as a

Secretary to the Council of Agriculture in Copenhagen. By training he was a lawyer and, as a reserve officer in the Guards, he had been recruited early on by the "Princes" as their reserve organiser. It had been due to his vigorous leadership that the Intelligence Organisation which had broken down after 29th August 1943, was rapidly set on its feet and functioned with considerably increased efficiency. Truelsen possessed a most persuasive manner and had considerably more shrewdness than his colleague Flemming Juncker. He quickly appreciated the difference in conditions in Copenhagen and London and his more diplomatic approach to problems frequently achieved results which the impetuous Juncker was unable to do himself.

It was about this stage that the lessons learned from the arrest of Christiansen were digested and applied. It had previously been the custom to correspond only with the telegraphists themselves, without regard to the subject matter of each message. The only exception to this practice was that Muus held a special code which was used for all matters of policy and particularly confidential messages. The disadvantage of this system was, to put it briefly, that the telegraphists knew too much, and it was accordingly decided to undertake a wide distribution of one-time pads, so that the various code holders could correspond with H.Q. in complete security. Codes were accordingly assigned to Bennike, "Toldstrup", Hecht Johansen, Muus's secretary, and Truelsen's successor, Captain F.B. Larsen.

The invasion of the Continent by Allied troops, although it caused a certain amount of disappointment among the Danes that their beaches had not been selected for this undertaking, provided a stimulus to the Underground Movement and to the population as a whole. Sabotage operations steadily increased culminating in the destruction, on 22nd June 1944, of Dansk Industri Syndikat. This was the signal for savage reprisals by the Germans; a record number of executions were carried out and martial law was proclaimed in Zealand and a curfew was introduced. These measures produced fresh demonstrations on the part of the population – disorders and shooting affrays taking place in the streets of Copenhagen. In the face of these demonstrations the Germans were obliged to give way and the curfew was somewhat modified.

As a result of D-Day the first large scale troop movement took place in Denmark with the despatch of the 20th Luftwaffe Division to Italy, where it was identified a week after its departure from Denmark. A new division arrived from Norway and took its place. In view of the comparatively short time within which these movements were accomplished due to lack of interruptions, S.O.E. issued precise instructions to Bennike that all such movements in the future were to be harassed and delayed as far as possible, and, in addition, in order to save time in the planning stage of these operations, Bennike was to be put into contact with Lieutenant Tillisch, local leader of the Intelligence Organisation in Jutland. The excellent collaboration which took place between these two men had the most fruitful results in the coming months.

There were at this time in London thirty-three agents in training, three of whom had been specially selected as operatives in underwater sabotage operations against enemy shipping. Another development of interest was that "Napkin", at the request of S.O.E., installed an automatic transmitter which enabled the W/T traffic from Copenhagen to be passed at the rate of eighty words per minute. This gave the telegraphists greatly increased security.

During June, 1944, the political situation in Denmark deteriorated still further owing to the provocative conduct of the Schalburg Corps – a Quisling [Waffen-SS] regiment recruited by the Germans from the criminal elements of the population and employed by them to carry out their campaign of counter-sabotage and murder. Affairs came to a head in the first week of July when a spontaneous General Strike took place in Copenhagen. It should be understood that the Strike was more an expression of public exasperation than an organised political manoeuvre.

The Freedom Council, however, saw the need for central leadership, and was intelligent enough to realise that in assuming that leadership, it had the opportunity to demonstrate its influence. It accordingly issued a proclamation to the effect that the Strike would continue until the Germans removed the Schalburg Corps from the streets of the Capital and lifted the curfew. An ineffective appeal by the leaders of the old political parties made no impression and the Strike continued until the Germans finally accepted the demands of the Freedom Council, when work was resumed. These events strengthened the position of the Freedom Council enormously, and its political leadership of the Resistance Movement was now indisputable.

During August some six-and-a-half tons of explosives were safely delivered by air and at last, after several months work which included four failures, a successful sea operation took place. The S.O.E. boat met two Danish fishing vessels at a rendezvous in the North Sea and was able to transfer four-and-a-half tons of stores, which were safely landed and distributed in Jutland.

W/T communications in the meantime had been greatly strengthened by three local recruits who had finished their training and were ready to begin work. Two agents had been dropped in the latter part of July. One of these was a telegraphist, but he was unfortunately arrested within a fortnight of his arrival. The local operators were more lucky, and all of them were sent to Jutland – one was stationed in Aalborg to work for the local Intelligence leaders, one in Randers, working for "Toldstrup", and the third in Aarhus also engaged on intelligence duties. The previous operator who had been working in Aarhus unfortunately had a bad attack of cold feet owing to the arrest of one of his comrades. S.O.E. was, however, able to replace him early in September by a first-class telegraphist called Jelgren. He was used for all communications between London and Bennike, the Jutland Resistance leader.

By the end of August, 1944, very considerable progress had been made in the organisation of a para-military movement. Some measure of decentralisation had been secured, local leaders appointed and communications both internal and external were greatly improved. By this time Muus had his hands full dealing with the leading personalities on questions of high policy and, as a further aid to decentralisation, he handed over the control of the Zealand sabotage organisation to Captain Ole Geisler.

It would be a wrong assumption to think that all the achievements mentioned above had been effected without casualties. German pressure increased, razzias, murders and mass arrests became an everyday feature of life in Denmark, and it was at the end of this month that S.O.E. suffered a particular blow in the death of one of its earliest friends – Robert Jensen – who was killed by the Gestapo while resisting arrest. Geisler, who was with him at the time, escaped by dashing off through a hail of bullets.

It had been Jensen's job to handle the Copenhagen end of the illegal traffic across the Sound between Denmark and Sweden, and it was many months before S.O.E. was able to get the service supervised in the efficient way that characterised the work of Jensen. This delay was also, in great part, due to Jensen's one great failing, about which he had been warned many times, namely, that of keeping a list of contacts.

When this list fell into the hands of the Gestapo it forced many good people to go underground and entailed a complete re-organisation of the Danish end of the despatch organisation. His immediate successor was almost immediately suspected by S.O.E. of being an enemy agent, and on the express instructions of the Danish Section, the case was investigated. S.O.E. fears proved correct and the man was liquidated.

Chapter 6

RE-ORGANISATION IN THE FIELD

At the beginning of September 1944, S.H.A.E.F. decided to form a special mission to represent the Supreme Commander in Denmark after the liberation of the country. The Mission, under the leadership of Major-General R.H. Dewing, formed in London at the beginning of the month and was largely dependent on S.O.E. for up-to-date information on conditions in Denmark. This move entailed the raising of a number of questions of policy and made it impossible for the Section Head, Pay Lieutenant Commander R.C. Hollingworth, R.N.V.R., to devote the amount of time to the supervision of daily operations which it had previously been possible to do, and a major re-organisation of the Danish Section therefore took place.

Major Lassen became Second-in-Command and Deputy Head of the Section, assisted by Major Winkelhorn, U.S. Army. The remainder of the Section was divided into two, the operational side being under Major Garrett, and the administration and supplies under Captain Taylor. Of these two officers, the former supervised the work of the following sub-sections, air operations (Flying Officer Townson, W.A.A.F.), operations in the Field (Captain Juncker), sea operations, intelligence (Captain Truelsen), signals (Ensign Schieldrop F.A.N.Y.), operations in Germany (Captain Strutt). The latter was responsible for training and finance, as well as administration (Captain Bowden) and supplies (Lieutenant A. Blanner, R.N.V.R.)

The liberation of France and Belgium enabled the Danish Section to get a considerably increased allocation of aircraft for Danish operations. Denmark now ranked in priority after Holland and Norway, and it was therefore of paramount importance to take full advantage of the new situation by drawing up a carefully thought-out programme for supplying the para-military groups with arms and ammunition. Their estimated strength at this date was 5,000.

Previously the major part of delivery by air comprised of explosives and sabotage accessories, in addition to a number of Sten guns and pistols for the personal protection of sabotage groups, and no effort had been made to undertake a large-scale supply of arms. In order to facilitate a long-term programme, it was decided to draw up three standard loads of arms, ammunition and sabotage material.

It was further decided that no ammunition loads would be delivered until a total of 15,000 men had been armed. (It should, of course, be understood that the standard arms load contained an initial supply of ammunition for each weapon). Sabotage loads were not to form a fixed percentage of overall deliveries but would be despatched as required in order to maintain stocks in the Field at a level which would permit the organisation to carry out current operations and to build up a reserve for "D-Day". The remaining loads were designed on the basis of equipping units of 100 men, and the scale of equipment selected for one unit was:

22	Sten S.M.G.s
75	.30 Carbines
4	Bren L.M.G.s
2	Bazookas or PIATs
200	Mills Grenades

The Section was greatly handicapped in being forced to select weapons for despatch more on the strength of their availability than on their suitability. Furthermore, those officers in the Section who had a good knowledge of weapons did not, unfortunately, have an intimate knowledge of the territory, whilst those who had lived for many years in the country had only a scanty knowledge of the different types of weapons available. It has been said that a larger proportion of long-range weapons should have been supplied, as the Resistance Groups would have been at a disadvantage if they had been called upon to fight a better equipped enemy at short range. This is a debatable point, but it is more probable that under the circumstances obtaining in Denmark, it would in any event have proved too hazardous to call the Resistance Groups into open battle and, as events turned out, they had no use whatsoever for long range weapons.

Mention must be made of two further factors. Firstly, the loads of all three types were effected by the fact that, since an aircraft flying to

Denmark did not carry more than twenty-four containers, arms for a hundred men were designed to be covered by twelve standard containers. Secondly, the proximity of Sweden and the possibility of infiltrating sub-machine guns of Swedish manufacture into Zealand led to a modification of arms loads delivered to Zealand. This modification entailed the substitution of Stens by an increase in carbines and Brens.

The new supply policy was speedily put into practice and during September twenty-six successful sorties resulted in a greater tonnage than in any previous month. Thirty-and-a-half tons were safely delivered to the Field including 1,800 lbs of explosives and arms for 2,000 men. A further successful sea operation also took place resulting in the infiltration of three special anti-shipping operatives and one liaison officer.

In their efforts to destroy the Resistance Movement, the Germans arrested a large number of officers with the object of removing potential leaders of resistance. They further deported nearly two hundred political prisoners to Germany, in spite of all undertakings they had given to the Danish Civilian Administration on this score. The result was a forty-eight-hour strike proclaimed by the Freedom Council, and to counter this demonstration the Germans disbanded the Danish Police Force on 18th September. Some two thousand police officials were deported to Germany and the remainder numbering about 8,000 went underground. Danish popular reaction expressed itself in a second forty-eight-hour strike held under the auspices of the Freedom Council.

No sooner had the Danish Police disappeared from the scene than the Gestapo redoubled their efforts against the Resistance Movement throughout the country. During the latter half of September, a meeting between Muus, his secretary and Captain F.B. Larsen, the chief of the Intelligence Organisation, had been arranged to take place at a certain flat. Arriving first, Larsen set about unlocking the front door when the key suddenly broke in the lock, and he was unable to gain admittance. He therefore decided that the meeting had better take place at another flat at 47, Bredgade, and before setting out for this new rendezvous, he informed Muus by telephone of the new arrangement. No.47 had not been used for some time by the organisation as it was believed to have become compromised. Muus and Larsen, however, felt that the risk of using it on one more occasion could be accepted.

This turned out to be a most unlucky decision as on entering No. 47 Larsen walked straight into the arms of the Gestapo and was arrested. Muus fortunately took the precaution of ringing up before arriving and so learnt of the danger just in time. The arrest of Larsen was all the more unfortunate as it led to a development which did not suit S.O.E. ideas at all. Larsen was succeeded as Intelligence Chief by another officer, Captain Svend Eriksen, who at the same time carried on with his former illegal duties of supervising the "import" of arms from Sweden and their distribution to the different groups.

The combination of these two jobs under one control caused S.O.E. considerable misgivings, which were subsequently justified, as Eriksen used his now considerable influence to further Army politics by securing the appointment of Army officers to the command of each of the six regions. The Danish Section felt that it would be unwise at this stage to raise objections as the question of appointments was recognised as being primarily a matter for decision by the Danes themselves. Unfortunately, there was a strong desire among these officers to keep the direction of underground warfare within their own small circle, which tendency was inclined to defeat London's efforts to decentralise.

In the normal course of affairs, S.O.E. would have relied on Muus to counter this influence. But Muus himself was suffering from the unwelcome attentions of the Gestapo, and this fact, together with his recent marriage to his secretary, Varinka de Wichfeldt, led to his withdrawal from intimate contact with the inner circle of Resistance leaders in Copenhagen. For security reasons this step was fully approved by the Danish Section although it meant that S.O.E. interests were not fully represented in the Freedom Council any longer.

The temporary retirement of Muus led to further adjustments. Geisler became the acting leader of the "Table" Organisation, and the control of communications with leading circles in Copenhagen passed into the hands of Herman Dedichen, a close and influential friend of Muus. It frequently appeared that Dedichen was not disinclined to further his own ambitions, but without doubt he placed the interests of his country first and foremost. It was largely due to his tactful and diplomatic handling that common sense was eventually established between the Freedom Council and the leaders of the official political parties. Muus was also obliged to relinquish the supervision of reception work in Zealand. This was now placed in the capable hands of Stig Jensen, a member of the "Old Guard" of Resistance, whose wide experience in practically every type of illegal work gave added impetus to the expansion of the Zealand reception organisation.

September 1944 was thus a month of great significance for the further development of Danish Resistance. The decisions taken in London and the re-organisation in the Field were later to have a far-reaching effect. Meanwhile, the Gestapo intensified its relentless campaign and the Resistance Movement was to face a period of greatly increased pressure by the enemy.

Chapter 7

FINAL PREPARATIONS FOR THE DANISH "D-DAY"

Early in October 1944, the German division stationed in the Aalborg area – 416 Infantry Division – left Denmark for the front in Holland. The movement was not, however, carried out unmolested, for the Resistance Groups in Jutland executed a series of well-planned and successful operations against the railways, which completely upset the enemy's timetable. These operations were not without loss to the patriots, and the intensive action initiated by the Gestapo in the previous month began to meet with some measure of success. As a diversionary measure destined to relieve the pressure on static sabotage groups, Jens Lillelund, alias "Finsen", who had been forced by Gestapo attentions in the Copenhagen area to evacuate to Sweden, was sent to Jutland as leader of a Sabotage Flying Squad which did excellent work, appearing unexpectedly at widely scattered places throughout the peninsula.

In Copenhagen, the arrest of Professor Mogens Fog, chairman of the Freedom Council, was a very serious blow for it deprived the Resistance Movement of its dominating political figure. In Jutland, action was more widespread. Groups in mid-Jutland suffered heavily and illegal work became much dislocated in consequence, while in South Jutland, which had always been the most difficult district for Resistance owing to the presence of a German minority, the organisation was virtually broken up.

There were, therefore, very cogent reasons which caused Lieutenant Colonel Bennike to send a special request to S.O.E. H.Q. asking for a bombing attack on the Jutland Headquarters of the Gestapo which were situated in a number of buildings at Aarhus University. This message was received by wireless on 15th October. The Danish Section at once set to work to produce a brief on the subject which, owing to the fact that it controlled the intelligence organisation in the Field, was a comparatively simple task.

Within a few days a most comprehensive description of the target was prepared. This included not only details of the target buildings themselves, but also the colour and full description of the materials used in their construction, anti-aircraft defences in the vicinity and suggestions as to the actual time of day at which an attack could be expected to cause most casualties to the Gestapo. With the approval of the Air Ministry and S.H.A.E.F. the operation was entrusted to 2 Group of the Second Tactical Air Force.

Some delay was inevitably caused owing to the incidence of unsuitable weather, but on 31st October the attack was successfully carried out by twenty-five Mosquitoes of the R.A.F. The attack was pressed home from rooftop height with exceptional accuracy. The target buildings were completely destroyed, together with all the cardexes so carefully compiled by the enemy; in addition, approximately one hundred and sixty-five Gestapo officials and between twenty and thirty Danish informers were killed or wounded. Furthermore, several Danish patriots who were being interrogated at the time of the attack were able to make good their escape. Among these was Ruth Dyre, the confidential secretary and courier of Lieutenant Tillish, Intelligence Officer for Jutland. She had been arrested on 7th October and her providential escape was a fitting recompense to her Chief who was responsible for providing the information on which the S.O.E. brief for the R.A.F. was prepared.

During October satisfactory progress was made with the delivery of supplies. Twenty-four successful sorties resulted in the safe arrival of thirty-two-and-three-quarter tons of stores, providing arms for a further 2,500 men.

During the first week of the month S.O.E. despatched nine liaison officers by air, all of whom reached their destinations in safety. The close of the fishing season had caused the temporary suspension of operations across the North Sea. During this period no fewer than 3,000 S.M.G.s of Swedish manufacture were infiltrated into Zealand from Sweden. Behind this operation there is a story of months of careful planning on the part of Ebbe Munck and his collaborators who controlled the routes, and of patient negotiations with the Swedes on the part of the S.O.E. Mission in Stockholm and its closest Danish collaborators in which Erling Foss played the leading part. It cannot be emphasised too strongly that the Swedes were far more prepared to risk their neutrality in such a way by

Danish request than they would have been as a result of a direct approach from the British.

Communications were strengthened by the addition of two locally trained operators and the establishment, after months of preparatory work, of the "Minestrone", i.e., a radio telephonic connection between Zealand and Sweden. In addition, and used for the sole purpose of reporting intelligence, the telephone cable between Sweden and Denmark had been tapped secretly in a way which provided constant communication between the Hamilcar Office in Stockholm and the Intelligence H.Q. in Copenhagen. The secret of this telephone line was very carefully guarded and the Germans have never suspected its presence. The "Minestrone" gave valuable respite to the Copenhagen telegraphists, but it did not afford a quick enough means of communication between London and Denmark for operational purposes. Recent air operations and the heavy traffic passing between S.O.E. and the Jutland reception leader, "Toldstrup", was placing a considerable strain on his own operator. Accordingly, one of the new recruits was ordered to join "Toldstrup's" staff and the other was established in South Jutland to provide a direct link between London and the local Intelligence Chief.

As far as the Intelligence Service was concerned, all its sub-headquarters were now in direct wireless contact with S.O.E. H.Q. and a steady flow of high-grade information was passed by S.O.E. to S.I.S. for dissemination. This happy state of affairs was marred by the arrest of the Intelligence telegraphist in North Jutland, which not only interrupted communications but necessitated the withdrawal of Lieutenant Bruun Petersen, head of the North Jutland sub-headquarters, from the scene of his activities. The telegraphist, who was severely pressed by his German interrogators, committed suicide rather than divulge information about his comrades.

It must not be supposed that the Gestapo had been able to arrest the progress of subversive operations during this period and the following table gives a broad outline of the number of successful operations which took place during the last quarter of 1944:

Target	Oct.	Nov.	Dec.	Total Successful Operations
Industrial	23	22	16	61
Railways	24	14	7	45
Shipping	7	10	3	20
Military	12	22	3	37
Total:	66	68	29	163

With the arrival in Denmark of the S.O.E. liaison officers a new factor was introduced into the leadership of Danish Resistance. Of the new arrivals, the following six were regular officers of the Danish Army: Helk, Vang, Kofoed, von Holck, Jensen and Bork Andersen. Of the remainder, Jebsen was a Norwegian who had made good his escape from a train of Norwegians being deported by the enemy through Denmark, Toft Christiansen had made his way to the U.K. from the Foreign Legion and Bangsboll had been recruited by O.S.S. from the U.S. Army. These liaison officers were attached as follows: Helk to Bennike, Vang and Kofoed to "Toldstrup" (in his then dual capacity of Jutland Reception Leader and Commander of the North Jutland Region), Toft Christiansen and Bangsboll to the mid-Jutland Region, Jebsen to South Jutland, Jensen to Fyn and von Holck to the Zealand Command and Bork Andersen to the Copenhagen Command.

It was the intention of S.O.E. that the liaison officers should strengthen S.O.E. control of the Resistance Movement by providing a personal link between S.O.E. and the several commanders in the Field, as well as giving technical assistance by way of instruction in weapon training and in the operation of special items of equipment. They were all fully conversant with the plans which had been prepared for action by Resistance Groups and before departure it was impressed on each officer that S.O.E. looked to each of them to provide full details of the organisation in his respective region. This was to be reported at regular intervals by means of film messages to S.O.E. H.Q.

The despatch of these officers had, of course, been agreed to in principle by the various leaders in the Field and S.O.E. had every reason to hope that it would be able to exercise a decisive influence at this somewhat critical stage. Certainly, the officers were well received and began work with great enthusiasm – everywhere, that is, with the important exception of Jutland. Here, unfortunately, the difference in temperament between Bennike and "Toldstrup" was causing considerable difficulties.

As reception leader, "Toldstrup" was responsible for all stores delivered to Jutland until they had been handed over to the various depots of which Bennike supplied the addresses. It was, therefore, necessary for Bennike to be kept informed as to the quantities delivered. As a double check, it later proved necessary to do this direct by W/T. The nature of "Toldstrup's" work was such that he was forced to take a number of security risks, whilst Bennike was prone to take exaggerated security measures which considerably held up the distribution and rendered a dovetailing and synchronising of the work of these two well-nigh impossible. This led to bad co-operation between the two and an exaggeration of independent action on the part of "Toldstrup".

At this time "Toldstrup" was still commander of the North Jutland Region of Resistance Groups and in such capacity was under the direct orders of Bennike, who again considered himself under the discipline of the military leadership in Copenhagen. As reception leader "Toldstrup" could, of course, only receive his daily orders direct from London since the time factor, and the risk of inaccuracy, would not have permitted the transmission of these daily changing orders by second-hand means; nor would this have been allowed on security grounds. This state of affairs caused considerable difficulties for the S.O.E. Liaison Officers in the Field. To "Toldstrup" were attached Vang on the reception side and Kofoed on the regional leadership of Resistance Groups. They were given considerable freedom of action as "Toldstrup" himself had no time for cumbersome staff work. The rest, however, attached to Bennike were unable to function efficiently so long as the dispute was in progress. They were obviously suffering from a lack of contact with London.

The Section, however, for the sake of maintaining the unity for which the whole country had been noted, felt it unwise, until a re-organisation had been effected, to press for this direct contact, bearing in mind that Bennike, who was over-inclined to adhere to strict military channels of command, would have felt his position ludicrous if, whilst he received his orders from Copenhagen, the Liaison Officers attached to him received theirs direct from London. There were two further factors to be taken into consideration, namely, that the W/T operators were already overburdened and the addition of extra code holders would have added to their traffic and, secondly, that the Section in London felt it unwise, with its more limited up-to-date knowledge of local conditions, to interfere too deeply in a domestic problem which the Freedom Council was closely watching.

In their desire to reconcile the various technical difficulties and maintain the unity on which everything depended, the Section in London eventually solved the problem, as will be seen later, by agreeing to "Toldstrup's" substitution as leader of Region I and placing him, as well as all the Liaison Officers, under the discipline of S.O.E.'s Chief Representative in Copenhagen, who was able to reconcile all differences of opinion with Bennike's superiors, the military staff in that city.

During November 1944, favourable weather greatly accelerated the delivery of arms by air, and no fewer than sixty-five successful sorties resulted in the delivery of eighty-six tons. This provided arms for an additional 6,800 men as well as seven tons of explosives.

December, however, was marred by continual bad weather and only seven tons of stores were delivered. Nor did January 1945, show a marked improvement, since the total delivery of stores dropped was only just over twenty-one.

In all, during these two months, a further six hundred men were armed. In September 1944, a first attempt was made to sail two motor vessels from England to Sweden with stores for trans-shipment by clandestine channels to Denmark. At first the operation looked like succeeding, but the vessels were recalled by the Admiralty owing to enemy dispositions in the Skagerrak after completing half the voyage. During October, November and December, although several further attempts were made to reach Sweden, none was successful.

The withdrawal of Muus from active participation in the direction of Resistance from Copenhagen has already been briefly described and, in the last quarter of the year, the lack of proper S.O.E. representation in Copenhagen began to make itself felt. The duumvirate of Dedichen and Eriksen was not regarded with any favour by S.O.E. as it was fast developing into a dangerous form of centralisation which constituted a great threat to the security of the Organisation. On the other hand, Eriksen in particular was unwilling to delegate the power which he held. He was, moreover, a leading exponent of Army politics.

Some improvement was obtained when post-liberation developments in Greece and Belgium became known in Danish Underground circles, and it became evident that a clear understanding must be reached between the moderate and extreme Right Wing elements on the one hand, and the Left Wing and civilian part of the Resistance Movement on the other. The Freedom Council was quick to take advantage of these developments and in its conversations with the leaders of the official political parties insisted that it should hold not less than half the Cabinet appointments in the first post-liberation Government. This the politicians were obliged to concede.

The political developments just described were certainly of some assistance to S.O.E., but it should be realised that S.O.E. was solely concerned with perfecting the Underground Organisation for action on the Danish "D-Day" and had nothing to do with post-liberation problems, although S.O.E. was acting as a channel for an exchange of views on such matters between the S.H.A.E.F. Mission (Denmark) and the leading Danish authorities.

It was abundantly clear that Muus must be succeeded by an officer who could give full weight to S.O.E. views in the highest councils of Resistance. To meet just such an eventuality S.O.E. had brought over to the U.K. Ole Lippmann, a young man whose previous illegal work was highly appreciated and whose contact with a number of the leading underground personalities in Copenhagen might be turned into a valuable asset by S.O.E.

Lippmann possessed a pleasant personality and the necessary drive and determination, but some misgivings were felt on account of his lack of years, a tendency towards over-confidence in his own ability and the readiness with which he advanced his own political opinions. It was, therefore, with a number of unspoken reservations that Lippmann was put into training for the position of S.O.E.'s Chief Representative in Denmark. To assist him to establish his position, three specially trained officers were earmarked for despatch as his personal staff. These were Jenk, Hammerich and Malling.

Towards the end of the year another important step was taken by S.O.E. Events in the Low Countries had made it clear that S.H.A.E.F. would be obliged to nominate a Commander-in-Chief of the Danish Resistance Movement prior to undertaking military operations on Danish territory. After a careful sounding of opinion in responsible underground quarters, it was decided by the Danish Section to recommend General Gørtz for this appointment. There were also technical reasons which rendered this appointment advisable.

The Danish Brigade in Sweden, or Danforce, which has been mentioned earlier, was by now fully equipped and trained for the task of supporting Resistance in its final stages, and it was clear that the duties of this task force would continue for some time into the post-liberation period working alongside the re-established Danish Army. Major General Knutson, its commander, was a regular army officer who naturally owed allegiance to his senior officer, General Gørtz. While there was no doubt the latter's appointment as C-in-C would be extremely welcome to the military clique as finally establishing the ascendency of the regular officers, S.O.E. was determined to ensure that it should neither lead to an over-controlled and cumbersome command in the Field nor to dissatisfaction amongst the civilian elements of Resistance.

By playing on the Danish officer's unquestioning acceptance of orders from his superior, S.O.E. hoped to achieve the golden mean. Accordingly, work was begun on preparing new plans and a special directive for issue to General Gørtz under the name of the Supreme Commander which would ensure a decentralisation of authority in the Field which security and the military necessity for the speedy execution of orders from London made necessary. It was intended that these new plans and orders should not be despatched before Lippmann had reached Denmark and that it would be the latter's first task to get these accepted by all concerned.

In completing the account of a most successful year, mention should be made of the daring operation planned and carried out by "Toldstrup's" groups in the first week of November. As a reply to the help given to the Resistance Movement by the R.A.F. attack at Aarhus, "Toldstrup" planned an operation with the object of destroying Luftwaffe planes at Aalborg Aerodrome. So sure was he of success that he informed H.Q. in advance of the intended operation, which was carried out on 3rd November with complete success. Twenty aircraft were destroyed, and some damage was occasioned to the buildings which housed the aerodrome staff, violent explosions continuing for a period of 48 hours. It was the most successful action which was ever carried out against German military establishments in Denmark.

One other series of operations by Resistance should also be mentioned. The disappearance in September of the Danish Police made it increasingly important to prevent the enemy laying his hands on the public registers of the population in order to make it more difficult for him to trace "wanted" members of Resistance and to hamper any move on his part to institute conscription of labour. Throughout the last quarter of the year, therefore, the Resistance carried out a systematic series of operations which resulted in the removal and safe concealment of these registers all over the country.

1944, therefore, came to an end with a reasonable expectation on the part of S.O.E. that the new year would see the successful completion of its task in Denmark.

Chapter 8

THE LAST MONTHS OF THE WAR IN EUROPE

During the last quarter of 1944 and the beginning of 1945, certain changes of personnel in the Danish Section took place. O.S.S. representation was increased by the arrival of Captain I. Verschoor and Lieutenant R. Snowden, both of whom assisted Major Taylor on the supply side. The latter, however, was shortly afterwards replaced by Mr. James Cross of O.S.S., Captain Bowden was replaced by Captain M. Foulds, F.A.N.Y., as Administration Officer and Mr. Spink re-joined the Section as Political Liaison Officer with the Foreign Office and P.W.E. In addition, Captain Brian Heddy, R.A. joined the Section as assistant to Major Garrett, and F/O Townson was replaced by Captain E. Burrus F.A.N.Y.

The first event of importance in the New Year was the successful delivery of stores by sea to Sweden. Under the command of Lieutenant Commander Bryan Reynolds, D.S.C., M.B.E., R.N.R. a convoy of three small motor vessels reached Lysekil on 15th January after many unsuccessful attempts, carrying a net weight of 35 tons of stores for the Danish Resistance Movement. These consisted of 1,046 carbines, 936 Stens, Bren guns, bazookas and over two million rounds of assorted ammunition. This cargo was camouflaged as ship's machinery parts and was safely unloaded to await shipment to Zealand by the clandestine channels which were now working smoothly and efficiently.

Subversive operations in the Field opened with something more than the proverbial bang by the destruction of Torotor Radio Factory on the outskirts of Copenhagen. It had been reported to S.O.E. H.Q. that this factory was making parts for enemy V-weapons, as well as gyroscopes for torpedoes, and the "Table" Organisation was accordingly charged with the task of destroying it. After many weeks of careful planning and one attempt which miscarried, the operation was eventually successfully carried out by eighty armed saboteurs.

During January, the number of successful operations carried out against industrial targets was twenty-four; against railway targets, twenty-two; and against various military establishments, five.

It was also a matter of considerable satisfaction that the supply programme drawn up in September 1944, which involved raising the armed strength of Resistance to 15,000 men by the end of January was, in fact, carried out ahead of schedule. Muus and his wife, who were evacuated to Sweden in December, were brought back to the U.K. early in January where they were shortly followed by "Napkin", whose presence was urgently desired in London to review the entire communications network in the light of probable operational commitments. His arrival also enabled him to meet Lippmann and thus get to know the officer who was to be his chief during the final months of the war.

Some concern was felt by the Danish Section regarding the provision of an adequate number of reserve personnel to cover the maintenance of communications with the Regional Commanders and the Intelligence sub-headquarters during active operations, and a comprehensive plan was agreed with "Napkin" by which these commitments would be covered. Time, however, did not permit these plans to be fully implemented before the liberation. There is, therefore, no point in describing them in detail. The purely technical side of the discussions was about the development of a new line of communication between Copenhagen and London.

It was planned to establish a receiving set in Sweden which would receive automatic transmission from Copenhagen on an ultra-high frequency. This would provide a valuable increase in security for the hard-pressed Copenhagen operators and, immediately upon "Napkin's" return to Sweden, steps were taken to implement these arrangements. During the first weeks, messages received in this way were re-transmitted from Sweden to London by ordinary cable, but as time passed and the attitude of the Swedish Government was influenced by Allied military successes in North West Europe, arrangements were made by which these messages were automatically relayed from Sweden to London at high speed by wireless, the actual keying being done in Copenhagen. The bulk of signals traffic was accordingly passed by this link and the burden on the direct Copenhagen-London wireless and on the radio telephone links across the Sound was materially lightened.

The opening months of 1945 saw a steady increase in the flow of troops moving from Norway to the Western Front via Denmark, and the efforts of the Jutland Resistance groups were redoubled against railway traffic with the object of disrupting these movements to the maximum possible extent. These operations were so successful that, to quote S.H.A.E.F., "results were striking and resulted in the reduction in the rate of movement from Norway from four divisions to less than one division per month.

"The intensity of these operations is well illustrated in the moves of 233 Reserve Panzer Division and 166 Infantry Division which were urgently needed on the Western Front. During the week 4th-11th February over a hundred successful sabotage attacks were directed against the transport provided for these divisions. By the end of the week more than half the forty-four trains involved were held up in Denmark and six of them derailed."

A further quotation from the same report is of interest: "In Denmark the steady interference of railways caused strain and embarrassment to the enemy over a considerable period. The striking reductions in the flow of troops and stores from Norway in 1945 undoubtedly had an adverse effect on the reinforcement and reforming of units which the enemy had to undertake for the battles both West and East of the Rhine."

Two further operations of note were the destruction of Lyac Accumulator Factory at Lyngby, whose production was entirely devoted to enemy U-boats, and the Darr Factory at Silkeborg, which was producing anti-aircraft guns for the Germans. The latter operation was organised by the S.O.E. agent Brandenborg, who had been operating since his arrival in November 1944, under Bennike's direction.

Meantime the problem concerning "Toldstrup" and Bennike, which has already been described, had reached an acute stage, and the Freedom Council itself had been obliged to send one of its members to Jutland to investigate and report. Towards the end of January, a special message was received from the Freedom Council asking for S.O.E. to approve the visit to London of one of its liaison officers, who had been fully briefed in all aspects of this question. This officer, Lieutenant Helk, took a passage on the packet boat from Copenhagen to the island of Bornholm, having managed with great good fortune to survive a Gestapo interrogation of the passengers before the boat sailed. As they passed through the Falsterbo

Canal, Helk quietly stepped on board the Swedish pilot boat which came alongside to enable the pilot to board the Danish vessel.

As Helk stepped off the Danish boat, Lippmann, who was being despatched to Denmark via Sweden – his three assistants being sent direct – took his place on board and he too was unlucky enough to have to face a Gestapo interrogation on his arrival in Bornholm. He had, however, been handed careful notes of Helk's cover story and was able to survive the ordeal at no more cost than a good deal of anxiety. He subsequently arrived safely in Copenhagen where he took up his duties as S.O.E.'s Chief Representative.

Helk was quickly brought over to London and, in the ensuing discussions, it was realised that his views were prejudiced by his close association with Bennike during the preceding six months. The position of "Toldstrup", who had now been dismissed by the Freedom Council from his position as Commander of Region I, but retained the leadership of the Jutland Reception Organisation was, as described above, settled once and for all by placing him directly under the orders of Lippmann. These changes secured a working arrangement between "Toldstrup" and Bennike and proved acceptable to the other parties concerned. Before returning to the Field, Helk was fully briefed on the new orders which were to be sent to Denmark with Lippmann's personal assistants Malling and Hammerich. These orders, although not introducing any new factors into the plans which had been made the previous summer, provided for a very considerable simplification in their execution, and when they reached their destination S.O.E. H.Q. quickly received appreciative acknowledgment that they were not only understood but also fully approved by all responsible Resistance commanders. General Gørtz, in fact, made it quite clear that he regarded S.O.E.'s written instructions as his "bible".

The military progress of the Allies on the Eastern and Western fronts gave added impetus to S.O.E.'s work, both at H.Q. and in the Field. The stage was about to be set for the grand finale.

During February forty-nine successful sorties resulted in the delivery of sixty-nine tons of stores which included arms for 1,600 men and fifty tons of explosives. The unusually large quantity of explosives was all the more necessary since intensified railway sabotage had reduced stocks to a dangerously low level. Jenk was safely dropped in Jutland during this month. In March, successful sorties were increased to ninety-six which included the successful dropping of the remaining two of Lippmann's personal assistants, one telegraphist and thirty tons of stores. Ammunition comprised the bulk of this weight though arms for 6,000 men were included.

The opening of the fishing season permitted the resumption of North Sea operations, and four tons of stores were successfully transferred to two Danish fishing vessels on the Dogger Bank, which delivered their cargo to "Toldstrup's" agents without incident. Although March had seen the arrival of supplies to Denmark on a hitherto unprecedented scale, this was surpassed by the results which were achieved in April. One hundred and fifty-five sorties were successful entailing the delivery of 238½ tons of stores. Over 5,000,000 rounds of assorted ammunition, 42,000 grenades and arms for 10,000 men reached Denmark safely.

In addition, a further four tons were successfully delivered by sea operations. These remarkable figures did not, however, comprise the whole story. Thirty-five tons of stores, which had, in the face of great odds been delivered to Sweden in January under the masterly direction of Lieutenant Commander Brian Reynolds, R.N.R., had by now been infiltrated into Zealand, owing to the patient efforts of Major Ray and his local Danish collaborators, particularly Colonel Nordentoft and Commander Mørch. By the end of April, making a generous allowance for loss of equipment in the Field, the Danish Resistance Movement could be conservatively estimated at a strength of 25,000 armed men, which was well in excess of the target which had been set.

At 11.00 hours on 21st March the 2nd Tactical Air Force carried out a bombing attack against another Gestapo headquarters on plans and intelligence provided by the Danish Section. This time the target was the Shell Building in Copenhagen.

After many weeks of delay, mainly due to weather conditions, the attack was pressed home by 18 Mosquitoes and 22 Mustangs. A total of 6,000 lbs of H.E. hit the building, as well as many incendiaries, and it was completely gutted.

One great difficulty to be met was that of saving the Danish hostages housed in the attic. These included many leading members of the Resistance, among whom were Professor Mogens Fog and editor Aage Schock. With the exception of a small number of fatal casualties, among whom was Admiral Hammerich, all the hostages were got away safely. Four Mosquitoes and 2 Mustangs were lost in the operation, which, although a tremendous success from the operational point of view and of vital significance to the Underground Movement, was unfortunately overshadowed by a tragedy which occurred when one of the machines hit a nearby school, killing a large number of children. As ill luck would have it, the majority of the senior German officials employed in the Shell Building decided to attend a state funeral at the time the attack was carried out and the enemy death toll was comparatively light.

At the request of the patriots, a further R.A.F. attack was carried out on 17th April against the last remaining Gestapo headquarters housed in the Husmands School in Odense on the island of Fyn. The building and records were destroyed.

The advance of Allied forces into Western and Eastern Germany caused material repercussions in Denmark. Pressure from the East resulted not only in a large influx of refugees and their subsequent distribution throughout Denmark, but also in a number of German naval units taking up their positions in Danish harbours; while towards the end of April the junction of Soviet and Anglo-American forces in Germany squeezed the remaining Nazi troops in North West Germany into the base of the Jutland peninsula. The loss of the Silesian and Ruhr coalfields caused the enemy to make increasing use of coal stocks in Denmark, to the dismay of the Danes who were dependent on these for providing power for their factories and heat for their houses.

The impending collapse of Germany entailed an intensification of planning work at S.O.E. H.Q., which had been instructed by S.H.A.E.F. to make preparations for assisting an Allied military drive into Denmark. The first step which was undertaken was the formation and training of seven teams of "Jedburghs", each under the command of a British officer with a specially recruited Danish officer as his assistant. The Danes in question were chosen from the ranks of Danforce. The exchange of telegrams concerning the employment of these teams in the Field was insufficient to give the Danish Resistance leaders a clear idea of S.O.E. intentions and, in addition, S.O.E. wished to acquire detailed knowledge concerning the extent of local contribution to be expected.

In the middle of March, therefore, Commander (S) Hollingworth paid a lightning visit to Sweden for a meeting with Lippmann, to whom he was able to explain the points at issue. Commander Hollingworth was also able to review all the arrangements which had been made for the final stages of the campaign before Lippmann's return to his post in Copenhagen.

With the possibility of the Allies having to fight their way up the Jutland peninsula, plans for co-operation by Resistance with the invading Allied armies had to be perfected, and particular efforts were made to ensure that, when the time came, the armies should be provided with a steady flow of high-grade tactical intelligence.

A special team under the command of Lieutenant Scavenius, an S.O.E. intelligence agent of some distinction, was trained and plans were made for its despatch by air. Provision had also to be made for liaison between the various bodies of Allied troops, which were expected to take part in the liberation of the country, the Danish Section at S.O.E. H.Q. and Resistance groups in the Field. Major Ray was selected as S.O.E.'s liaison officer for Danforce, and in the middle of April Major Garrett paid a short visit to 21st Army Group H.Q. to discuss with the S.O.E. representatives at this H.Q. the means of effecting efficient liaison with the force designated for operations in Denmark. It was accordingly decided that a small team headed by Major Garrett should, in due course, be despatched to the H.Q. of the Army in Denmark.

Events now began to move with extraordinary rapidity. British forces had reached Lübeck by the last week in April and the Jutland peninsula was thus successfully sealed off from the remainder of Germany. Major Garrett and his team, to which was added Lieutenant Scavenius and Lieutenant Lyck, were placed on short notice to move, and on 4th May flew to North West Germany, completing their journey to 2nd Army H.Q. by road. The capitulation on the same day of all German forces facing 21st Army Group came as a considerable surprise as, although it was recognised as being imminent, it had not been expected that it would take place quite so quickly. Wireless messages were immediately sent to all Resistance leaders instructing them to execute their plans for safeguarding important installations throughout the country.

Simultaneously, S.H.A.E.F. had decided that a small advance party of its Mission to Denmark should be flown to Copenhagen at the first opportunity and, on receiving a wireless message from Lippmann that the aerodrome at Kastrup was safe for landing, General Dewing and his party, accompanied by Commander (S) Hollingworth, R.N.V.R., flew to

Kastrup on 5th May, where they were followed two days later by the remainder of the S.O.E. Mission.

Early in the morning of 5th May, Danforce made a successful unopposed landing at Helsingør, Major Ray having the honour of being the first British officer to set foot on liberated Danish soil. Throughout the country resistance had come out into the open and had successfully established control in the name of King and Government. Denmark was again free.

Chapter 9

AFTERMATH OF LIBERATION

During the first few days after 4th May and the formal capitulation, the population were able to give expression to the feelings which had been pent up for five long years. Everywhere Allied personnel received a tumultuous welcome from the Danes. Resistance came out with flying colours. No less than 20 cars awaited the arrival of General Dewing's party at the airport, and there was numerous transport of all kinds throughout the country and large stocks of petrol looted from the Germans were placed at the disposal of the Allied Forces.

General Dewing and Commander Hollingworth drove in state through streets lined with armed Resistants to see the Prime Minister, and two days later M.J. Christmas Møller arrived to take up his post as Foreign Minister in the new Government. The Danish police were non-existent and the entire country was in the hands of the Resistance who, considering the fact that they had waited five years to use their arms, showed magnificent discipline throughout all ranks.

It cannot be over-emphasized how much General Dewing's Mission and all other Allied Forces in Denmark were dependent on the Resistance in these early days. However, S.O.E.'s representatives had a hard time preventing friction which subordinate members of the S.H.A.E.F. Mission were apt to cause by their unwillingness to accord to the Resistance their due recognition.

While the capital was much taken up with flag flying, feasting and song, Resistance, especially in Jutland, had the most important task to fulfil. The suddenness of the surrender, when the "cease fire" order was given on 4th May, had precluded Resistance from implementing plans which had been made to apprehend Gestapo officials, war criminals and Danish collaborators, who all seized their chance to flee to Germany without delay.

The delay by the 2nd Army forces in closing up to the Danish frontier placed the entire burden of frontier control on Resistance, although

Resistance had not the transport at its disposal to facilitate a rapid concentration of the forces necessary to establish a close control of the frontier. Their task was further complicated everywhere by the fact that, in making the surrender, the Germans were successful in making it clear that as far as their troops in Denmark were concerned, the surrender was to 21st Army Group and not the Danish Government, which was technically non-belligerent, nor to the Danish Resistance forces. This meant in practice that local German commanders were able to refuse the "requests" of the Danes unless they were presented by an Allied officer. During the early days, therefore, S.O.E. liaison officers filled a most valuable function in acting as a buffer between Resistance and the enemy garrisons, and since they were in uniform, they were able to act with full authority as Allied officers.

S.O.E. having completed its operational task in Denmark, the S.O.E. Mission devoted its energies to carrying out liaison duties with the S.H.A.E.F. Mission, although this seriously delayed the increasingly large amount of administrative work in connection with the liquidation of the organisation in Denmark. The collection of special equipment, account of S.O.E. financial transactions and problems arising out of the disposal of agents composed the bulk of the work.

At the same time, opportunity was taken by Commander Hollingworth and his staff to make extensive personal contacts among Resistance personnel, and thus to foster the goodwill which was based on the comradeship in arms of the past five years. Denmark was fortunate in not having to undergo political upheavals, which in some other countries followed close on the heels of liberation. Credit for the comparative smoothness with which political life was resumed was due, not so much to the sagacity of the political leaders whether in the Resistance Movement or outside it, but to the innate common sense and respect for law and order which is characteristic of modern Denmark, and to the magnificent discipline displayed at all levels.

The Resistance Movement had secured for its representatives half the Cabinet portfolios, and developments were characterised by a forbearance which had been expected of the Danes. The Government wisely made no immediate move to disarm the Resistance forces and, by committing them to carry out extensive military duties such as the guarding of installations and dumps of enemy material, in the course of two months a large percentage of Resistance men were only too anxious to return to their normal vocations and take up the pen, hammer, or sickle in exchange for Sten guns and carbines.

It is therefore expedient to review the story of five years subversive activity in Denmark and to examine the conclusions which may be drawn from the experience that S.O.E. has gained.

First place should be given to the question of communications since it was over 18 months before S.O.E. was able to establish direct communications with Denmark, and until that happened the work of building up Resistance could not begin. There is much truth in the argument that the first necessity was to create a favourable atmosphere for the growth of an Underground Organisation, but this demanded an infiltration of agents to establish communications and send back operational intelligence on which planning could be based. It was a vicious circle which had to be broken.

Another very valuable lesson which has been learned is that whoever controls a wireless link to London has a power which H.Q. can exploit to advantage. That power should never be allowed to get into the wrong hands. If provisions had been made prior to the occupation of Denmark for the provision of wireless links and the establishment of a secure advance post, much valuable time and effort could have been saved.

By skilful planning of the W/T network, not only could S.O.E. direct the energies of local factions to mutual advantage, but they could also compel a practical method of decentralisation. It was particularly noticeable in Denmark that, while internal communications were difficult, as soon as a proper measure of decentralisation was achieved, concrete results quickly followed.

Careful consideration should also be given to the possibilities of effecting interchange of views between the staff officers at S.O.E. H.Q. with those at the advance base and with agents in the Field. Whenever this did take place the results were extremely beneficial to all concerned. It was found that personal contact provided not only a clearer understanding of the problems which had to be faced whether in London, Stockholm or the Field, but also an increase in mutual confidence which produced a most useful stimulus to the work of S.O.E.

Nothing has been mentioned in this narrative of the constant difficulties S.O.E.'s representatives had in Stockholm with S.I.S. representatives, who appeared to resent S.O.E.'s Danish organisation's unchallengeable position in the field of intelligence. It can be emphatically stated here, however, that Denmark is too small a country for two separate secret organisations to be maintained and directed without grave security risks. In practice the Resistance organisation and the Intelligence service overlap at many points, and so long as there is only one department in London controlling the two organisations, the problems arising from any clash of interests between Intelligence and Resistance can be carefully considered by officers who have an intimate knowledge of both organisations.

Experience has shown that the selection of personnel for the Field is one of the most vital problems to be faced. Quite apart from technical and other qualifications, it has been found in Denmark that a high social standing or an air of such is one of the greatest assets in dealing with all sections of the population. Much discussion has taken place on the question of the term of duty of an agent in the Field.

While allowances must be made for the character of each individual, it is considered that, as a general rule, six months is the longest period an individual should remain in the Field. It was generally the case that after this period the value of a particular agent steadily depreciated, nor is this surprising when one considers the tax on an agent's nerves imposed by the continual strain of a clandestine existence.

Finally, no real success is possible unless the right psychological attitude towards the country in question is adopted from the very beginning. In Denmark it paid to emphasize that Denmark's struggle was a Danish show entirely, for which S.O.E. was providing the tools, liaison officers, communications and directives. Even though this line was sometimes taken with "the tongue in the cheek", it paid never to hint that S.O.E. was in control.

One thing is certain, and this is probably true of all other countries where S.O.E. has operated, that the attitude of the majority of the population towards S.O.E. was that "never have so many owed so much to so few", and this vast amount of goodwill, if properly followed up, can be a tremendous moral asset to Great Britain.

APPENDICES

LIST OF APPENDICES

Appendix I

ANALYSIS OF AGENTS

| Year | Number of Agents | Casualties | | | |
		Evacuated	P.O.W.	Killed	Total
1941	2	1	-	1	2
1942	7	-	3	2	5
1943	20	1	4	2	7
1944	20	7	6	1	14
1945	8	2	-	-	2
Total	57	11	13	6	30

Appendix II

LIST OF AGENTS

Name	Date Despatched	Duties in Field	Further History
1. Bruhn C.J.	26/12/41	Chief Organiser	Killed Jumping.
2. Hammer M.	26/12/41	W/T Operator	Returned '42, went 18/10/42, evacuated Apr. '43 and trans. R.A.S.C.
3. Rottbøll	16/5/42	Chief Organiser	Killed 26/9/42
4. Lok-Lindblad P.	21/5/42	Sabotage Instructor	Captured 12/3/44, escaped 19/3/44, Sweden 6/6/44, returned Denmark July '44, P.o.W. 4/9/44
5. Mikkelsen	16/5/42	W/T Operator Copenhagen	P.o.W. 5/12/42
6. Nielsen A.P.	31/7/42	Sabotage Instructor	U.K. 9/8/43, joined S.A.S.
7. Pedersen K.E.	31/7/42	Sabotage Instructor	P.o.W. 5/12/42
8. Hansen H.F.	31/7/42	Sabotage Instructor	P.o.W. 5/12/42
9. Johannessen	16/8/42	W/T Operator	Killed 5/9/42
10. Larsen A.T.	16/2/43	Sabotage Instructor	P.o.W. 28/3/43
11. Larsen H.H.	16/2/43	Sabotage Instructor Copenhagen	Died 30/5/43
12. Christiansen G.	16/2/43	W/T Operator Copenhagen	P.o.W. 27/4/44
13. Geisler O.	16/2/43	Sabotage Instructor Zealand	
14. Jensen J.P.	11/3/43	Sabotage Instructor	Returned U.K. 27/3/44, and attached to S.A.S.
15. Balling E.	11/3/43	Sabotage Instructor	Evacuated Sweden, U.K. 27/3/44
16. Muus F.B.	11/3/43	Chief Organiser	U.K. 15/10/43, returned 11/12/43. U.K. Jan '45

Name	Date Despatched	Duties in Field	Further History
17. Johansen V.	11/3/43	Sabotage Instructor	Sweden 31/3/44
18. Lund K.R.	21/4/43	W/T Operator Jutland	P.o.W. 14/12/43
19. Carlsen	11/5/43	Sabotage Instructor	U.K. 27/9/44. Pioneer Corps.
20. Hansen P.	11/5/43	Sabotage Instructor	Evacuated Sweden 8/10/43, Danforce.
21. Johansen H.R.P.	17/5/43	Sabotage Instructor Fyn.	Died 27/7/44
22. Jensen J.	17/5/43	Sabotage Instructor	P.o.W. 14/12/43
23. Petersen V.	17/5/43	Sabotage Instructor Zealand	U.K. 27/3/44
24. Boelskov E.	22/7/43	Sabotage Instructor	Died 25/8/43
25. Christensen A.M.	26/7/43	Sabotage Instructor	Sweden 11/3/44, joined Danforce.
26. Petersen E.J.P.	26/7/43	Sabotage Instructor Zealand	
27. Ibsen H.H.F.	11/12/43	W/T Operator Mid-Jutland	U.K. 27/3/43, 4/8/44, P.o.W. 3/9/44
28. Junker J.B.	11/12/43	Sabotage Instructor	P.o.W. 14/12/43
29. Fink K.	5/2/44	Sabotage Instructor	Evacuated Sweden 9/7/44
30. Lassen F.	5/2/44	Sabotage Instructor	P.o.W. 4/9/44
31. Herschend K.	31/3/44	Propaganda Agent Copenhagen	P.o.W. 4/9/44
32. Johansen J.E.H.	31/3/44	Reception Organiser, Fyn.	
33. Hansen C.A.	1/5/44	*Minestrone* [secret radio link] expert	
34. Vang	4/8/44	Liaison officer to Toldstrup	
35. Christensen H.P.	23/9/44	Underwater Operative	
36. Holm-Hedegaard	23/9/44 by sea	Underwater Operative	
37. Ryder H.E.	23/9/44 by sea	Underwater Operative	
38. Kofod	23/9/44 by sea	Liaison officer to Toldstrup	
39. Helk J.	30/9/44	Liaison officer attached Bennike	U.K. Feb. '45, returned 3/3/45

Name	Date Despatched	Duties in Field	Further History
40. Von Holck	30/9/44	Liaison officer Zealand	
41. Bork-Andersen	30/9/44	Liaison officer Copenhagen	P.o.W. 27/4/44
42. Jensen E.H.	30/9/44	Liaison officer Fyn.	
43. Jebsen P.	30/9/44	Liaison officer South Jutland	
44. Sorensen V.B.	4/10/44	Liaison officer	
45. Toft-Christensen	4/10/44	Liaison officer Mid-Jutland	
46. Bangsboll L.	4/10/44	Liaison officer Mid-Jutland	
47. Stemann Petersen	6/10/44	Liaison officer	Evacuated Sweden 6/1/45
48. Brandenborg	30/11/44	Sabotage Instructor	
49. Boge	4/2/45	Penetration of Slesvig Holstein	Arrested March '45 but Escaped.
50. Jenk J.R.	7/2/45	Personal Assistant to Lippmann	
51. Lippmann O.L.	10/2/45 via Sweden	Chief Organiser	
52. Thyregod J.	3/3/45	W/T Operator North Jutland	
53. Hammerich P.	4/3/45	Personal Assistant to Lippmann	
54. Malling J.	4/3/45	Personal Assistant to Lippmann	
55. Birkelund	11/4/45	Penetration of Slesvig Holstein	
56. Munter	12/5/45	Penetration of Kiel area	
57. Pedersen J.S.		Trained Stockholm Penetration of Kiel area	

Appendix III

WIRELESS COMMUNICATIONS

It is not the purpose of this Appendix to give a detailed history of the building-up of wireless communications between Denmark and the U.K., but rather to give a general picture of the organisation as it existed in 1944/45 with short notes on different aspects of the organisation.

Telegraphists

Only a small percentage of Danish telegraphists were trained in S.O.E. schools and despatched from the U.K. The majority were locally recruited by "Napkin", (who it will be remembered, was himself a local collaborator) from both amateur and professional circles. It is a remarkable tribute to "Napkin's" ability that, although he had never been trained by S.O.E., he was able to instruct local recruits in S.O.E. procedure. Although "Napkin" himself operated for some months, the work of training new recruits, construction of sets, and the distribution of spare parts and signal plans made such demands upon his time that he was eventually obliged to give up transmitting himself. "Napkin" was, in fact, the S.O.E. Chief Signal Master in the Field. At the close of the campaign S.O.E. had in Denmark twelve working telegraphists.

Disposition of Telegraphists

In April 1945, S.O.E. telegraphists were distributed and employed as follows:

(a) Zealand.
A team of two telegraphists and three assistants handled all signals traffic in Zealand including that of the S.O.E. Chief Organiser, the leaders of the Resistance Groups in Copenhagen and Zealand, the Chief of the Intelligence Organisation, the S.O.E. Paymaster and the reception leader for Zealand.

(b) Fyn.
One telegraphist handled traffic for the Resistance Commander and the reception leader, and a second telegraphist handled traffic for the Intelligence sub-headquarters covering South Jutland and Fyn.

(c) Jutland.
In North Jutland one telegraphist was at the disposal of the North Jutland Intelligence sub-headquarters and a team of three telegraphists handled traffic for "Toldstrup" the reception leader, while in central Jutland one telegraphist transmitted for Bennike, the Jutland Resistance Commander. Two telegraphists working one plan, transmitted for the Jutland Intelligence Chief and the remaining telegraphist was to work for the South Jutland Resistance Commander but only came up on the air on the day of the German surrender.

It will thus be seen that, except in Zealand, the Intelligence Organisation had its own whole-time telegraphists, the remainder were shared by the Resistance Commanders and Reception Leaders throughout the country.

The build-up of this organisation as has been explained in the narrative, took many months to achieve. The initial contact was between Zealand and the U.K., and the next development was the establishment of a telegraphist early in 1944 in Fyn. A run of bad luck hampered the development of communications in Jutland but from the middle of 1944, when the first telegraphist was established there, steady progress was made.

Signal Plans and Broadcasts
Two types of plans were used by S.O.E. telegraphists in Denmark – the "V" and the "Z" plans. By January 1945, the latter was universally used as the "V" type proved insecure, since after three months it repeated itself. This necessitated a large supply of plans being available in the Field in order that the change over from one plan to another could be made in good time. There was, in addition, a plan to introduce a special type of signal plan known as "Marker Channel" for use by the Intelligence telegraphists. One of the S.O.E. telegraphists, Thyregod, who was dropped in March, 1945, was specially briefed in the use of this type of plan, and it had been arranged that he should pass on his knowledge to the

telegraphists in the Field. However, the speed with which events moved precluded this arrangement from being carried out, and this type of plan never came into operational use.

In 1942, until the last quarter of 1943, it was the practice to handle all incoming and outgoing traffic on the two-way skeds [schedule] of the "V" plans, but with the increase of wireless traffic and the difficulties of operating in the Field owing to the activities of enemy mobile detector squads, a more secure procedure was adopted. The two-way sked was only used for transmission from Denmark. Only in circumstances of exceptional urgency were outgoing messages passed on a two-way sked.

From the end of 1943 onwards, outgoing traffic was transmitted on broadcast plans. These plans did not necessitate any contact between the Home Station and the telegraphist in the Field, but were received "blind" by the latter. He then acknowledged the safe receipt of the broadcast the next time he was transmitting on his two-way sked. To ensure safe reception each broadcast transmission was repeated on two consecutive days. In 1945 S.O.E. operated three broadcast plans to Zealand, one to Fyn and seven to Jutland.

Ultra-High Frequency and "Minestrone"
With the development of the S.O.E. organisation in the Field and the continual efforts of the enemy to locate and capture telegraphists, it became necessary to develop supplementary methods of transmitting information from the Field. After many months of preliminary planning, the "Minestrone" connection was finally established in October 1944. This was a shore-to-shore radio telephone contact by S-Phone between Helsingør in Denmark and Helsingborg in Sweden. From Helsingborg the messages were passed to Stockholm and then sent by cable to London. On the whole, however, this channel proved to be too slow for operational use and was devoted to handling administrative traffic and political intelligence. In March 1945, the ultra-high frequency link began to operate.

A special set had been installed in Copenhagen capable of transmitting messages to Malmö in Sweden by means of an ultra-high frequency operating in the 200-400 megacycles band. From Malmö the traffic was relayed direct to London by cable. A transmission took place at the speed of five hundred letters per minute and was automatically recorded at the receiving end in Malmö.

This link proved so satisfactory that it eventually handled the bulk of traffic between Zealand and the U.K. and a further development was the installation in April 1945, of a relay transmitter in Malmö. Whilst the home station in England was receiving the message from Sweden the actual keying of that message was being carried out in all safety in Copenhagen. At the same time the Copenhagen operator was able to listen in to the home station and satisfy himself that his relayed message had been properly acknowledged.

Codes
At first S.O.E. agents in Denmark did all their coding by means of poems, but these were soon replaced by one-time letter pads which gave 100% security. All codes were initially held by the Chief Organiser in Copenhagen, but in order to save unnecessary trips by couriers carrying this compromising material, codes were later infiltrated direct into Jutland where they were held by "Toldstrup" and Bennike, who distributed them at the orders of S.O.E. H.Q. In April 1945, no fewer than thirty-three one-time pads were in current use.

Conclusions
In conclusion the following comment by Captain K.C.R. Howell, Royal Corps of Signals, who was at one time Chief Signal Master at the Home Station and later Signals Officer in the Danish Section, gives an expert opinion of the S.O.E. communications network in Denmark:

"The general standard of the Danish operators has been a very high one. Indeed, it is the opinion of the majority of operators who have worked for them, that they were of a better all-round standard than those of any other Section, though there may have been a few outstanding individuals amongst these latter. This standard was consistently maintained during their period of operations, and was a great factor in the success of communications from Denmark by making the work of the Home Station correspondingly easier than would have been the case had outstations operating been as 'sticky' as experienced with certain other nationals. It would appear that without exception all the Danish operators possessed the requisite confidence both in their own sets and in the Home Station which is so necessary for successful work. In this respect it is interesting to note that their sets were home produced and great credit must certainly go to those responsible for their production."

Appendix IV

INTELLIGENCE

In 1940 and 1941, while the main effort of the S.O.E. Danish Section was to establish wireless communications with Denmark, a concurrent effort was also made to form a para-military organisation – perhaps it would be more accurate to describe it as one of exploring the possibilities in this direction. It thus happened that towards the end of October 1941, Turnbull established contact through a cut-out with some officers of the Danish General Staff. The cut-out was a reliable man but under a promise not to divulge the names of the officers, and all that was known about them was that among their other connections, they did a certain amount of intelligence work.

The contact was carefully fostered with the idea of making use of these officers to build up a para-military organisation and, when it was found that they were able to provide intelligence material, this was accepted by S.O.E. from the "Princes", the code name by which these officers were known. This was done not because S.O.E. had any direct interest in obtaining intelligence at that stage, but because it was not felt politic to oppose the delicate relationship then existing between S.O.E. and the "Princes" by apparent lack of interest on the part of S.O.E. in what was the chief function of the "Princes" themselves. It was in this manner that S.O.E. first came into contact with an Intelligence Organisation in Denmark, which it was later to control and direct with considerable success.

The "Princes" were composed of the following officers: Oberstleutenant Nordentoft, Director of Military Intelligence, Kaptajn Winkel, Ritmester Lunding and Kaptajn V. Gyth. As their contact with S.O.E. developed, a steady flow of intelligence covering Danish territory and parts of North Germany came into the hands of Turnbull in Stockholm, and was then passed to S.O.E. H.Q. and S.I.S. This state of affairs continued until 29th August 1943, when the crisis resulted in the flight to Sweden of Nordentoft, Winkel and Gyth, and the arrest of Ritmester Lunding.

While it was now possible to establish a close contact with Nordentoft and his colleagues in Stockholm, who immediately set up an officer in Denmark to continue their work on Intelligence, the whole organisation in Denmark was virtually broken up. Nordentoft had, however, made preparations for just such an eventuality, and a Reserve Officer, Lieutenant S.A.P. Truelsen, now stepped into the breach to re-construct the Intelligence Organisation and to preserve continuity.

This plan had the full approval of the Danish Commander-in-Chief, General Gørtz, who stipulated however, that on no account should regular officers be used, as these were not only well-known to the enemy, but there was always the risk that the discovery by the Germans that regular officers were indulging in Intelligence activities, might result in the internment of the entire Officers Corps. This would have seriously compromised the Danish Army's plans to form illegal para-military groups. Truelsen, therefore, had to start from the beginning, and there was consequently a marked, though temporary, diminution in the flow of Intelligence reports to Stockholm.

At the same time, it should be appreciated that Nordentoft himself had considerable difficulties to overcome in establishing illegal routes across the Sound. It may be said here that the "Princes" were extremely cautious in committing themselves to supporting subversive operations in Denmark, and this, together with the Army's plan for an illegal organisation and the cover story which was widely circulated to preserve secrecy, led S.O.E. to entertain considerable suspicions that the "Princes" were a small clique of officers who were set to further their own ambitions as appearing as the ultimate saviours of Denmark. It was not fully understood that in fact the "Princes", as the leaders of the Military and Naval Intelligence Departments of the Danish General Staff, were working with the full approval of the Danish Commander-in-Chief. Fortunately, S.O.E. suspicions were finally allayed in the beginning of 1944, and from then onwards a full and complete collaboration was established with Nordentoft and his staff, not only on Intelligence matters, but on all forms of underground work inside Denmark.

By the end of March 1944, Truelsen had made sufficient progress with his organisation to produce the most satisfactory results, and Intelligence reports once more began to reach Stockholm in considerable bulk. It was at this juncture that Truelsen, who was already in contact with the S.O.E.

Chief Organiser, Muus, was allowed a code of his own and given access to S.O.E. wireless communications. This step brought about a radical change in the direction of the Intelligence service as S.O.E. H.Q. were now able to send Intelligence directives direct to the Field instead of using the former method of working through Nordentoft in Stockholm.

The arrival in the U.K. in July 1944 of Truelsen and his subsequent integration into the Danish Section made S.O.E. control absolute. Fortunately, the good relations with Nordentoft were in no way impaired as Truelsen possessed his full confidence, and although the centre of gravity shifted from Stockholm to London, a very close liaison was maintained with Nordentoft on all Intelligence matters. At S.O.E. H.Q. the Danish Intelligence sub-section was considerably expanded in order to enable it to produce Intelligence summaries based on material received from the Field on a large and diverse number of subjects. It was in fact the only Intelligence department which specialised in collecting and collating Intelligence from Denmark.

The Intelligence service in the Field was organised as follows: a headquarters was set up in Copenhagen covering Zealand and the German-Baltic seaboard. This H.Q., which was in wireless communication with S.O.E. London, also forwarded its reports to Nordentoft in Stockholm. Under this H.Q. a central sub-headquarters was set up in Aarhus covering mid-Jutland and also for receiving reports from local sub-headquarters at Prederikshavn and Kolding which covered North Jutland, South Jutland and Fyn respectively. Each sub-headquarters had its own wireless communication with S.O.E. in London.

In the main the service was excellent, providing the most detailed reports on all German dispositions inside Denmark, and the excellent coverage given to troop movements and arrivals from Norway was not only of strategic importance to S.H.A.E.F. but of tactical importance to S.O.E. in planning operations against enemy troop movements inside Denmark. A direct liaison was established with the Norwegian Intelligence Department and this collaboration yielded valuable results in assessing the probable intentions of the German command in moving troops from Norway through Denmark to the Western Front.

The Intelligence service did, however, have two weaknesses which made themselves felt as the war progressed. The first of these was the lack of drive in organising the naval part of the service. This was largely due to the fact that the chief of the service in the Field was always an Army officer, and military rather than naval influence predominated. The second weakness was in communications. It must be frankly acknowledged that the failure to appreciate the need for a special type of signal plan was not appreciated soon enough at S.O.E. H.Q., with the result that when the "Marker Channel" plans (which were more suitable for passing intelligence traffic "Z" type plans) were sent out to the Field, they arrived too late to be put into operation.

Mention must be made of S.O.E. relations with S.I.S. It was soon apparent to S.O.E. that Denmark was too small a country to contain two secret organisations under separate control, and the Danish Section policy towards S.I.S. was dominated throughout by the desire to prevent compromising the various organisations S.O.E. had built up. Although a gentleman's agreement had been reached with S.I.S. on this score, continued attempts were made on the latter's part to infiltrate agents who invariably got picked up by one or other of S.O.E.'s organisations which, having received no advance warning of their arrival, treated them with utmost suspicion.

Eventually, S.O.E. was bound to adopt the same attitude with regard to the Intelligence Service which it controlled. To emphasise this point it should be understood that in the field of Intelligence there are very often only one or two sources which can provide a particular piece of information. In nearly every case satisfactory arrangements had been made by the local Intelligence people to establish contact with these sources by methods which embraced the security of the source and of the Intelligence Service. The arrival of an outside agent who had instructions to procure information of a certain type would inevitably lead him to contact the source already in use. There was thus a hundred per cent increase in the security risk to the source and through him to the local Intelligence Organisation. The folly of this procedure is very well illustrated in the circumstances which led to Truelsen's evacuation form the country.

A particularly brilliant Intelligence operation had resulted in the penetration of the enemy experimental U-boat station at Høruphav. This operation had been carried out as a result of instructions which had been issued by S.O.E. H.Q., which in turn had been requested by S.I.S. to make every possible attempt to obtain the information required. At the same time, unknown to S.O.E., an S.I.S. agent was also trying to secure this information, and his lack of caution led to the arrest of Truelsen's local contact, who was unfortunately in a position to compromise his chief. Truelsen, therefore, had to be evacuated in order to preserve the security of the Organisation. It is needless to emphasise the irritation caused to the local Intelligence Organisation by the attempts of S.I.S. to maintain its own agents in Denmark.

The Danish Section was, therefore, obliged to act in a screening capacity to protect the interests of S.O.E. people in the Field. In Stockholm difficulties also arose from the activities of the S.I.S. officers concerned with Denmark with whom Turnbull was not always in full agreement. Continual apprehensions, which were felt by the Danish Section, made co-operation difficult. The relationship between the two Departments in London was frequently being upset by the reports of minor "incidents" from Stockholm.

From the S.I.S. side much irritation was felt that no direct contact was established between the S.I.S. officers in Stockholm and Colonel Nordentoft. In the early stages of the war the relationship between S.O.E. and the "Princes" was too delicate to admit any possible confusion arising in the minds of Nordentoft and his colleagues about the functions and interests of the two British Departments, and S.O.E. consistently refused to permit S.I.S. officers contact with Nordentoft.

Later, as collaboration between Nordentoft and S.O.E. developed, and mutual confidence was securely established, S.I.S. again reopened the question but it was apparent that Nordentoft had no wish to have contact with the S.I.S. officers in Stockholm. Indeed, during a visit to London in December 1944, Nordentoft was introduced to S.I.S. H.Q. and a meeting took place at which no S.O.E. officers were present. S.I.S. was able to ask Nordentoft personally for direct contact with his office in Stockholm. This, however, was flatly refused.

In spite of these difficulties the Section in London was determined to work for the best possible co-operation with S.I.S. and accordingly instituted a series of regular meetings. These meetings eventually bore such good results that when Allied military operations into Jutland appeared to be imminent, no difficulty was encountered in reaching an agreement to set up a joint S.O.E.-S.I.S. team to assist the Allied Task Force, and S.I.S. unreservedly placed their officer under the control of the Danish Section representative. In many ways it was a pity that this team never had an opportunity to function and give concrete proof of the goodwill which was established between the two Departments in the later stages of the war.

As stated in the narrative, Denmark is too small a country for two separate Allied organisations to operate there without crossing each other's lines and adding to the local risks.

Appendix V

AIR OPERATIONS

During 1941 and 1942 the indifferent state of communications between Denmark and the U.K. made planning of air operations a difficult and protracted affair. Another contributing factor to the difficulties which existed was the lack of experience of the embryo S.O.E. organisation and its local collaborators. Points were selected and sent to the U.K. by film message via the Stockholm Mission, and this slow process resulted in very few air operations taking place during the first two years.

In 1943, however, there was some improvement. Concurrently with the growth of the Underground Organisation, wireless communication was established on a more reliable footing, though owing to the fact that the telegraphist worked in Copenhagen while the majority of dropping points were in Jutland, delays were inevitably caused by the necessity of passing instructions from one end of the country to the other.

The dropping point was described in a wireless message to S.O.E. H.Q. A repetition of this description was then sent back to the Chief Organiser asking for confirmation by crack signal that this was in fact correct. At the same time the B.B.C. code name and recognition signals for the Reception Committee and the aircraft were forwarded to the Chief Organiser, who again had to acknowledge receipt of these by further crack signal. Not only did this cause some delay but the entire procedure was somewhat insecure and clumsy. It obliged the Chief Organiser to contact the leader of his Reception Committee an unnecessary number of times in arranging a single dropping operation and, furthermore, since the messages were usually encoded in the telegraphist's code, it meant that an operation could be compromised in the event of the telegraphist being arrested.

Once this procedure had been completed, a code message in the form of, for example, "Greetings to Maria" (Maria being the B.B.C. code name allotted to the point in question) was broadcast at the end of the B.B.C. 6 p.m. Danish News Bulletin. The Reception Committee on hearing the name would stand by at the point on the same night as the broadcast took place. In the event of the operation being cancelled due to bad weather (or some other reason) after the broadcast had taken place, there was no means of informing the Reception Committee, and on occasions committees were obliged to stand by when no attempt was made to carry out the operation.

During the last quarter of 1944 when it became apparent that air operations would be materially increased, the whole procedure was examined with a view to simplifying it and ensuring better security. The first step that was taken was to de-centralise the Reception Organisation in the Field and the country was divided into three Reception areas – Jutland, Fyn and Zealand – each under a separate Reception leader. These leaders were "Toldstrup" (Jutland), Hecht Johansen (Fyn) and Stig Jensen (Zealand), each of whom had his own code for wireless communication with S.O.E. H.Q.

In this way no one outside the Reception Organisation could learn of the operations which were being planned. It then became apparent that something must be done to cut down the number of wireless messages relating to anyone dropping operation and also to reduce to a minimum the number of contacts necessary between the Reception leader and his committee.

Accordingly, S.O.E. H.Q. dispensed with the procedure of requesting the Reception leader to confirm his initial description of the point. A further simplification was effected by allotting to each Reception leader a large number of B.B.C. code names and ground signals which he himself allotted without reference to London H.Q. This resulted in effective reduction in the contact between the Reception leader and his committee.

In order that the broadcasting of operational B.B.C. code messages should avoid giving any indication to the enemy of the operations which were to be attempted on any one particular night, a comprehensive deception plan was put into practice. It was understood that the code names which had been issued to each Reception leader would be used for dummy broadcasts, although in order to avoid confusion it was expressly made clear that a B.B.C. code message would not become operational until forty-eight hours after the transmission of the wireless message to S.O.E. H.Q. This enabled the code names to be repeated indefinitely and gave added security to the operations.

The system of describing dropping points was based on the use of the Danish General Staff 1:100,000 maps of Denmark published in book form and comprising three volumes. The system evolved by the Danish Section, which proved to be most accurate and favoured by the R.A.F., appeared extremely amateurish but turned out to be most reliable in view of the large numbers of mutilations that crept into the W/T messages. It consisted merely of the number of the book, page and square in which the point was situated. It then gave a cross-bearing in kilometres from the first letter of easily identifiable place names printed in that square.

As a finishing touch to the operational procedure, it was arranged to repeat all B.B.C. code messages on the second Danish News Broadcast at 8.0 p.m. and, in the event of operations being cancelled after the first broadcast had taken place, a special B.B.C. code message was used in the second broadcast to indicate this cancellation. This reduced the number of occasions on which Reception Committees had to turn out unnecessarily.

A refinement in operational procedure was the use of fixed and mobile Eureka Beacons. The former were operated on every night on which air operations took place and, in order that the team responsible for each Beacon should know when to turn out, five B.B.C. code messages were allotted to each Beacon – the broadcasting of any of these code names bringing the Beacon into operation. As far as mobile Eurekas were concerned the country was divided up into twenty zones, the plan being to have three or four mobile Eurekas available for use on the dropping points in any particular zone. These mobile Eurekas used the same recognition signal as the Reception Committee and the Reception leader informed S.O.E. H.Q. on which points Eurekas would be operating. In all there were four fixed Beacons situated on the West Coast of Jutland as follows:

1. 56°43′ 00″   North
   08°34′ 40″   East
2. 56°21′ 35″   North
   08°33′ 48″   East
3. 56°06′ 09″   North
   09°00′ 10″   East
4. 57°05′ 05″   North
   09°01′ 02″   East

Fifty-four mobile Eurekas were dropped by air and on 8th May 1945, thirty-six were in operation – the remainder having been either smashed on landing, or destroyed to avoid being compromised or captured by the enemy.

One further development is worthy of mention. After much planning and delays due to hard weather, a successful water drop was carried out on 28th February 1945. It was unfortunate perhaps that the difficulties of producing a sufficient number of the special type containers required for water dropping prevented this method from being fully exploited. The Reception Organisation in the Field were greatly impressed by the increased security afforded by water dropping as it enabled the Reception Committee to choose its own time to collect the containers, although this advantage was to some extent offset by the difficulties involved in retrieving the containers from the water. The second and last water drop took place on 23rd April 1945.

The methods employed on the ground in each of the three Reception areas were by no means uniform – the size of the Committee varying greatly, as did the number of containers delivered to each point. For example, owing to the difficulties of transporting containers away from the point, it was rarely practicable to deliver more than twelve containers to any one point in Jutland, whereas, in Fyn, a dropping operation always comprised twenty-four containers. The same applied to Zealand, where Stig Jensen also successfully introduced the novel idea of arranging for the reception of the loads of as many as three aeroplanes at one point, thus on several occasions seventy-two containers were successfully handled at one place.

The situation on the ground was usually controlled by the number of men available for reception work and, more particularly, the transport at their disposal. At the end of April 1945, Jensen went so far as to plan an operation in which ten aircraft were to deliver 240 containers at a point situated alongside a railway; a special train manned by members of the Underground was to stand by ready to convey the containers to their destination in Copenhagen. However, the surrender of the Germans on 4th May prevented this operation ever being carried out.

There follows a table giving a short summary of air operations to Denmark:

Date	Sorties		Men	Tons	A/C Missing	Remarks
	Attempted	Successful				
1941	1	1	2	-	-	-
1942	4	4	12	-	-	3 packages
1943						
Jan-Mar	4	2	8	1	-	4 containers 5 packages
Apr-Jun	4	4	7	2	-	14 containers 3 packages
Jul-Sep	9	8	3	7	-	61 containers 8 packages
Oct-Dec	8	5	5	2	1	21 containers 2 packages
1944						
Jan-Mar	3	3	2	3	-	24 containers 3 packages
Apr-Jun	8	7	3	8	1	72 containers 10 packages
Jul-Sep	12	12	2	15	-	144 containers 6 packages
Oct-Dec	104	71	10	143	3	1402 containers 54 packages
1945						
Jan-Mar	83	54	5	109	4	1059 containers 59 packages
Apr-May	174	114	-	330	8	3098 containers 409 packages

Totals

Date	Sorties		Men	Tons	A/C Missing	Remarks
	Attempted	Successful				
1941	1	1	2	-	-	-
1942	4	4	12	-	-	3 packages
1943	25	19	21	12	1	100 containers 18 packages
1944	127	93	17	169	4	1642 containers 73 packages
1945	257	168	5	439	12	4157 containers 468 packages
1941-45	414	285	57	620	17	5899 containers 562 packages

Appendix VI

SEA OPERATIONS

At the beginning of 1944, it was agreed that D.D.O.D.(I) [Deputy Director of Operation Division (I)] would earmark two of their fishing vessels for operating in conjunction with Danish boats in the North Sea. Preliminary investigations of the possibility of sending supplies via this method were successfully concluded, and the skipper of the fishing boat "Aladin" based in Esbjerg agreed to carry out the job.

Contact, however, between the skipper and Muus through various cut-outs was not altogether successful, and the disappearance of the cut-out in Esbjerg led the skipper to believe he might be compromised. The boat, having been held up by bad weather, eventually sailed in the middle of March but, on finding no British boat at the rendezvous, ran into Grimsby without waiting. The absence of any British boat was assumed by the skipper to confirm his misgivings that the operation had been compromised on the Danish side. Unfortunately, he had received no instructions about waiting at the rendezvous. Thus, the first attempt ended in failure.

Not discouraged, S.O.E. pursued its efforts and a few days later Muus was able to report that a second fishing boat was ready to make a further attempt. The proposed operation had to be cancelled at the last moment owing to the reaction of the Danish skipper to the broadcast in which it was officially announced that the "Aladin" had been captured by the British Navy. The Danes, of course, had not realised that this broadcast was put out on purpose in order to ensure that the enemy would not suspect the skipper of the "Aladin" of escaping on purpose.

Delays of one sort or another held up operations during the spring. The arrival of Flemming Juncker in the U.K. provided the Danish Section with a great deal of information which had been lacking earlier in the year, and the establishment of wireless communications with Jutland made the planning of further operations considerably simpler. A series of meetings held with D.D.O.D.(I) reviewed the previous procedure employed and considerable improvements were devised. This included the provision of a crack signal to signify the departure of the Danish vessels from their home ports as well as code messages for broadcast on the B.B.C. Danish News, which would be received by the Danish skipper while he was at sea. It was considered more secure for the Danish vessel, on proceeding to sea in company with the fishing fleet, to carry out normal fishing during the first two or three days.

By the means of the B.B.C. code message the skipper would then be instructed to be at the rendezvous within twelve hours of the time of the broadcast, where he was to await the arrival of the British boat. This was a considerable improvement in the procedure and in fact worked most successfully. Further delays in the early summer were caused by the invasion of the Continent and S.H.A.E.F.'s ban of fishing vessels operating in the North Sea, and it was not until 11th August that the first successful operation took place and four-and-a-half tons of stores were successfully transferred at sea.

The rendezvous chosen for these operations was on the North side of the Outer Silver Pit, 54° 08′ N and 02° 09′ East. This rendezvous was selected as it could be easily recognised by any professional fisherman by sounding methods and did not necessitate the use of navigational instruments which might not be in the fisherman's possession.

The stores were packed in watertight tin containers placed in fish boxes. The transfer of stores from one vessel to another was, of course, not an easy matter, more particularly if any sea was running. The usual method employed was for the Danish vessel to lie a short distance astern to the British boat from which stores could be transferred by a warp. As well as arms, diesel and lubricating oil had to be supplied to the Danish boats as stocks in Denmark available for the fishing fleet were extremely limited. On arriving at the rendezvous, the Danish vessel then returned to the fishing ground and sailed back to its home port in company with other fishing vessels.

The next successful sea operation took place towards the end of September, when 4 agents and stores were successfully transferred to two Danish fishing vessels. This was the last operation undertaken in 1944 as the fishing season closed at the end of September.

Until the opening of the fishing season early in the New Year planning both in the Field and at H.Q. proceeded at full speed and a further successful operation took place in the middle of March. This was followed by another successful operation in the middle of April. The next transfer of stores was planned for the first week in May, but the surrender of the German Army brought these operations to a close. In all 16½ tons of stores were shipped to Denmark by means of these operations.

The lesson which was learnt in connection with these operations was that the organiser in the Field must be stationed close to the port of departure and must have a telegraphist near at hand. In the beginning of 1944 endless delays were caused by the failure of wireless messages relating to sea operations to reach the skippers in time. The delays were caused by the distance between the telegraphist and the organiser, and between the organiser and the skipper. Once messages could be passed direct to Jutland "Toldstrup" was placed in charge of sea operations.

The practice of using aircraft for reconnaissance and assistance to establish contact between the British and Danish boats was well justified though it would not have been possible to operate this aid unless enemy air activity over the North Sea had been reduced to a minimum. The most difficult phase in these operations was naturally that of unloading the compromising cargo and getting it safely ashore in the face of enemy controls, but fortunately the Reception Organisation in Jutland was always able to devise ingenious methods by which the enemy were outwitted, and no stores were ever lost while being unloaded.

There were, of course, a large number of sea operations between Sweden and Denmark but no mention of this is made here as full details can be found in the history of the Stockholm Mission.

Appendix VII

FINANCE

Unlike other countries in which S.O.E. conducted subversive operations, there was no Danish authority outside the country with whom a financial agreement could be concluded, and since Danish assets in the U.K. were subject to the Trading with the Enemy (Occupied Territory) Orders, means had to be devised for ensuring that the S.O.E. Organisation in the Field was not prejudiced by lack of funds. It was, therefore, the object of S.O.E. to maintain a separate organisation in Denmark composed of business men who would be prepared to supply funds to the S.O.E. Organisation, but who would not engage in any other form of illegal activity. This object was most successfully achieved.

Every S.O.E. agent who was despatched from the U.K. to Denmark carried a certain amount of Danish currency which had been obtained in the U.K., either from funds already in possession of H.M. Government or from those which were brought into the country by escapees from time to time. Danish currency was also purchased in and infiltrated direct from Stockholm, where the S.O.E. Mission supplied Danish currency to the Chief Organiser and, at a later date, to "Toldstrup", the Jutland Reception leader, as well as to a number of local employees who were engaged in illegal traffic across the Sound between Denmark and Sweden.

The method by which the greater part of funds required by the S.O.E. Organisation in Denmark were raised was by securing contributions from Danish business men on the security of an equivalent sum in sterling being placed to their credit in the U.K. This method was successfully introduced by Mr. Turnbull of the Stockholm Mission, who, during the period 1940 to 29th August 1943, was able to make contact with various Danes who travelled to Sweden for commercial reasons.

It was found expedient to appoint a Paymaster in the Field, whose responsibility it was to raise such money as was required from time to time. The first Paymaster was Landretsagfører [District Attorney or Prosecutor] Mr. Federspiel, who carried out these duties until his arrest in January 1944.

He was succeeded by Jonas Colin who, unfortunately, however, became compromised two months later, and the third holder of this appointment who continued to function until the liberation was Count Adam Moltcke.

The Paymaster was not only responsible for the raising of sufficient funds to meet the requirements of the S.O.E. Organisation, but also for seeing that these funds were disbursed in accordance with instructions of S.O.E. H.Q. In order to exercise some control over expenses, a list of numbers was furnished to the Paymaster by S.O.E. H.Q. These numbers, which were of three digits, were unknown to anyone else in the Field. The procedure was that when the S.O.E. Chief Organiser notified H.Q. by wireless that he needed a certain sum of Danish currency for a purpose which he specified, S.O.E. instructed him to apply to the Paymaster for the release of certain specified numbers on the list in the Paymaster's possession – each number being valued at 5,000 kroner – which covered the amount in question. Later this system was abandoned when Count Moltcke was issued with his own one-time pad and given contact to the S.O.E. wireless communication. Instructions were then issued direct to the Paymaster.

A further method used for raising funds was the infiltration into Denmark of diamonds which were subsequently sold for cash on the instructions of the Paymaster.

In 1943 a special system was introduced for raising money from Danes who might not have sufficient confidence in lending money without any written acknowledgment regarding security. To meet this and to enable the Chief Organiser to raise money quickly in emergencies, a number of small cards known as "Promissory Notes" were issued to him. These had to be filled in by the Chief Organiser and entitled the bearer to be refunded the sum of £500 on presentation in a certain room at the War Office.

The following figures show the amounts of Danish kroner raised by the different methods:

	Kr.	Kr.
Direct infiltration from the U.K.	510,203.00	
Direct infiltration from Stockholm	274,142.00	
		784,345.00
Sale of smuggled diamonds		415,919.00
Against sterling credit at Headquarters		5,117,489.00
Promissory Notes		350,219.00
	Total	6,667,972.00

In order to exercise a system of general control over finance with the minimum of correspondence between S.O.E. H.Q. and the Field, the Chief Organiser submitted to H.Q. a monthly budget. This budget was carefully scrutinised by the Danish Section, who then submitted it to the Finance Officer for his approval. When this approval was obtained, the Paymaster in the Field was authorised by S.O.E. H.Q. to make certain fixed monthly payments to persons such as Regional Commanders, Reception leaders, the Chief Organiser etc., and only if the monthly budget was exceeded, had the sanction of S.O.E. to be obtained prior to paying out the amount in excess.

While the system was not absolutely watertight, it did enable S.O.E. H.Q. to keep a check on expenditure in the Field, and it may be said that the liquidation of the Financial Organisation and the meeting of all claims against S.O.E. was cleared up without any difficulty.

Finally, it should be stated to the credit of the Danes that they honoured their word, given in the early days, to repay all cash outlays in Denmark made by S.O.E. and, on 25th September 1945, the Danish Finance Minister's cheque for the total amount was handed over.

Appendix VIII

THE STOCKHOLM MISSION

In reviewing the history of the Danish Section of the Stockholm Mission it is essential to divide the history into two distinct periods, a) prior to 29th August 1943, and b) subsequent to 29th August 1943.

In March 1941, Mr. Turnbull arrived in Stockholm to take over his duties as Danish Section Head. At the time he left England, communications with Sweden were so bad that it was necessary for Turnbull to travel via the Middle East, and his journey took him three months.

Before leaving London, he had been given the name of Ebbe Munck as his sole contact in Stockholm. Sir Charles Hambro, K.B.E., M.C., had visited Sweden in October 1940, had sounded out Ebbe Munck and this latter had offered to assist in every way.

At that time communications between Denmark and Sweden were most irregular. There were practically no illegal routes and all messages were carried by bona fide travellers. The work of the Danish Section was, therefore, limited almost entirely to that of being a post office.

Contact with the "Princes" Organisation existed through Ebbe Munck and irregular but valuable intelligence reports came through this channel and were forwarded to London. At that time Turnbull had the assistance of N. Petersen, who acted as chief factotum but who was subsequently transferred to assist in the Gothenburg office. Turnbull had also responsibility for outposts in Helsingborg and Gothenburg.

The Helsingborg Office was under the direction of E.T. Grew, who had consular cover and who was assisted by Mr. Blakeley. In point of fact the Helsingborg office carried out little or no S.O.E. work. Mr. Grew produced a fortnightly report on Danish political and commercial matters but this report was primarily for the Foreign Office. Mr. Blakeley carried out ship watching in the Sound and his reports were telegraphed direct to the Naval Attaché in Stockholm. An additional service carried out by this office was a daily weather report which was telegraphed direct to the Air Ministry. It had been hoped that the Helsingborg office would have been used in connection with the "Minestrone" project, but subsequently this project was turned over to our O.S.S. colleague, Mr. Hass, who operated from American Consular cover in Helsingborg.

The Gothenburg post was under the command of Mr. A.E. Christensen who also enjoyed consular cover. Prior to the development of the illegal routes in the autumn of 1943 the work of the Gothenburg office had been limited to infiltrating into Zealand, via Danish cargo vessels, small consignments of operational stores, black and white propaganda and occasional operational messages. However, after the development of the illegal routes the Gothenburg post became of the greatest importance in that the illegal routes operating from Sweden to Jutland were centred in Gothenburg. The operations which later became known as "Creep" operations were handled by the Gothenburg office. The "Creep" operations are dealt with in full under a separate heading.

The Danish Section in Stockholm acted as agents for P.W.E. in the procuring of Danish political intelligence and in assisting in the infiltration of black and white propaganda into Denmark.

Up to 29 August 1943, the main sources of political intelligence were Erik Seidenfaden, who was at that time the Stockholm correspondent of the leading Danish daily, "*Politiken*", the weekly reports prepared in Denmark by Erling Foss, infrequent reports written by Ebbe Munck and, lastly, a very irregular flow of clandestine newspapers.

One of the main developments arising out of the German action in Denmark in August 1943, was the escape to Sweden of certain members of the "Princes" Organisation. Colonel Nordentoft, Captain Gyth and Captain Winkel succeeded in reaching Stockholm safely – but unfortunately Ritmester Lunding was arrested and subsequently deported to Germany.

The "Princes" then decided to set up an Intelligence Office in Stockholm under the cover of the Danish Legation and they were joined by Commander Mørch, the Danish D.N.I. Colonel Nordentoft and Commander Mørch became Service Attachés and enjoyed full diplomatic cover.

Their Intelligence office, which was called the "Hamilcar" office, was set up with the full approval of the Swedish Intelligence Service who co-operated in providing facilities for couriers and in assisting in the establishment and maintenance of illegal routes and other forms of communication with Denmark.

In the early part of 1944, the "Princes" Organisation which had been taken over by Truelsen, began to make its weight felt, and a regular and voluminous flow of Intelligence reports were sent to the "Hamilcar" office where these reports were analysed, co-ordinated and then sent on to the Danish Section at the British Legation for onward transmission to London by Diplomatic Bag. In addition to these detailed and somewhat voluminous reports the "Hamilcar" office arranged for secret telephone links between Malmö, the island of Hven, and between Elsinore and Helsingborg for the transmission of most urgent Intelligence items. There is no doubt that much of the success of the "Hamilcar" office must be attributed to the co-operation of Swedish officials, particularly Captain Walqvist of Malmö, who rendered outstanding service in giving his blessing and help to the illegal routes operating from his town.

K-Committee
In the summer of 1944, a body named the "K-Committee" was formed under the joint chairmanship of Erling Foss and Ebbe Munck, with one representative from all the larger Danish Resistance Organisations. The objects of the Committee were: a) to co-ordinate the illegal routes, ensuring a maximum efficiency with the minimum of duplication and the pooling of resources; b) to endeavour to prevent the return to Denmark of persons whose journey was not approved by the Committee. It was arranged that none of the illegal routes would carry persons who were not supplied with a "laissez passer" by the K-Committee.

This was a most important step as many young Danes who had been seriously compromised and evacuated to Sweden found it difficult to reconcile themselves to a life of inactivity in Sweden and endeavoured to return, ignoring the possible consequences. The Danish Section of the S.O.E. Mission was consulted when personnel evacuated by the "Table" Organisation attempted to return to Denmark against orders.

Klip Office
This office started simultaneously with the K-Committee and performed a most useful function in co-ordinating the despatch of British propaganda material to the Field. The Committee included representatives from all the more important Resistance Organisations.

Prior to the formation of this Committee there had been a deplorable tendency on the part of some of the local organisations, particularly the "Dansk Samling", to monopolise propaganda material for their own organisation. All propaganda material, leaflets, newsreels, newspapers etc., sent from the Danish Section in London were passed over to this Committee and a really satisfactory dissemination was achieved.

Liaison with Outside Departments: SIS
Although the procurement of Danish Intelligence was included in the S.O.E. charter and S.O.E. were carrying out this charter to the fullest satisfaction of the Service Departments, there was no doubt that S.I.S. were occupying themselves with obtaining Danish Intelligence. Innumerable attempts were made with the local S.I.S. officers to reach a gentleman's agreement on this matter but the attempts were unsuccessful in that the S.I.S. officer concerned claimed that they were not working in, but through, Denmark. The inability or unwillingness on the part of S.I.S. to co-operate was a source of great disappointment, not only to the Danish Section but also to our "Hamilcar" friends whose Field Organisation was compromised on several occasions by S.I.S. agents. Our relationship with the local Section V officer was, however, cordial, and harmonious liaison was maintained.

Liaison with Outside Departments: Service Attachés
There was little or no liaison with Service Attachés except on perfectly "straight" matters, but all three Service Attachés were at all times helpful and courteous, and a particular vote of thanks is called for to the Military Attaché, Brigadier Sutton Pratt, who gave his official and unofficial support on many occasions.

Creep
Owing to the difficulty in obtaining airlift during the early part of 1944 it became increasingly desirable for the Danish Section in Stockholm to assist in the transporting of stores to Denmark. Stockholm had been able to cope with the despatch of small packets of wireless components, etc., but no real attempt had ever been made to try and infiltrate large quantities of explosives and weapons.

At that time the most urgent need was for explosives in Jutland in order that the sabotage organisations might be able to implement the London directives to carry out large scale operations on the Jutland railway network. An agreement was reached with certain Danish refugees domiciled in Gothenburg that the Danish Section would assist them in the purchase of a boat and would cover the maintenance and running charges. After some negotiations and many disappointments this route finally became a most dependable service and was successful in transporting the stores listed at the end of this Appendix.

Although Jutland had priority for stores there was, nevertheless, a strong demand for stores, particularly small arms, in Zealand, and it became necessary to establish some satisfactory and regular route between Sweden and Copenhagen. A start was made with two or three local routes operating from Malmö, but it was finally decided that the route directed by two former Field collaborators, Madsen and Dinesen, should be used exclusively for "Creep" operations. Madsen and Dinesen maintained a first-class service, and a large quantity of stores and equipment were successfully infiltrated to Zealand from Malmö.

Welfare

Prior to the pogrom in the autumn of 1943 the number of Danish refugees in Sweden was very small and there was little or no provision for maintaining them. The Danish Minister, Mr. Kruse, who was notoriously weak and apathetic to Danish refugees, would not assist them, and accordingly a considerable number of refugees made their way to the Danish Section of the Stockholm Mission. Even before the establishment of the Danish Refugee Office in Stockholm in October 1943, many Danish refugees who had been intimately connected with the "Table" Organisation came to the Section for financial assistance. During the last twelve months prior to the capitulation the Section was paying out approximately £2,000 a month in allowances.

Although this welfare activity entailed a considerable amount of work it was of considerable importance as many of the people we were helping had been evacuated from the Field on the instructions of local agents who were often obliged to promise them financial assistance in order to secure their evacuation. If the Section had not been able to implement these promises there is no doubt that many of these evacuees would have returned to the Field with disastrous consequences to the Field Organisation.

D.P.T.

Prior to the establishment of the Danish Press Service in the spring of 1944, P.W.E. were dependent on the following sources for the political intelligence necessary for their keeping the Foreign Office fully informed on the Danish political situation and for their servicing the Danish Section of the B.B.C. with broadcast and background material:

a) A weekly report compiled by Erling Foss in Denmark and forwarded by clandestine channels to Stockholm.
b) Political reports prepared by Erik Seidenfsden.
c) Casual items of political intelligence obtained by Ebbe Munck.

The mass migration from Denmark arising out of the German action of 29th August 1943 rendered some form of controlled news agency highly desirable, if only from a security point of view. Leading Danish journalists, therefore, resolved to form a news agency with the object of maintaining an accurate news service combined with some degree of voluntary censorship. Starting with a staff of 4 journalists, under the leadership of Erik Seidenfaden, it gradually developed into the unofficial press department of the Royal Danish Legation in Stockholm, and in the last six months had a staff of some 40 journalists and secretaries under Sten Gudme who was brought over from London specifically for this purpose.

At the request of the Stockholm Mission, P.W.E. agreed to subsidise the Danish Press Service and, in return for this financial assistance, P.W.E. obtained a daily telegram and a regular flow of all illegal publications, also a 24-hour priority in release of news. This tie up with the D.P.T. was a decided asset to S.O.E. from an operational point of view, as it was most desirable that Danes in Denmark should cultivate and retain the habit of listening to the B.B.C.'s Danish broadcasts through which they might one day receive operational instructions.

Danforce

After 29th August 1943, the last remaining units of the Danish Army were disbanded by the Germans and many of the officers interned for a short period. Subsequently, a large number of these officers fled to Sweden and were used to establish a unit which was eventually to return to Denmark.

The formation and training of this unit, which came to be called "Danforce", was carried out at the instigation of General Gørtz, the Danish C.-in-C., and with the connivance of the Swedish authorities, who placed various facilities at the disposal of "Danforce". General Knutzon, who had managed to escape to Sweden, was placed in command of "Danforce".

From among the younger and more active refugees who arrived in Sweden during the last four months of 1943, a further number of recruits was drawn and "Danforce" was organised and trained as a Regiment of two Battalions capable of carrying out coup-de-main operations with particular reference to street-fighting and guerilla warfare. The fact that "Danforce" might be used to assist the Allies in ejecting the Germans from Denmark was known only to a few of the "Danforce" senior officers, certain Allied Departments and to the Swedish Government. On security grounds it was impossible to enlighten the rank and file of "Danforce" as to its true mission and the cover story used was that they were being trained to assist in the carrying out of police duties in a liberated Denmark.

In later discussions and conferences in London, in which attempts were made to assess the conditions in which "Danforce" could be used, it was decided that the situation in Zealand must be such that German forces were prepared to surrender before it would be possible to bring "Danforce" into Denmark.

As there was now a tacit understanding in London that "Danforce" would be used ostensibly for post-hostility watch and ward purposes, it was not an S.F.H.Q. [Special Forces Head Quarters] responsibility to supervise its training and to undertake its equipment. It was agreed that General Dewing should be responsible to S.H.A.E.F. for assisting in the training and reporting on the state of efficiency and capacity for operations of "Danforce". The functions of the Danish Section of the Stockholm Mission were limited to acting as a liaison body between General Dewing and the General Staff of "Danforce".

Towards the end of August 1944, discussions took place between leading members of the Swedish Government and Danish representatives, the latter acting on behalf of the Danish Prime Minister and other Danish authorities in Denmark, which resulted in the Swedes agreeing in principle that "Danforce" might leave the country to take part in the liberation of Denmark and that it might do so as a fully equipped military unit as soon as a desire to this effect was expressed by S.H.A.E.F.

In December 1944, General Dewing, Head of the S.H.A.E.F. Mission in Denmark, paid a visit to Stockholm where he held discussions with General Knutzon and his staff. After an exchange of talks on the potentialities of "Danforce" and an inspection of the camps and training methods, General Dewing recommended that everything be done to increase the strength of "Danforce", which at that time numbered about 1,800 men.

As the result of an intensive recruiting campaign the strength of "Danforce" was increased to 3,500 fighting personnel with an additional 1,500 auxiliaries, drivers, medical units etc. To assist in their training, arrangements were made for two British officers to be attached to "Danforce" to assist in the infantry training and in instruction in mine lifting and booby traps.

To transport "Danforce" to Denmark a small fleet had been built up from vessels which had either escaped from Denmark or had been chartered from the Swedes. The fleet, which was based on several Swedish harbours on the Sound comprised:

70 fishing cutters
80 small landing craft
3 minesweepers
6 steamers
1 ferry boat

In considering the role to be played by "Danforce" it was apparent that "Danforce" must co-operate very closely with the Danish Resistance Movement, particularly in the operational stages. To assist in this co-operation, it was essential to have speedy lines of communication. S.F.H.Q. were asked to provide an Officer whose responsibility it would be to establish and maintain lines of communication between "Danforce" and the Resistance Movement and between "Danforce" and 21st Army Group via S.F.H.Q.

Major Ray, of the Stockholm Mission, was recalled for briefing as Communications Officer and returned to Sweden on 31st March 1945.

At the end of April 1945, General Dewing made another visit to Stockholm and discussed the final arrangements by which "Danforce" would receive its orders to proceed to the Field.

In April, owing to the developments on the Western Front, "Danforce" was moved up to the Swedish coast to be in a position where they could embark with the minimum of warning.

On 4th May, 21st Army Group instructed "Danforce" to move into Zealand immediately in order to assist in the maintenance of law and order. This order from 21st Army Group coincided with an order from the Danish Prime Minister instructing "Danforce" to proceed to Zealand.

At approximately 10.00 hours on 5th May two light battalions embarked at Helsingborg for Elsinore and by the evening of the 5th the whole of "Danforce" with its equipment was on Danish soil.

After some delay, two battalions were sent to the frontier to undertake patrol and control duties and the remainder were garrisoned in Copenhagen and assisted the Resistance Movement in the general preservation of law and order.

"Moonshine"

The "Moonshine" Operation was a major contribution of the Danish Section to compensate for the insufficient airlift. An important part was played by Colonel Nordentoft and Commander Mørch who were responsible for negotiating with the Swedish authorities.

When Ebbe Munck returned from the U.K. with news of the "Moonshine" operation a committee under the chairmanship of Major Ray was set up to discuss methods of approach to the Swedish Government and the practical means by which the stores could be trans-shipped to Denmark. It was decided that Mr. Erling Foss, Colonel Nordentoft, Commander Mørch and Ebbe Munck should approach their high-placed Swedish political friends and that Major Ray should discuss with Mr. Christensen at Gothenburg the questions of transportation, security, etc. One of the former Field agents, Lieutenant Scavenius, was appointed as liaison officer between the local Swedish authorities in Gothenburg and the S.O.E. office in Gothenburg.

Analysis of 1944 Creep

Plastic   5,620 lbs.

W/T Equipment   3 Vibrators
                             6 rolls of tape
                             Electrical wire recording equipment (for Scala)
                             Power packs and W/T equipment
                             Valves, cables and vibrator packs
                             1 S-Phone set
                             Valves
                             6 M.C.R.
                             1 box wireless equipment
                             50 valves
                             Time Pencils: 1,000
                             Tyre Bursters: 1,000
                             Detonators: 200

Sundries   1,000 compasses

Guns, Revolvers etc.   6 silent Stens and ammo.
                             9 Stens and ammo.
                             8 Colts plus mags. and ammo; 20 mills
                                 grenades and detonators
                             80 automatics and 4,000 rds.
                             14 Stens and 2,800 rds.
                             1 box hand grenades

General Stores   250 fog signal igniters
                             1,200 detonators No. 27
                             14 tins primers
                             10 boxes primers
                             360 primers and 480 detonators
                             750 primers
                             100 detonators
                             1,500 feet Cordtex
                             1,440 ft. Safety fuse
                             100 ft. Cordtex

4 rolls Khaki tape
6 tubes Bostik
2 yds. Rubberised fabric
40 C.E. primers
12 Magnets
84 ampoules
12 A.C. delays
12 bursters
6 cases special underwater charges
328 igniters fuse fog signals
500 igniters strikers
10 boxes fuse matches
100 lbs. Vulcastab

Creep – January 1945

Plastic H.E.	540 lbs.
Primers	2,370
Detonators	2,440
Slide stores	6 cases.
Stens	18 and 3600 rds. ammo.
Large quantity of W/T equipment	A. Mk. II sets, M.C.R.s, Valves
	Vibrator packs
	Signal plans etc.
In addition:	1,000 Sylva Compasses were purchased in Sweden and sent to the Field.

Creep – February 1945

Plastic H.E.	2,304 lbs.
New type composite pack: P.E. and Dets.	38 tins
Various W/T equipment	8 hand generators
	2 S-Phones
	Electrical equipment
	Power packs
Waterproof bags for rifles	20 cases
Abrasive powder	100 lbs.
Commando knives	25

50 tins of this new pack were despatched each week.

Creep – March 1945

Plastic H.E.	1,777 lbs.
Primers C.E. 1 oz.	5,550
Detonators in mags. Mk. II	5,550
Limpets Mk. II	32
Clams M.D.1	64
Switches No. 10 black	1,615
Switches No. 10 red	1,615
Switches No. 5	196
Switches No. 4	132
Cordtex	8,810 ft.
Fuse safety No. 11 Mk. II	6,806 ft.
Fuse A.C. delay (D. 2) with	
Bursters Type 6 Mk. II	64
Igniters, fuse, fog signal	1,860
Igniters, safety fuse	
striking Mk. I/L	1,040
Tool, crimping ICI	22
Tape, adhesive, khaki	742 rolls
Striker boards	44 packets
Balloons long	264
Trap wire .014″	132 reels
Luger automatics	36
Luger spare magazine	36
Vulcastab	20 lbs.

W/T Equipment

M.C.R. sets	31
SCR/195 sets	9
S-Phones	18
Hand generators	4
Receiving and transmitting	
sets AR. 88	1
Nicolls sets	12
Petrol charger, 250w No. 1	
DC/AC type Bo 12 A	1
Radio valves type 7H7	20

Microphones	1 carton
Accumulators 6 x 30 AH dry	10
Aerials, telescopic for SCR/195 AN 30b	10
Headphones, crystal	15
Fluxite	8 tins
Resin core solder	12 reels

Other Equipment

Message containers, Type "R"	12
Typewriters, portable	6
Typewriter ribbons	54
Abrasive powder	100 lbs.

Photographic Equipment

Leica cameras, f 3.5 lens	2
Leica supplementary lenses	
No. 1	2
No. 2	2
Leica cable release	2
Pocket thermometer in case	2
Reloadable Leica cassettes	8
Developing tanks 35 mm	2
Magnifying glass (x 8)	2
Microfile Pan film (35 mm)	200 ft.
D.76 Developer	16 packets
Acid fixer	4 lbs.
Cellophane tape	2 reels
Supplementary lens tables	
Lippmen plate	8 packets
Mat glass 3" x 2"	3 pieces
D.8 Kodak developer	1 packet
Microscope with 2/3" objective lens	1

Creep – April 1945

Plastic H.E.	3,301 lbs.
Primers C.E. 1 oz.	1,320
Detonators in mags., Mk. II	660
Limpets Mk. II	18
Clams M.D.1	36
Switches No. 10 black	1,095
Switches No. 10 red	1,095
Switches No. 5	84
Switches No. 4	212
Cordtex	7,490
Fuse A.C. delay D.2 with	
Bursters type 6 Mk. II	36
Igniters, fuse, fog signal	1,220
Igniters, safety fuse striking	
Mk. 1/L	1,060
Tools, crimping I.C.I.	42
Tape, adhesive, khaki	452 rolls
Striker boards	284 packets
Balloons long	464
Trap wire, .014	152 reels
Fuse, sealing, Mk. III	120 tubes
Fabric rubberised	80 yards
Vulcastab	80 lbs.
Abrasive powder	100 bs.
Tree Spigot operational sets	20

W/T Equipment

S-phones, Admiralty type 868	8
S-phones, ground	3
Valves, radio, type HY 114.b	10
Tape, German recorder	3 reels
Film, microfile pan	24 rolls

Other Equipment

Syringes	48
Iodine	101 bottles
Message containers	
(fountain pens, pencils)	Various

Appendix IX

ACTS OF SABOTAGE

The following acts of sabotage were carried out by the Danish Resistance Movement under the control of S.O.E. H.Q.

20 Feb 43	Frederikshavn	Burmeister & Wain's large Iron Foundry gutted.
15 May 43	Copenhagen	Madsen Machine Gun Factory destroyed by fire.
17 May 43	Lycavej	Accumulator factory "eliminated".
18 May 43	Svendborg	Shipyards destroyed by fire.
	Esbjerg	Shipyards destroyed by fire.
	Aalborg	Shipyards destroyed by fire.
9 Apr 43	Copenhagen	Explosion in a coastal mining vessel under construction at Nordbjaerg & Weddels shipyard. Damage estimated at 88,000 Kr. (Approx £4,400).
4 Apr 43	Skadvinge	Explosion at Flax Scutching Factory. Watchman overpowered by 4 men and bomb placed in dynamo. Considerable damage caused. Factory was left in flames and dynamo, power house and stocks of raw materials totally destroyed.
5 Apr 43	Copenhagen	Violent explosion at Hartmanns Maskinfabrik. Explosives were placed on the roof of an adjacent transformer station. The roof was torn off and much damage done to the transformer station itself.
	Copenhagen	Fire in the hardware stores belonging to Dansk Svensk Staal Co. The method used was to bore a hole in one of the window frames and spray the interior with inflammable liquid, the liquid then being set alight.

8 Apr 43	Copenhagen	Violent explosion at the motor repair shop "Super Service", Blegdamsvej. Considerable damage to machinery estimated at Kr. 100,000 (£5,000).
	Copenhagen	H.E. bomb on roof of a transformer belonging to the engineering firm of Petersen & Wraae. Transformer damaged.
11 Apr 43	Copenhagen	Explosions at workshops belonging to Heiber & Co. Considerable damage to workshops, machinery and motor vehicles.
3 May 43	Holte	Badminton Hall burnt out. This building was used by the Germans for testing barrage balloons. Considerable damage was caused.
5 May 43	Copenhagen	Explosions followed by fire at Nordbjaerg & Wedells shipyard. Considerable damage caused, also to adjacent yards of Eriksen & Grøn. At N. & W. 2 speed boats and a motorboat were burned, as well as a number of spare parts for speed boats. 30-35 Danish yachts in the vicinity of the yards were also destroyed.
9 May 43	Bagsvaerd	Explosion at Maskinfabrikken "Kik", which caused considerable damage.
1 May 43	Aalborg	Explosion in the Rørdal Cement Factory. Cement house blown up. Fires spread to oil storage where about 450 litres of oil destroyed.
2 May 43	Lyngby	Explosion at Accumulator Factory. Gas and water pipes destroyed by 2 H.E. bombs and building damaged.
10 May 43	Svendborg	Fire at Shipyard. Engine room and machinery completely destroyed, also all spare parts. The damage is estimated at approximately £100,000, and repairs will take 2-3 months.
	Copenhagen	Explosion at Danish Machine Gun Factory (Dansk Industri Syndikat). An electrical distributor was completely destroyed and a number of adjacent workshops were damaged. Many drawings and plans were lost. There were 12 sabotage guards on duty.

13 Apr 43	Ringe	Efte Furniture Factory burnt out. Damage estimated at several hundred thousand kroner.
	Aalborg	Piles of timber belonging to German Army fired. Estimated damage £500.
11 May 43	Aalborg	Explosion at shipyards pumping station. Considerable damage caused.
12 May 43	Aarhus	Two explosions on 2 German ships. One (a transport) sprang a leak, the other (an armed merchant vessel used as a "Sperrbrecher") was heavily listing. Both vessels were undergoing repairs and were inside the closed German area under German guard.
21 Jun 43	Copenhagen	Glud & Marstrand, manufacturers of tinplate and enamelled articles, considerably damaged.
23 Jun 43	Odense	Thrige, electrical machinery, considerably damaged.
	Aarhus	Aarhus Motor Co. considerably damaged, transformer station completely wrecked.
1 Jul 43	Randers	Skandia Railway Carriage Shops. This factory had just received an urgent order for 300 coaches for the Germans. It was decided that the best method of attack was to blow up the transformer station. After two unsuccessful attempts to penetrate the factory, the sabotage guard was heavily reinforced, but a third attempt was a complete success. One transformer was totally destroyed, the other so seriously damaged that it had to be sent away for repairs. By way of diversion, incendiary attacks were made on several smaller factories, one of which (Langaa Iron Factory) was burnt out.

2 Jul 43	Aalborg	This factory, the Rørdal Cement Factory, supplies the bulk of the rapid-hardening Portland cement used for the construction of German bunkers in Denmark. The two main targets were the transformer station and 4 rotating packing machines with a capacity of 67,000 sacks daily. There was an armed sabotage guard of 18 men. 1 transformer and 3 of the packing machines were completely wrecked.
5 Jul 43	Aalborg	Aalborg Shipyards. The pumping station was wrecked and the wall of the dry dock torn open from top to bottom. The attack caused the dock to be put out of commission for a fortnight, and then it was worked with the aid of small mobile pumps which took 2-3 days to empty the dock of water, whereas previously the dock was emptied in less than 3 hours.
8 Jul 43	Odense	Nordisk Gimmi Rubber Factory successfully attacked.
9 Jul 43	Odense	Smith & Co. Ironware Factory successfully attacked.
10 Jul 43	Copenhagen	A.T. Hansen, Joinery. This firm was working solely for the "Wehrmacht" and turned-out various articles manufactured from wood. The factory and stores were totally destroyed by fire. The value of the stores was assessed at about £400,000.
14 Jul 43	Aalborg	Hemp Factory. This factory was owned by a Danish Nazi and was working solely for the Germans. The warehouse contained a large stock of German feeding stuff and building materials.
18 Jul 43	-	German merchant vessel S.S. *Duisburg* damaged by limpet.
Aug 43	Elsinore	German auxiliary cruiser sunk. Skandinavian Motor Factory. Transformer destroyed and capacity of factory reduced by 50% for eight months.

This firm was engaged solely on the manufacture of spare parts for the Wehrmacht.

Skandinavian Gummi. Stock of rubber clothing intended for Wehrmacht destroyed by fire. Loss valued at £10,000.

Finnish vessel *Gottfred* (3,500 tons). Sunk. Two Dutch vessels, one carrying parts for U-boats and diesel motors. Sunk.

A large number of attacks on German transport including the blocking of 29 goods locomotives in a depot.

Sep 43	Odense	Thrige, electrical machinery, transformer station destroyed by a bomb (2nd attack).
	Odense	Shipyards. German minesweeper sunk, followed by a strike of 3,400 men as protest against German sabotage guard.
	Odense	Sorensen. 12 German cars destroyed by fire.
	Odense	Fehr. Garage with 30/40 German vehicles destroyed with explosives.
	Aarhus	Boat Yards. Four speed boats destroyed with explosives.
	Copenhagen	Nordisk Radio. Destroyed by bombs.
	Aalborg	Private Railways. 6 locomotives destroyed. 6 Transformer Stations – supplying power to the Germans in various parts of the country – blown up.
	Jutland	Various attacks on railway network.
Oct 43	Aalborg	German Military Headquarters blown up.
	Copenhagen	The closely guarded Gestapo Headquarters badly damaged by dropping bombs through the ventilators. Various factories producing aircraft accessories have been attacked, and a hangar at Kastrup aerodrome was burnt down.
		An electrical workshop producing jamming equipment was blown up.

Nov 43	Jutland	9 transformers were simultaneously destroyed in South Jutland. Entire border district in Flensburg was without electric power and light for days.
		The train ferry *Sjaelland* from Nyborg to Kørsor was burnt out. It will take over 12 months to repair, damage estimated at Kr. 1,500,000.
	Copenhagen	Radio equipment factory was completely destroyed by bombs and incendiaries – 700 radio sets were burnt out.
	Aarhus	Main switch box controlling the railway station and marshalling yard destroyed.
	Jutland	Railway network linking up Aarhus, Aalborg and Silkeborg was cut and all bridges blown up. Silkeborg was at this time the headquarters of General Hanneken.
	Aarhus	Motor Works and transformer destroyed and main plant attacked.
	Aarhus	German minesweeper seriously damaged in harbour after being attacked with limpet.
	Aarhus	German motor torpedo boat blown up crossing the harbour.
	Copenhagen	Naval yard attacked with incendiaries where Danish commandeered aircraft were kept. The fire destroyed most of the buildings and their contents.
	Copenhagen	A/S Siemens. Workshop and stores buildings completely destroyed by explosion and fire. Factory production stopped.
	Copenhagen	Globe Shoe Factory and a Furniture Factory. Factory buildings burned down by largest fire seen in Copenhagen for many years. Thirteen people hurt and large stores of valuable wood, irreplaceable machinery and stores of leather destroyed. Damage estimated at Kr. 1,000,000.

	Copenhagen	American Apparat Co. Completely destroyed by fire. Damage estimated at Kr. 1,500,000. Large stores of wireless sets and irreplaceable machinery destroyed. Production has ceased.
	Aarhus	Electrical signal control tower at Aarhus Station blown up and points and rails blown up north of station. Damage estimated at Kr. 1,000,000 for tower alone. Rails round Aarhus also blown up.
Dec 43	Copenhagen	K.A. Hartmann's Machinery Factory. Two storey building torn apart by explosions. Nearby shoe factory also severely damaged. Production stopped.
	South Jutland	Varde Steel Works. Large scale attack by 50 armed saboteurs. New power plant completely destroyed, as were two compressors and blast furnace. Many machines irreplaceable. Damage considerable. Steelworks were producing castings for submarine parts and tank wheels.
	Copenhagen	Burmeister & Wain. Power plant in engine shops completely destroyed by violent explosion, followed by a large fire.
	Copenhagen	Dansk Industri Syndikat. Largest modern arms factory in Denmark. Most important building producing A.A. guns and parts totally destroyed by explosion and fire.
Jan 44	Horsens	Acetylene Gas Factory severely damaged by bomb.
	North Jutland	Railway system cut in three different places.
	Copenhagen	Three explosions at Burmeister & Wain. Main shop and transformer completely destroyed.
	Esbjerg	Branch of Aarhus Oliemølle destroyed by fire. Several hundred tons of mustard seed destroyed.

	Copenhagen	Allways Radio Works completely destroyed by fire.
	Odense	Ship sunk by sabotage.
	Copenhagen	General Motors – main transformer blown up and completely destroyed.
Feb 44	Copenhagen	Bomb explosion destroyed large ammonia plant belonging to big Copenhagen works.
	Copenhagen	Extensive damage was done when bombs exploded in Bro's Houlberg's Factory (Slaughterhouse and sausage factory) in Kødbyen (Meat City). This concern was put out of action for some time.
	Ringe	Ringe Asphalt Factory distillation apparatus destroyed by fire.
	Holbaek	Engine and several coaches derailed at Station.
	Holbaek	Scadinavisk Mobelvarksted destroyed by fire. Damage estimated at Kr. 100,000.
	Aalborg	The large German ship *Dorpat* sunk after a violent explosion which took place on board the ship during the day. The *Dorpat* was just about to leave Aalborg after a major overhauling and reparation.
	Aarhus	A rail track south of Aarhus was blown up in several places.
Mar 44	Nastred	Toy Factory of P.A. Skroeger, making patterns for Germany, completely destroyed.
	Aarhus	German telephone exchange seriously damaged by explosion.
	Jutland	Main telephone exchange of the Jutland Telephone Co. severely damaged by explosion.
	Odense	Husmands School, German Police H.Q., attacked with H.E. bomb.
	Aalborg	Dangerous fire at shipyard.
	Aalborg	H.E. bomb caused very severe damage to the printing presses in the premises of Aalborg Stiftstidinde.

	Copenhagen	Group of factories at Ørholm destroyed by fire.
	Copenhagen	Copenhagen Gas Works severely damaged by explosion.
Apr 44	Copenhagen	German ship *Minna Corda* wrecked by explosion.
	Copenhagen	Ufa Film Co. Offices and stores completely destroyed.
	Copenhagen	H.Q. of D.N.S.A.P. labour office, Østerbro, blown up.
	Copenhagen	Skandinavisk Motor Co. completely destroyed by bombs and fire.
	Copenhagen	Himmerland Electricity Supply Co. Transformer wrecked – local consumption severely cut.
	Copenhagen	Carltorp Factory, Roskildevej. Damaged estimated at Kr. 750,000.
	Fredericia	Transformer Station wrecked by fire.
	Helsingør	Shipyards, smithy, boiler room and foundry burned out. Total damage Kr. 1,000,000.
	Limdershov	Railway Fredericia-Esbjerg line cut.
	Rødovre	Transformer Station destroyed.
May 44	Copenhagen	Klostergade Printing Works badly damaged.
	Copenhagen	M. Nielsen's Factory. Foundry and metal factory damaged.
	Copenhagen	Power Station at Free Port. This station supplied power to a number of adjacent factories employed on German orders. Its destruction caused a complete cessation of work for over 3 weeks in all the factories except Industri Syndikat which was able to arrange an alternative supply.
	Glostrup	Globus Machine Factory. This factory was engaged on production of cartridge cases, tail fins and steering gear for the Wehrmacht. An attack by 30 saboteurs caused serious damage.
	Copenhagen	P. Sørensen's Engine Factory employed on German orders. The main workshop was entirely destroyed.

	Copenhagen	Kløvermarksvej Airfield. Saboteurs disguised as workmen successfully held up the special guards and destroyed all the workshops and one hangar.
	Copenhagen	Burmeister & Wain. This is Copenhagen's biggest shipbuilding concern and has been extensively exploited by the Germans. It has been attacked on a number of occasions and on this particular one, the compressor shop was destroyed.
	Copenhagen	Burmeister & Wain. A further attack by 25 saboteurs resulted in the destruction of a 4-storey building containing dies and machine tools, and a number of diesel and aero-engines.
	Copenhagen	Pedersen's Radio Factory destroyed.
	Copenhagen	Adler Motor Services severely damaged by 10 saboteurs.
Jun 44	Utterslev	Neutrofon Radio factory. This factory was producing parts for enemy radio location devices. The first attack was not successful but a second operation achieved the complete destruction of this factory.
	Glostrup	Globus Machine Factory. As an extension of the operation in May a further attack was staged by 50 saboteurs. The factory was completely destroyed, damage being assessed at Kr. 2,500,000.
	Copenhagen	Petersen & Wraae's Machine Factory. This operation was not at first successful as some of the bombs failed to explode. A second attempt resulted in the greater part of the factory being destroyed.
	Svendborg	German Naval Units. An attack was made on 4 enemy naval vessels consisting of 2 auxiliary cruisers of 2,000 and 1,000 tons respectively and 2 patrol vessels. 3 of the vessels were sunk and the remaining one badly damaged. This operation was carried out by two men.

	Odense	Holm Nielsen's motor shop, containing 30-40 German military vehicles. A successful operation caused the building to collapse on the German vehicles.
	South Jutland	During the move of 363 Inf. Div. from Bramminge to Dixmude a greater part of the division was successfully delayed for 18 hours by sabotaging the railway.
	Copenhagen	Dansk Akkumulator og Elektro Motorfabrik, a factory working for the Germans, was successfully attacked and great damage resulted.
	Copenhagen	Dansk Industri Syndikat. This factory was engaged in the manufacture of machine and anti-tank guns for the Wehrmacht. It had successfully survived the operation earlier in May so another attack by 80 saboteurs was staged resulting in its complete destruction. This is one of the biggest and most successful sabotage actions ever carried out in Denmark.
Jul 44	Hillerød	Railway Station sabotaged. Damage estimated at Kr. 1,000,000.
	Aarhus	Jensen Bros., Petrol Store. Petrol store, 3 lorries and large consignment of fuel destroyed. Damage estimated at Kr. 100,000.
	Randers	24 hours delay caused by sabotage on main mid-Jutland lines.
	Aarhus	Locomotive sheds – Danish State Railways. 3 bombs exploded causing considerable damage.
	Copenhagen	Englandsvej Armament Factory severely damaged.
	Copenhagen	Clothing factory at Kongensgade making German uniforms, destroyed.
	Aalborg	Svend Overgaard's factory making camouflage materials for the Germans was destroyed.

Aug 44	Kaerby	Transformer Station. Explosion broke German telegraph and teleprint connections with Norway.
	Vejle	Dam and railway embankment near Davgaard. Newly built dam blown by saboteurs. Rail traffic across dam obstructed for some considerable time.
	Copenhagen	Jorgensen Bros. Garage. Building blown up and set on fire.
	Aarhus	Motor work shop belonging to Willy Andersen Aaryhøy. Three explosions followed by fire wrecked the building. Kr. 250,000 damage done.
	Aalborg	Motorcentralen. Workshop and garage wrecked and burned.
	Aarhus	Auto-lager. Motor workshop blown up – other premises in same block also gutted by fire. Damage estimated at several hundred thousand kroner.
	Aalborg	Nordjysk Elektro. Building wrecked by bombs and all installations rendered useless.
	Frederikshavn	A German ship in dock was blown up upon completion of repairs.
	Odense	The S.S. *Røsnaes* which was carrying supplies for the Germans, and had just completed repairs, seriously damaged.
	Vejle	Vejle-Skandenborg railway line blown up and all traffic in both directions temporarily suspended.
	Aalborg	Explosion on double railway track south of Aalborg dislocated all traffic.
Sep 44	Aalborg	Engineering workshops at 72 Hobrovej completely destroyed. Several switchboards, 25 electrometers and other machinery put out of action.
	Kolding	Steil's machine shop working for the Germans was destroyed.
	Randers	The machine shops of Ravn & Fagerlund completely wrecked.

	Aarhus	Universal Factories completely gutted after being blown up and set on fire.
	Aalborg	Mekaniske Vaerksted. A German ship under construction had her after-part destroyed.
	Randers	The shipyards sustained extensive damage when five bombs exploded.
	Copenhagen	The 3,000-ton ship *Irene Oldenburg* being built on the Hansa programme by Burmeister & Wain was sunk the day before she was due to be delivered.
	Aarhus	Derby's shipyards in the Nordhavn were attacked. A bomb exploded in the power station destroying a transformer supplying the engine works. Work suspended until a new power unit was established.
	Herning	A German train carrying troops and material to Karup was attacked at Sunds Station. A large part of the train was derailed. One German soldier was killed and 10 wounded. The line was blocked for at least 48 hours.
	Kolding	Railway line cut at Sejstrup and Ejstrup. Several German patrol trucks blown up and 1,000 litres of petrol set on fire.
	Viborg	German ammunition train derailed. 3 wagons remained intact, and the rest were demolished.
Oct 44	Aalborg	Electrical plant destroyed cutting off power to several German factories.
	Aarhus	Mattress factory destroyed. Damage estimated at 500,000 Kroner.
	Copenhagen	Nazi owned premises "Weinox", Nørre Voldgade, destroyed by fire.
	Aarhus	Schroeder & Rasmussen's motor repair and vulcanising works destroyed by fire following explosions. Fire spread to State Rubber Centre, seven hundred tyres burnt. Damage estimated at Kr. 2,000,000.

Copenhagen	Two violent explosions at motor works Jørgensen & Jensen. Cars in repair shop destroyed.
Aarhus	Considerable damage caused by two bombs in machine shop in southern harbour.
Aarhus	Two bombs exploded in Diana Motor Service Station.
Roskilde	Maglekilde machine factory and iron foundry damaged by violent fire. Many casting models destroyed.
Aarhus	Foundation of 15-ton crane, excavator destined for Germany and three German cars blown up.
Nørresundby	Explosion took place in workshop of Bak's Auto-Ophug. Stores of generator fuel and workshop destroyed.
Copenhagen	Ford Factory damaged. Two German motorships and patterns to the type destroyed.
Copenhagen	Bendix Motor Repair Station partly burnt down after explosions destroying several German cars and motor-cycles.
Copenhagen	Retort House of Maskinhallen Gosch, which makes ignitions for Germans, partly destroyed. Works must remain idle for some time.
Vojens	Goods train blown up and derailed.
Aarhus	Turn table at Frich's Fabrik. Newly built engines temporarily immobilised.
Hjortkjaer	German Military Express blown up between Hjortkjaer and Røde Kro. Engine and 3 coaches destroyed; 24 coaches overturned. 5 persons killed, 25 injured. Line blocked for three days.
Fanø	Ferry between Esbjerg and Fanø blown up and put out of action for some considerable time.
Aarhus	Explosion on German ship *Sharnhorn*. Ship had to be beached.

	Esbjerg	O.T. Offices in Skolegade, 17, attacked by 4 saboteurs. Whole of ground floor collapsed, injuring 3 Germans.
	Esbjerg	12 lorries supplying Wehrmacht blown up.
	Aarhus	Bomb exploded in German watch tower.
	Odense	Public registry offices raided and registers burnt.
	Kauslunde	One armoured car and four German lorries blown up in guarded car-park. Three of the guards injured, two being taken to hospital.
	Copenhagen	Engine sheds at railway goods station were attacked. 15 locomotives were derailed, blocking 25 others. This operation caused the cancellation of a number of goods and passenger trains all over Zealand.
Nov 44	Kaas	3 bomb explosions destroyed motor repair shop.
	Vejle	2 bomb explosions destroyed South Jutland Raffin Olies Anlaeg (Refined Oil Depot).
	Jyderup	4 armed men held up explosives factory and removed 22,000 detonators.
	Copenhagen	10 armed men removed six new private cars from Ford Works, South Harbour.
	Aarhus	Soerensen's Motor Car Workshop completely destroyed. Entire building collapsed destroying all machinery and about 10 cars. Damage estimated at 1,000,000 Kroner.
	Aarhus	3 bombs caused fire which completely burned down Lufttoerringsvaskeriet. Damage 2-300,000 Kroner.
	Copenhagen	Armed saboteurs removed pistols and ammunition from Valby Maskinfabrik.
	Aarhus	Armed men placed bombs in De Forenede Autovaerksteder, which works for the Germans, destroying 10 cars.
	Horsens	Joinery factory "Ebon" including stores and machinery completely destroyed by fire.

Buddinge	Parachute factory considerably damaged.
Copenhagen	Explosion in "National" chemical factory. Fire spread to greater part of building.
Esbjerg	Rope factory working for Germans sabotaged and transformers blown up.
Copenhagen	3 bombs exploded in automobile works of Herning Motor Co., destroying 5 cars and damaging building.
Aarhus	Egequist's Cylinder Reboring Works seriously damaged. Most of valuable machinery damaged.
Roskilde	Much damage to pro-Nazi O. Poulsen's straw-goods factory.
Hornslet	Bomb exploded under car in service station destroying building.
Aarhus	Service Station at Randersvej destroyed by explosion.
Vejle	5 German cars blown up in workshop.
Copenhagen	Saboteurs carried out daring raid on Army's weapon factory at Amager Boulevard and took away 1,200 machine pistols and ammunition.
Odense	5 explosions at Mechanical Company. Building severely damaged and engines and machinery considerably damaged.
Aalborg	Building of contractor firm, C. Carlssen, destroyed by bombs and fire. All drawings destroyed.
Odense	Armed men placed charges in tinned milk and cream factory seriously damaging building and machinery.
Frederiksvaerk	United Iron Foundry buildings severely damaged by explosion in large compression plant.
Randers	Cog factory totally destroyed.
Aarhus	2 bombs exploded in Deularen's plant transformer in harbour. Firm deals with Germans.

Copenhagen	Machine joinery works of Hans Andersen, Taarnby on Amager, has been completely destroyed by fire. Andersen worked exclusively for the Germans.
Aalborg	Railway signal system destroyed by sabotage.
Odense	2 heavy bombs exploded at England Quay at a jetty normally used by six German speed boats. Same night bomb also exploded in harbour basin off Naesbyhoved Forest.
Nakskov	Shipyards attacked and engine rooms of large vessel about to be delivered to Germans destroyed.
Aarhus	2 bombs exploded on slipways in South Harbour. Engine house for slipways collapsed.
Aalborg	Large installation at Skibsvaerft blown up.
Odense	Newly built ship of 3,000 tons ready for delivery to Germans completely destroyed at Staalskibsvaerft.
Halsingborg	Ferry *Store Baelt* taken over by patriots on way to Copenhagen and taken to Sweden.
Svendborg	German naval craft blown up and sunk at Skibsvaerft.
Kattegat	Steamer *Frederikshavn* severely damaged by explosion.
Copenhagen	Extensive sabotage in Burmeister & Wain shipyards. 2 newly built ships of 5,000 and 3,500 tons sunk and later explosion sank third ship.
Copenhagen	Armed saboteurs destroyed two newly built speed boats in the Ford factories at South Harbour.
Lillebaelt	To prevent Danish customs boats from falling into German hands saboteurs blew up *Maagen* and *Leif* in Lillebaelt and sank *Ternen* and *Neptun* in Vordingborg Harbour.

Aalborg	2 enemy patrol ships sunk in harbour.
Aalborg	Ship's gun lying in goods wagon at Station blown up.
Aarhus	Fire on Skovbakken, presumably in German huts by tower. Fire lasted 3 hours.
Copenhagen	Armed men entered Varedirektorat and removed card indices in order to prevent Germans using them to conscript labour.
Kastrup	Saboteurs robbed German patrol depot at aerodrome by attaching pipeline and drawing off 4,000 litres.
Kastrup	2 men removed uniforms and equipment from Fire Station.
Kastrup	3 German aircraft destroyed by explosion on aerodrome.
Copenhagen	Lorry containing 500 German uniforms held up and stolen.
Aalborg	Aerodrome "Vest" attacked by saboteurs. 2 hangars, about 30 aircraft, special aero-mechanical workshop with all tools, and a car containing special tools destroyed. Officers' canteen blown up and many Germans killed and injured. Chief of dismantling party killed in attempt to dismantle charge on oil tank.
Amager	Fire destroyed German wooden barracks at "Faste Batteri".
Aalborg	20 armed men removed all card indices from Municipal Registry after Germans had demanded them.
Roedovre	Number of filo-index cards removed or destroyed at municipal offices.
Horsens	108,000 file-index cards destroyed at Registrar's office.
Helsingor	Aalsgaard bathing hotel, requisitioned by Germans, destroyed by fire.
Gentofte	Municipal registers and files destroyed at Town Hall.
Copenhagen	Fire again broke out at German occupied "Faste Batteri" on Amager. Workshop destroyed.

	Silkeborg	Files at Registry Office removed by 8 armed men.
	Silkeborg	Records in office used by A.R.P. Service destroyed by fire.
	Aarhus	Slipway recently repaired and transformer supplying light and power to ships blown up, making speedboat repairs impossible.
	Copenhagen	80 saboteurs forced their way into Public Registrar's building in Frederiksberg and destroyed papers and records by fire. Similar sabotage at Hvidovre.
	Randers	Card index files at Registry Office removed by armed men.
	Lemvig	7 lorries engaged in excavation work at Gammelbjerg near Lemvig completely destroyed.
	Aalborg	Slipway for seaplanes completely destroyed.
	Tikjoeb	Records of Registry, including 10-15 parishes in North Jutland destroyed.
	Horsens	Armed men removed 10,000 record cards from Employment Office.
	Kalundborg	Public register stolen from Town Hall.
Dec 44	Randers	Cement factory of J. Søndergaard destroyed by bombs.
	Aalborg	Richard Svendsen's textile factory destroyed.
	Copenhagen	Magneto Factory destroyed.
	Copenhagen	Factory of Standard Electric blown up.
	Aarhus	C.E. Thumand's electro-mechanical factory destroyed by bombs.
	Odense	Echhoffs' Odense tinned goods factories damaged by bombs.
	Grenaa	Explosions at Aarhus Stone & Gravel Works destroyed accumulator station, 3 locomotives and 2 excavating machines.
	Copenhagen	Bohnstedt Petersen's Factory, working for the Germans, blown up, destroying large stock of aeroplane parts, varnish and lacquer.

	Naestved	Plywood factory making aeroplane parts blown up.
	Copenhagen	Rixen Machine Factory damaged by explosions.
	Copenhagen	Astra engine works completely destroyed.
	Copenhagen	Workshop and warehouse of Wegamo Gas Motor Co., destroyed.
	Nakskov	Damage caused to S.S. *Lilieborg*.
	Copenhagen	3 ships attacked at Burmeister & Wain's wharf, 2 torpedo boats and a lighter sunk and sea cocks opened of *Girginia* and *Louisiana* of the United Shipping Co.
	Frederikshavn	French steamer under repair blown up.
	Svendborg	2 patrol boats under repair in harbour sunk.
	Odense	S.S. *Lindenau* with cargo of pork damaged by bomb on way through canal.
	Bøjden	Transformer blown up supplying German Naval Experimental Station in Norne Peninsular near Faaborg. 2 barges carrying material to the Station were destroyed.
	Sølund	30 bombs exploded in Asylum area taken over by Germans, destroying transformer station, 4 engineers' offices and 25 cars.
	Copenhagen	Contents of railway van at Goods Station taken consisting of machine pistols, automatic rifles, hand-grenades, hand-bombs and ammunition.
	Aalborg	Transformer supplying Vest aerodrome blown up. No supplies of current for four days.
	Copenhagen	German jamming station in Amager Faelledve blown up.
Jan 45	Copenhagen	Ejco Factory making parts for German guns attacked. Stocks and finished goods destroyed.
	Copenhagen	Engine Factory Haparanda destroyed by bombs.
	Copenhagen	Tybring radio factory, Søborg, manufacturing submarine detectors, completely destroyed.

Copenhagen	Premises of engine works at 108 Store Kongensgade destroyed by explosion.
Copenhagen	Caltrop motorcycle factory working exclusively for Germans blown up.
Charlottenlund	Torotor Radio Factory attacked by eighty armed saboteurs and whole building blown up. Factory produced parts for German V weapons and gyroscopes for torpedoes.
Copenhagen	Machine Factory Praecision, working for Germans, damaged by heavy explosion.
Copenhagen	G. Johansen's machine factory, Nørrebro, completely destroyed by explosion.
Køge	Ørum Hansen's machine factory blown up. The factory was producing bomb parts, and had recently obtained a special machine for making parts of V1 and V2. The factory was entirely destroyed.
Copenhagen	Automobile firm A/S Motor Jensen, blown up. Saboteurs returned later in month and blow-up machines which had not previously been damaged.
Kastrup	Wood factory of Lars Rendal & Sons and Kastrup Engine Factory damaged.
Høgh Rasmussen	Machine factory in Copenhagen has been destroyed. 2 unsuccessful attempts had previously been made.
Kastrup	Furniture factory of Messrs. Rendal & Sons destroyed by sabotage.
Copenhagen	10 armed men placed bombs in the Aluminium Industry Co. at Englandsvej 32, Copenhagen, a great deal of damage done.
Copenhagen	Emmeche metal goods factory in Grundtvigsvej, belonging to the well-known Nazi sympathiser Junggren, was blown up by saboteurs and completely destroyed.
Copenhagen	The radio factory owned by Mauritz Andersen in N. 6. Ørstedsvej, was completely destroyed by a fire which broke out after 2 bombs had been placed in it.

Copenhagen	The premises of Siemens at Blegdamsvej 124, were raided by armed man who demanded and obtained drawings and blueprints of work done for the Germans.
Vejle	Brickett factory at the North Station was destroyed.
Copenhagen	C.A. Stub's cog-wheel factory blown up by saboteurs.
Horsens	Sabotage includes the Horsens Radio Factory Ltd., Burchardt Nielsen's Motor Accessories Factory and Møller & Jochumsens Machine Factory.
Copenhagen	The explosions at Hans Just's Stores on the 22nd Jan caused severe damage also to Electro-Mechano Ltd., on the third floor, and completely destroyed Skandinavisk Radio Valve factory which was also on the third floor.
Copenhagen	Armed patriots recently overpowered a lorry driver who had just collected 30 boxes containing special instruments for V2 and valuable blueprints from a German factory at St. Pedersträde 26.
Roskilde	Poul Møllers machine factory at Borup, was damaged by a bomb explosion after 3 armed men had entered the factory, disarmed the guards and placed a couple of bombs.
Slagelse	Serious damage was done to a machine factory at Slotsgade by a bomb which exploded in the 2 storey machine shop.
Aarhus	The lightship at the entrance to the harbour was blown up.
Holbaek	Armed saboteurs held up guard at German radio location station and blew up radio-location installation, warehouse and machine shed.
Hjørring	Storage building containing lorries blown up at Lendum.

anish police officers display a parachute recovered at an SOE drop zone at Trend Hede, Denmark.
he drop involved took place on the night of 31 July-1 August 1942. The three agents who jumped were
ans F. Hansen, Peter Nielsen and Knud Erik Pedersen. (All images courtesy of the Freedom Museum/
anish National Musuem)

Danish policeman is pictured wearing an agent's jump suit, with other equipment laying around,
1 the drop zone at Trend Hede following the supply mission and agent drop on the night of 31 July-1
ugust 1942.

Recovered SOE parachute containers pictured at Ranum following the SOE drop at Trend Hede on the night of 31 July-1 August 1942.

A Danish police display of equipment recovered from the drop at Trend Hede on the night of 31 July-August 1942.

Members of the Danish Resistance manhandle a supply container away from a drop zone in Central Jutland.

A garage and warehouse building in Middelfartgade, Copenhagen, after it was the target of a sabotage attack by the Danish Resistance on 6 October 1942.

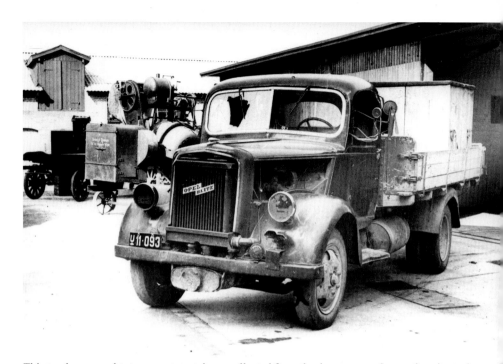

This truck was used to transport containers collected from the drop zone and reception site to the sout of Madum Lake, the largest lake in the Himmerland peninsula of Jutland, Denmark, on 17 August 194 During the journey from the drop site, the vehicle encountered German troops and a fire fight ensue Damage and bullet holes from that engagement can be seen. One of the Danish Resistance men presen Niels E. Vangsted, was killed. A second, Poul Kjær Sørensen, was injured and subsequently capture He was taken to Copenhagen, where he was sentenced to death the next day by a German court. He wa executed ten days later. He was the first Danish resistance fighter who was sentenced to death.

Civilians gather to watch as a pall of dense smoke rises into the sky following an attack by the Danis Resistance on fuel storage tanks at Holbæk on 12 March 1945.

The smoking ruins of part of the Burmeister and Wain factory after it was attacked by a force of 25 Resistance fighters on 24 May 1944. The sabotage resulted in the destruction of a 4-storey building containing dies and machine tools, as well as a number of diesel and aero-engines.

derailed train in Odense railway station after the track was sabotaged in 1944.

A German patrol boat sunk in Frederikshavn Harbour after a Resistance attack on 9 August 1944.

An RAF Short Stirling pictured at low-level dropping supply containers at Annebjerg, south of Gre
on 30 September 1944.

copy of the Sten gun pictured whilst being locally manufactured for the Danish Resistance. Many of ese copies were fitted with a pistol grip so that they were easier to conceal under a coat.

railway bridge at Haderslev, in Southern Denmark, after it was attacked by members of the Danish sistance.

A smiling Resistance fighter, Visborg Helsingør, is pictured by defaced portraits of Hitler following Denmark's liberation in 1945.

Members of the Holger Danske Resistance group pictured in Lyngby in May 1945.

	Aarhus	Saboteurs threw a bomb down the refuse chute into the cellar of the Handels & Landbrugsbank in Aarhus, where the Germans recently installed a DF and teleprinter station.
	Nørresundby	A Wehrmacht straw depot was destroyed by bombs. The entire store burnt down. A Wehrmacht straw depot was destroyed by bombs. The entire store burnt down.
	Beldringe	Saboteurs fought their way to the airfield where the Germans were building hangars. Locomotives of the tip-up trains and six excavators were blown up.
Feb 45	Korsør	Saboteurs stopped a supply train at Forslev, overpowered the guard and carried away all the arms and ammunition from the train.
	Lyngby	The transformer station of the Lyac Factory which had been making accumulators for German submarines, was destroyed on orders from this H.Q.
	Silkeborg	The Dars Factory, which was making nose sections for aircraft and supports for A.A. guns was destroyed by sabotage.
Mar 45	Copenhagen	Johannesen & Lunds engine works at Ryesgade 55 were completely destroyed.
	Copenhagen	The shutter factory at Bleedamsvej 50, destroyed by saboteurs.
	Copenhagen	A workshop at 62, Smallegade, which had been making cartridge cases was destroyed.
	Kolding	Irreplaceable machines and tools and several motor cars were destroyed when Karl Jacob Jensen's motor car workshop was destroyed by fire by saboteurs.
	Falster	Møller's furniture factory was burnt down by saboteurs. Most of the furniture in the factory was ready for delivery to Germany the next day.

Copenhagen	Machinery was destroyed when 14 armed saboteurs, who arrived in a petrol driven car, attacked the strongly guarded firm Heiber Service at Lyngbyvej 165.
Glostrup	The accumulator factory Wootan was blown up.
Copenhagen	Danaco's Store House at Scandiagade badly damaged.
Aarhus	A food store at Jaegersgaardsgade 142 destroyed by sabotage.
Copenhagen	The Triangel Repair Shop, which was taken over by the Germans some time ago, was blown up. The patriots gained access to the workshop through a sewer.
Copenhagen	Violent explosions and fires occurred in the repair shop of Heinberg's Motor Service, and a number of cars were burnt.
Copenhagen	Bombs exploded in the "Dan" Engine Works at Bragesgade 10. Considerable damage was caused.
Aarhus	There were heavy explosions at J.P. Jensen's Steel and Iron Shop.
Nykøbing F	4 violent explosions occurred in the "Petrol Harbour" where NAFTA, DDPA, Shell and KKKK have their tanks. Fires which broke out in 3 of the tanks were not extinguished until 8 hours later.
Naestved	Stocks of oil and paraffin were set on fire. Several buildings were destroyed and 400 metres of the Fabriksvej were at one time in flames. The fire was under control 3½ hours after it had started.
Naestved	Oil fires spread to the Coal Importer Co., where irreplaceable cranes and spare parts were destroyed to the value of Kr. 100,000.
Hellerup	An oil and petrol tank in the DDPA Harbour were blown up. The quantity of oil destroyed is estimated at between 400,000 and 500,000 litres.
Amager	An accumulator factory in Vaermlandsgade was blown up.

Kastrup	A store of benzol was blown up at the Syrefabrik.
Vejgaard	E.C. Nielsen's metal workshop was destroyed by bomb explosions.
Aalborg	Messrs. Abel's coal crane, which was being used to remove Danish stocks of fuel, was destroyed by bomb explosions.
Copenhagen	1,400 litres of petrol were taken away from a chemical factory at Amager Strandvej.
Vejle	Wittrup's wool factory was attacked by saboteurs. The machine shops and the building containing the looms were destroyed and the damage has been estimated at Kr. 1,000,000. The Thomas Kongsbak Motor Repair Works, which had been reconditioning German vehicles, was destroyed by sabotage.
Aabenraa	A fuel tank was blown up in the area of the Danske Petroleum A/S and BP's premises. The fire spread to neighbouring buildings which were burnt down.
Odense	A warehouse was blown up by saboteurs.
Refshalevig	A factory used for screwing threads on breach-blocks for A.A. shells was blown up.
Kastrup	65,000 litres of petrol have been removed from the harbour. Together with amounts previously destroyed here, this should exhaust the petrol supply at Kastrup.
Aalborg	Damage estimated at between one and two million kroner is said to have been caused when the Hygaea Factory was destroyed by sabotage.
Skanderborg	The sawmill of Voer Ladegaard belonging to merchant Brodersen of Horsens, who was producing generator wire for the Germans, was blown up.
Holstenbro	Motor car workshop destroyed.
Kolding	Motor car workshop destroyed.

Copenhagen	The Factory "Allways" was completely destroyed by bomb explosions. This factory, which was one of the largest working for the Germans, had been manufacturing parts for submarines and V-weapons and two-way radios for planes which were an exact copy of those used on Flying Fortresses. The factory had been attacked several times before and was partly destroyed in Jan 44, but it had been rebuilt.
Copenhagen	Resistance workers seized seven anchors for U-boats from a workshop where they were ready for deliver.
Gedser	The ferry boat *Danmark* was sunk by saboteurs in the harbour. It had come to the knowledge of members of the Resistance Movement that the ferry boat was again to be put under steam. The crew were evacuated before the boat was sunk.
Helsingor	The Danish ferry boat *Odin* which was withdrawn from service by the Germans and taken to Korsør for overhauling was subjected to an attack by Danish patriots on its way from Helsingør. The patriots tried to get command of the ship and take her to Sweden, but they were overpowered by the Germans and taken back to Helsingor under arrest. The Danish pilot was killed.
Copenhagen	Bombs exploded on the Langebro and fires started at the centre of the bridge. Street fights followed and 12 persons were taken to hospital. The swing control mechanism of the bridge was destroyed and it cannot be opened, so that a number of ships are now bottled up in the South Harbour.
Copenhagen	20 armed men forced personnel of the Goods Station to hand over 34 large boxes addressed to the Wehrmacht. The boxes were loaded on two lorries and driven away.

	Charlottehøj	Patriots have destroyed 2 cement mixers which were being used to build fortifications.
	Odense	A big roller, which was to be sent to Lunde airfield has been destroyed.
	Lunde	Cables were cut on direction finders, listening posts and transformers at the airfield.
	Bornholm	The masts of a jamming station which were under construction at Elemensker have been sawn through by saboteurs. Telephone and telegraph lines were cut between Taastrup and Vridsløse and on Fyn.
	Copenhagen	Patriots destroyed A.A. and searchlight equipment on the upper floor of the annexe to the Royal Theatre.
	Trustrup	Bomb explosions destroyed three cement mixing machines at the station.
	Nørre Uttrup	Stores of timber and partly made huts were destroyed when saboteurs placed 20 bombs on the premises of Contractor Fuchs.
	Naestved	Patriots recently seized and set fire to two railway wagons containing 40,000 litres of petrol at the station. The petrol was on its way to Aarhus for the Wehrmacht. Land mines and time bombs were recently placed in the German defence trench from Bellevue near Risskov to the Grenaa high road. Yellow posters warned the workmen who were sent home.
	Aarhus	The transformer station in Marselisboulevard was blown up by saboteurs.
Apr 45	Hjørring	The Cooperative pig slaughter house and sausage works were damaged by a bomb explosion.
	Aalborg	Saboteurs have recently made several attacks against hauliers working for the Germans. Several lorries have been stopped and the engines blown up.

Nørresundby	Transformer blown up.
Christiansholm	Saboteurs stormed the machine factory of Brycomann et Nielsen. Several bombs were placed, many valuable machines destroyed and the factory completely ruined.
Faster	The West Jutland Drying Works were destroyed by bombs.
Frederikshavn	A motor car repair shop has been destroyed by saboteurs.
Copenhagen	A bomb exploded in a garage at the corner of Øresundsgade and Randersgade and extensive damage was caused.
Aalborg	Armed men forced their way into the premises of "Gas Accumulators", which was producing acetylene for welding purposes. The compressors were completely destroyed by bomb explosions.
Rødding	The cooperative slaughterhouses and sausage works were completely destroyed by bomb explosions. 50,000 Krs' worth of pork and sausages were lost.
Tindbaek	Saboteurs destroyed the workshop and furniture store belonging to the sawmills.
Lindholm	About a dozen bombs exploded in a block of mechanical workshops. Considerable damage was done.
Aalborg	A coal crane at the harbour belonging to Messrs. Abel was destroyed by the two bombs.
Copenhagen	A large factory making wheels for tanks has been blown up on Amager Boulevard.
Copenhagen	The marmalade factory Sunda has been blown up.
Esbjerg	A motor workshop, belonging to Filip Petersen, a Nazi who had been supplying the Wehrmacht, has been blown up by patriots.
Aarhus	Aage Neidemann's motor works have been attacked by saboteurs. All motor cars in the factory were destroyed.

Aalborg	Herman Schaffer's mechanical workshop has been blown up. It had been working exclusively for the Germans and was making spare parts for German locomotives.
Kolding	The Nimmus Motor Workshop, which was making cylinders for German speed boats, has been attacked by patriots and machinery was destroyed.
Esbjerg	Philip Petersen's motor workshops, which were making diesel motors, have been destroyed.
Bogense	The Arken restaurant, which had been requisitioned by the Germans two days previously, has been burnt down.
Vejen	Schluenzer's saw-mill was destroyed by bombs.
Copenhagen	Halejaer's furniture factory was burnt down and destroyed. The factory had been making beds, radio cabinets and pre-fabricated garages.
Middelfart	Johannes Poulsen's motor workshop has been destroyed by bombs. 5 German motor vehicles, lathes, machinery and a cement mixer were destroyed.
Copenhagen	A violent explosion destroyed a transformer of the Titan engine factory. No one was hurt but considerable damage was done.
Risskov	10 lorries were destroyed at contractor Helbo's garage.
Copenhagen	P. Hansens's woodwork factory was burnt to the ground.
Copenhagen	The transformer station outside 24, Sydhavnsgade, was blown up recently. There were 150 soldiers acting as guards.
Lillebaelt	Several bomb explosions occurred at the beam signal stations.
Copenhagen	25 cases containing finished parts for U-boat motors were destroyed by patriots at the "Transmotor" engineering factory at Finsensvej.

Aarhus	Patriots boarded the M.S. *Godtfred Hansen* 397 tons, belonging to the KKKK Company, ordered the crew to leave her and placed bombs which caused the ship to sink in 10 minutes. The *Godtfred Hansen* was loaded with 600 tons of fish and was on her way from Norway to Germany.
Sønderborg	There were several loud explosions in the area of the town and a large part of the main quay was blown up. It is believed that saboteurs sent drifting mines over from the other side of Alsund.
	The entire Danish salvage fleet and a great part of the tugboat fleet made its escape to Sweden. The operation was carried out with the approval of the Ministry of Trade and the Danish Admiralty.
Copenhagen	Patriots smuggled themselves aboard the *Røsnas*. The next day the *Røsnas* sailed and dropped her pilot. The patriots then came out of hiding, held up the captain and crew and took charge of the ship grounding her on the southern tip of the island of Nven. They called for help by wireless. As the tugs approached the crews were put under armed guard. The next morning the *Røsnas* was re-floated and sailed with her convoy of 18 tugs for Landskrona.
	The S.S. *Tula*, 1,251 tons, passenger boat, which normally sails between Copenhagen, Oslo and Gothenburg, was hailed by a yawl which had hoisted an SOS signal. The *Tula*, came alongside and the 5 members of the crew of the yawl boarded the *Tula*, held up the captain and crew and took the ship back to Gothenburg.
Olyngøre	The drawbridge of the railway ferry was blown up and fell into the water.

	Patriots sank the United Shipping Company's vessel *Ejøbenhave*, 1,668 tons. The vessel which used to sail on the Copenhagen-Aalborg route, was to have been put on the Gedser-Warnemunde line as a passenger steamer.
Aalborg	Patriots have sunk a large German naval craft East of the Limfjord. Only the mast heads are above water.
Randers	Patriots have thrown a bomb into the engine room of the tug *Bjørn* which had been requisitioned by the Germans and was due to sail.
Middelfart	A guiding light indicating the fairway in the Lillebaelt has been blown up.
	All the pilots of Copenhagen and Helsingør have escaped to Sweden with their boats.
Knippelsbro	2 vessels have been sunk here at the entrance to Copenhagen harbour. This has prevented a collier, which the Germans wished to use, from getting out.
Copenhagen	During the attack on the Titan Engineering Works cases containing 6 large dynamos for U-boats were destroyed.
	2 Danish inspection vessels, the *Løvenørn* and the *Argus* of 253 and 618 GR respectively, which were seized on their way to take up positions at Store Middelorunden and Anholt Knob, have been seized by patriots who boarded them from speed boats. The vessels were taken to Swedish ports.
Faaborg	The power unit of the Faaborg-Mommark ferry boat was recently destroyed.
Copenhagen	A tugboat was sunk by patriots in the harbour. The crew were uninjured.
Aalborg	25 lorries, which were being driven for the benefit of the Wehrmacht, were destroyed.

Aalborg	Saboteurs blew up a Heinkel 109 on a rail car at the station. The plane was totally destroyed.
Horskrød	Materials and equipment being used for fortification work were blown up.
Plovstrup	A German listening post was completely destroyed by explosions the day after its construction had been completed.
	Resistance workers removed a store of bedding and blankets from the Hareskov Kuranstalt which the Germans had requisitioned for use as a hospital.
Aarhus	Bombs exploded in the telegraph station, serious damage being done to telegraph and telephone cables. For the rest of the day only 2 cables were in use, one to Copenhagen and one to North Jutland.
Esbjerg	According to the German Press Office the Wehrmacht HQ was attacked by saboteurs. As a result, a curfew is now in force from 2000 hours to 0600 hours.
Vonsild	Patriots blew up the workers' hutment. Other attacks were also made on German places of work.
Copenhagen	Patriots broke into the gaol at Blegdamsvej and seized parts of radio transmitters which were being stored there.
Aabenraa	Concrete mixers belonging to contractor Weiss, who was working for the Germans, have been destroyed.
Aarhus	A warehouse belonging to the Corn Fodder Co., which was being used for storing German uniforms, has been burnt down.
Copenhagen	Several schools, including the Øresundsskolen, have been sabotaged just as refugees were about to move into them.
Nastva	Two farms were burnt down. Notices were stuck up on telegraph poles saying, "This is the fate of all informers".

Copenhagen   Patriots entered the German Chamber
                    of Commerce at Nørrevold, held up the
                    German and Danish staff and made a
                    thorough examination of all papers.
                    Everything of interest was packed in boxes
                    and taken away in a removal van 3 hours
                    later. The patriots also removed typewriters
                    and duplicators.

RAILWAY SABOTAGE

Since June 1944, acts of railway sabotage occurred on an ever-increasing scale, as shown below:

1944

July	10 successful operations
August	26 successful operations
September	34 successful operations
October	30 successful operations
November	34 successful operations
December	7 successful operations

1945

January	12 successful operations
February	Nil
March	53 successful operations
April	90 successful operations

EVALUATION OF S.O.E. ACTIVITIES IN DENMARK

Summary

S.O.E. work in Denmark was conditioned by the following adverse factors:

(i)   The geographical division of the country into the mainland and various islands makes internal communication more difficult than it is in most countries.

(ii) The long passage across the North Sea and the unsuitable coast of West Jutland makes clandestine communications between Great Britain and Denmark almost impossible.

(iii) The people of Denmark are peace-loving and unaccustomed to war. During the last century they have gained a high level of social prosperity. In consequence they did not at first realise the necessity for opposing the occupying enemy.

(iv) The lack of effective Danish diplomatic representation in Britain during the war.

(v)   The small number of men available and suitable for recruitment in Britain at the beginning of the war.

On the other hand, there were several favourable factors from the point of view of S.O.E. work:

(a)   The standard of intelligence, education and loyalty amongst the population was high.

(b)   The propinquity of Sweden to Denmark facilitated communications and travel.

(c)   The fact that SOE made a very early (although unwitting) contact with the Danish military intelligence organisation. As a result, all clandestine activities in Denmark were controlled by SOE and there was little of that friction and confusion with SIS that unfortunately took place in some other countries.

The account of SOE operations in Denmark shows what an intelligent people assisted by an efficient SOE organisation can achieve in combatting an occupying power. The Danish resistance movement carried out a very large number of successful operations against a variety of targets and undoubtedly caused the enemy grave difficulties.

These were the more acute in that the Germans had hoped to use Denmark as a model of what a state should be under German control. Furthermore, Denmark was a vital link in the enemy communications to Norway and operations in Denmark had an important effect on his activities in that country.

In addition to the harm done to the enemy, the efficiency of the resistance movement and its work after the enemy collapse undoubtedly helped the country to minimise the evil after-effects of enemy occupation.

Summary of Operations

Date	Sorties Attempted	Sorties Successful	Men	Tonnage	A/C Missing	Containers	Packages
1941	1	1	2	-	-	-	-
1942	4	4	12	-	-	-	3
1943	25	19	21	12	1	100	18
1944	127	93	17	169	4	1642	73
1945	257	168	5	439	12	4157	468
Total	414	285	57	620	17	5899	562

D-Day Plans

(a)   Several informants stated that they felt that the orders for D-Day were received too late. However, this seems to be because they did not realise the necessity for security and the need for these orders to be in accordance with the actual situation.

(b)   The majority of informants agree that the orders received were clear, although one or two complain that they were too complicated.

(c)   All agents were emphatic that the Resistance should not be called out more than 72 hours before the arrival of Allied troops. The Country Section agrees with this point.

Briefing and False Papers

(a)   The majority of the agents interrogated stated that they were satisfied with the briefing which they received. Only three men had any complaints about their briefing and these complaints related to lack of information on the relationship between the different Resistance groups in Denmark. The Country Section comment that these men were briefed by one of the Danish local leaders who used his discretion as to the amount they should be told. Nevertheless, it seems unfortunate that these men should feel that they had been inadequately briefed.

(b)   Most of the agents reported that they were very satisfied with the false papers which they received and in at least one case these papers withstood Gestapo examination.

(c)   The Country Section comment that all agents were informed that the papers issued were only for immediate use and should be changed as soon as possible for papers made out in agreement with false entries in the official registers.

Political Role

Agents agree on the importance of thorough briefing for those who will deal with political matters. With one exception the agents who were interrogated on this point state that their briefing was adequate.

Intelligence

It is of importance to note that, at the request of the Danish Intelligence Service themselves, all Danish intelligence was handled by SOE and not SIS. It was found essential that in such a small country as Denmark only one secret organisation should operate and, as SOE was established and had the confidence of the Danish authorities, it fell to them to act in both roles, and this in effect proved most successful.

Training

1. W/T.

Only seven W/T operators were trained in England and all except one of these were captured or forced to flee. Nevertheless, an operator was recruited locally who trained additional operators with great success. Owing to the technical aptitude of the Danes this system caused no difficulties at all.

2. General Training.

(a)   SOE training was generally considered to be good.

(b)   The majority of agents expressed particular appreciation of the training received at STS XVII (Industrial Sabotage) and at Group 'B' (Agents' Training).

(c)   Most agents emphasise the importance of training in foreign weapons.

(d)   Those agents who are likely to take part in guerilla warfare should receive special courses in this subject. The courses should include instruction in street fighting if the operator is likely to be employed in urban areas.

(e)   Agents who need it should receive instruction in driving and servicing motorcars and motor bicycles.

(f)   Agents should receive plenty of practice with the actual weapon which they will take to the field with them.

(g)   Propaganda training should only be given to those students who need it. This entails an early decision by the Country Section on the work to be done by the agent.

Despatch

(a)   All agents were supposed to be searched before despatch, but two report that they were not searched. The majority realised the necessity for searching and approved of it. The failure to search two men might have been serious and some system must be established by which this cannot happen.

(b)   All agents agree that the arrangements for despatch were satisfactory.

(c)   The password did not always work satisfactorily. Sometimes the reception committee were not aware of the correct password.

Arrival

(a)   One agent was killed because his static line came unhooked. This tragedy led to improvements by the Air Force in the safety hooks for static lines.

(b)   With one exception agents interviewed expressed satisfaction with their arrival.

(c)   One man stated that the reception committee to which he had been dropped expected stores but no agents. The reason for this error has not been discovered, but the system employed should be such that similar mistakes cannot arise.

(d)   Denmark provides the best example of the successful dropping of an agent into water. A very heavy agent, who had been injured on previous drops, was successfully dropped into the sea about 150 yards from the shore. He reached the land without difficulty. He was equipped with a waterproof suit and an R.A.F. fighter dinghy and also wore a "Mae West".

Signal Communications

(a)   The Danes showed outstanding ability in the field of W/T communications. Six out of the seven operators infiltrated from England were either arrested or forced to flee. Nevertheless, through the outstanding ability of a W/T operator recruited in the country, further men were recruited locally and trained so well that communications with Denmark were always most efficient.

(b)   At the close of the campaign there were twelve W/T operators working in Denmark.

(c)   Where possible the Intelligence Organisation was given its own operator.

(d)   Signal Plans. (i) The "V" Plan was used first, but was found insecure. The "Z" Plan was then adopted and found satisfactory. (ii) Later the "broadcast" system was used and found very secure. Ten such plans were operated in all. (iii) For Intelligence purposes arrangements were made to introduce the "Marker Channel" plan, but, owing to the enemy surrender, this was never put into operation.

(e)   S-Phone Link. An S-Phone link was established between Denmark and Sweden, messages being relayed to London by cable. This link proved too slow for operational messages, but was used for administrative and intelligence traffic thus taking a load off other links.

(f) U.H.F. Link. An U.H.F. link working on 200-400 megs. was established between Copenhagen and Malmö, operating at 500 letters per minute. The traffic was relayed by cable direct to London. Later a relay transmitter was installed at Malmö so that the operator in Copenhagen could check the safe receipt of his message by the British station. This link proved of very great value.

Codes and Cyphers

One time pads were used throughout the war and were secure and efficient. Those printed on silk were found to be the most convenient.

Secret Inks

There is no report of the use of secret inks in Denmark.

Pigeons

Pigeons were not used by the Danish Section.

Internal Communications

Couriers were used. Messages were sent by word of mouth or on films in RS containers. Messages sometimes encoded by Playfair or Innocent Letter.

S-Phone

(a) Several reports speak of S-phones being valuable for reception committee work, for which they were frequently used.

(b) A permanent S-phone link was established between Denmark and Sweden (see Signal Communications).

(c) A number of S-phones were damaged when dropped by plane. Replacements were smuggled in from Sweden.

(d) There seems little doubt that the technical aptitude of the Danes made them more successful with S-phones than some other nations.

Eureka

(a) A good system of both fixed and mobile Eurekas was established in Denmark and proved invaluable for reception committee work, enabling the RAF to operate in the non-moon period.

(b) As with the S-phone, the Danes' natural aptitude assisted them in using the Eureka.

Stores Reception

(a) At the outset slow communications and too great centralisation of control in the field caused delays and consequently operations were less frequent than they might have been. These drawbacks were gradually removed and improved communications coupled with decentralisation of control in the field permitted a steady increase in the number of operations.

(b) Container dropping technique seems to have been generally satisfactory although there are occasional reports of wide scatter.

(c) Some complaints were received of stores being delivered to the wrong reception and in one case of a load being dropped 5 kms. away. In one instance an agent received 24 containers, although he had stated that he could only deal with twelve. These instances seem to indicate some failure in the Air Liaison Section and the system should be so devised that such mistakes cannot occur.

(d) Complaints were received that the scatter of packages was frequently excessive. On one occasion packages were scattered over 2-3 kms.

(e) Local torches were generally used for reception committees. SOE torches were proved satisfactory when used. Black cardboard shields were used to cut out side glare and aid security.

(f) A percentage of parachute failures was reported and this percentage appears to have increased just before the liberation. At this time it is reported that many parachutes became detached from the container. Such failures are probably due to the use of ground crews who were not accustomed to the work.

(g) Pilot 'chutes were frequently found detached.

(h) There are several complaints that the 'planes circled the reception committee several times before dropping their load, thus endangering the committee.

(i)   There are frequent complaints of containers opening in the air. This applies to both 'C' and 'H' type containers. These mishaps were probably due to faulty construction as it is known that A.I.D. inspection was at one period insufficiently thorough and representations were made to M.A.P. on this point.

(j)   Packing of containers was on the whole satisfactory. Stores packed in 'H' type cells suffered less damage than those packed in 'C' types. Packing of packages was less satisfactory. One explosive container burst in the air and one incendiary cell caught fire on the ground. Both accidents must have been due to faulty packing.

(k)   The only damage in cells due to damp was to a few time pencils and to some arms which became superficially rusty. Nevertheless, it is clear that waterproof cells would be an advantage.

(l)   Complaints were received that the 'C' type container is difficult and noisy to open. The carrying handles should also be improved.

(m)   Numerous reports state that the total load as marked on the containers was seldom accurate. This points to a lack of system at the aerodromes and should be remedied.

(n)   There were several complaints that the handbooks packed in the containers were written in French. This was of course due to the mass packing problem and the use of standard containers. Although this may be difficult to remedy, efforts should certainly be made to overcome the trouble, if only on the grounds of morale.

(o)   K-Type Container. This container was used on two operations in Denmark. (i) Both operations were successful. The containers were collected from the sea after two days in one instance and after five days in the other. In both cases the stores were undamaged. The scatter was only 150 metres. (ii) The reception committee were much impressed by the additional security afforded by this method. The reception committee made the following points:
Advantages:
(i)   The enemy was unfamiliar with this technique.
(ii)   The 'planes, if spotted, would probably be taken for minelayers.
(iii) The risk for the committee is much reduced.
(iv)   The containers can be left until convenient and sunk after emptying.

Disadvantages:
(i)   The container lid is difficult to open.
(ii)   The container is difficult to unload.
(iii) There are too many buoys.
Suggestions:
(i)   One buoy only per container.
(ii)   Buoys to be shaped like ducks.
(iii) 48-72 hour delays on the buoys.
(iv)   Easier opening lids.

Amphibious Operations

(a)   The first attempt at making a rendezvous between one of
       DDOD(T)'s fishing boats and a Danish vessel failed because
       the time taken in passing messages to the Danish skipper was
       excessive. This was due to paucity of W/T links with Denmark at
       that time.
(b)   A second attempt failed because the Danish skipper was
       disheartened on hearing of the failure of the first operation.
(c)   The method of communication was improved by using BBC code
       messages and as a result two successful operations took place in
       the Autumn of 1944 and two more in the Spring of 1945.
(d)   The total number of men infiltrated by this method was four and
       16½ tons of stores were shipped to Denmark by means of these
       operations.
(e)   The rendezvous was fixed in a spot which could be found by the
       Danish craft using normal fisherman's methods.
(f)   The stores were specially packed in watertight containers and
       camouflaged in fish boxes.
(g)   One attempt was made to attack German ships in Aarhus by
       swimmers.

The two swimmers used swim suits with warm underwear and breathing
apparatus. They used U.S. swimfins. Each man carries two 2lb. limpets
with buoyancy bags. The apparatus functioned well and they placed the
charges. Unfortunately, none of the charges fired. An enquiry has been
held but no reason for the failure to fire has yet been found. The limpets
used were standard and of the type which has been used without failure
on many operations.

Stores

General.

   (a)   Several complaints were received that the proportions in which the stores were received was not satisfactory. Since the agents themselves differed in their opinions as to the ideal proportions it is probably true to say that those supplies were as good as could be devised but that naturally they could not be ideal for all situations.

   (b)   There were very general complaints that incendiaries were not supplied in sufficient quantities in spite of repeated requests. The Country Section comments that, since railway sabotage was of prime importance, P.E. was more useful than incendiaries. Nevertheless, the insistence by the agents that they needed and could have used incendiaries indicates that such requests from the field should not be ignored by HQ.

   (c)   There were few complaints as to the reliability of the stores and devices received. The complaints received were mainly on the score that the time pencil was not accurate. From an examination of the reports it seems that these complaints were usually due to a lack of appreciation of the temperature co-efficient of time pencils.

   (d)   Several complaints were received that the white colour of cordtex renders it too visible. Cordtex is a War Office store and, at the request of SOE, the War Office attempted to produce coloured cordtex, but without success.

Arms

   (a)   It is generally agreed that the best personal arm for clandestine operators is the Colt .32 Automatic.

   (b)   Several agents reported that they would have liked more Welrods and Silent Stens.

   (c)   It is generally agreed that pistols and Stens and also the US M.1 carbine are not suitable for guerilla warfare. For guerilla campaigns the Bren, rifle and Bazooka are essential. The 2″ mortar would be very useful if air supply could be arranged.

   (d)   The Sten, .45 pistol and No. 36 Grenades are useful to covering parties.

   (e)   The M.1 carbine is too large for clandestine operations and has too short a range for guerilla operations.

Drugs
- (a) Agents were able to vouch for the efficacy of the 'L' tablet.
- (b) Several agents suggested that the 'L' tablet if found is very compromising and suggest camouflage in the form of a button.

Cameras
- (a) Cameras of the 35mm. and 'Minox' type were used a good deal in Denmark since messages could be sent on film via Sweden to London.
- (b) Cameras should be supplied only to agents who require them and are capable of using them to advantage.
- (c) A good self-destroying film container of the RS type would supply a real requirement.

Camouflage and Disguise
- (a) Several agents used minor disguise with success, such as growing moustache, using glasses, parting hair differently.
- (b) Two men considered that insufficient care had been spent on selecting their clothes, which did not fit well with their cover story.
- (c) One man suggested that poison can be placed in a small glass phial in the muscle of the left upper arm and can be broken by a hard blow by the person carrying it.
- (d) Agents have pointed out that the lack of any marks on clothing is very suspicious. Therefore, clothing must bear marks of origin. Information must be obtained showing what marks of origin are permissible in any country. For instance, in Denmark, British markings were quite harmless.

Enemy Stores and Weapons
The resistance groups stole enemy stores and weapons and used them with success.

Use of Dogs
The enemy definitely used dogs to track suspects and, on one occasion at least, with success. Some means of defeating this method is desirable.

Sabotage

Sabotage in Denmark was extremely vigorous and widespread. It is worthy of note that many successful attacks took place on the following types of target:

Factories, particularly armament factories; radio installations; numerous ships; railways and rolling stock; enemy establishments, such as military and Gestapo headquarters and airfields; stocks of rubber, timer and oil; shipyards; electric power transformers and industrial installations of all types. In addition, large numbers of civil records were destroyed or removed in order to prevent checking of resistance personnel.

It is interesting to note that wherever operators used the techniques advised by STS XVII they proved successful. An examination of the reports shows that in a large number of instances the operators worked in comparatively large groups and destroyed factories by using large charges placed in the buildings. This method succeeded in the small factories found in Denmark and with a friendly population, but it is doubtful if they would have been so successful in larger installations and with less help from the local people. Under these more difficult circumstances the STS XVII methods would be far more certain.

A further point of interest is the use which the Danes made of incendiary methods. They undoubtedly employed fire to a greater extent than any other nation. This may be attributed to the better education and intelligence of the Danes since the successful use of incendiarism requires careful preparation.

Counter-Scorching

The German surrender obviated the necessity for counter-scorching, but plans had been prepared to minimise the effect of enemy demolitions if attempted.

(a)   The radio station at Kalundborg was prepared for protection with the co-operation of the manager. The latter arranged a system by which he could cut the telephone lines between the station and the town, blow some special valves and blow up the German guardhouse, all by dialling certain numbers on his house 'phone.

(b)   Plans were made to sink the block-ships at Helsingør before they were in position.

(c)   Plans were made to prevent the port demolitions at Esbjerg.

Propaganda

The underground press printed posters showing Allied successes and had them displayed in order to discourage the Germans and encourage the Danish population. German notices were mutilated and counter-manded in the name of the Freedom Council.

Bribery and Blackmail

(a) Insecure persons were threatened by sending presents of revolver bullets with threatening letters.

(b) Enemy officials were bribed by promising safety for themselves and families in the event of Allied success.

(c) Bribery of enemy personnel always involves risks and must be carried out skilfully by suitable personnel.

Financial Operations

Since there was no Danish authority with whom HMG could make financial agreements, it was necessary to take special steps to provide funds for SOE work in Denmark. A separate organisation of business men was set up whose only function was to provide financial facilities. This system, which was assisted by smuggling from Sweden and by infiltrating diamonds, was most successful. The special organisation was controlled by a Paymaster in the country who later had his own W/T contact. Promissory notes, guaranteeing payment in London, were prepared for use in an emergency to raise money from individuals who had not sufficient confidence to lend on other terms.

The following figures show the amounts of Danish kroner raised by different methods:

	Kr.	Kr.
Direct infiltration from the U.K.	510,203.00	
Direct infiltration from Stockholm	274,142.00	
		784,345.00
Sale of smuggled diamonds		415,919.00
Against sterling credit at Headquarters		5,117,489.00
Promissory Notes		350,219.00
	Total	Kr. 6,667,972.00

Personal Attack

Traitors were usually liquidated by shooting. The use of a car using the sign 'Doctor' proved effective in kidnapping traitors.

Appendix XII

OPERATION MOONSHINE

Operation *Moonshine* was mounted primarily for the purpose of carrying urgently required supplies for the Danish resistance movement in amounts greater than could conveniently be dropped by air, and of bringing back most important material required by the Ministry of Supply from Sweden.

Two of the Bridford vessels, M/Vs *Nonsuch* and *Hopewell* were loaned by the Admiralty to the Ministry of War Transport for this purpose, and loaded with 26 tons of Danish cargo. During the summer they had been undergoing trials and modifications to try to improve the reliability of the engines.

The operation looked like succeeding at the first attempt made in the September no-moon period under ideal weather conditions, but the vessels were recalled by the Admiralty owing to enemy dispositions in the Skagerrak, after completing half the voyage. M/V *Hopewell* returned with a broken crankshaft.

On the assumption that the engines seemed no more reliable, a third Bridford vessel, the M/V *Gay Viking*, was loaned by the Admiralty to try to ensure that at least two vessels should reach their destination. She was loaded with a further fourteen tons of Danish stores.

During the October, November and December no-moon periods weather conditions were such that although several attempts were made to reach Sweden none was successful.

All three vessels eventually arrived at Lysekil, their port of destination in Sweden, on the morning of 15th January 1945, during the middle of the no-moon, carrying 44½ tons of cargo. On the return voyage, made in February, the M/V *Nonsuch* reached the United Kingdom loaded with 33 tons of cargo for the Ministry of Supply. The M/V *Gay Viking* was lost in collision with M/V *Hopewell* during very thick weather in the Skagerrak. No lives were lost and M/V *Hopewell* put back to the Swedish coast. She eventually returned to the U.K. at the end of the February no-moon period, carrying 30 tons of Ministry of Supply material.

On their return to the U.K. *Nonsuch* and *Hopewell* were each loaded with a further 20 tons of supplies for the Danes, and made several abortive attempts to reach Sweden, but, owing to weather or engines, were always forced to return.

Due to the lateness of the season the operation was finally abandoned in the middle of March.

Although at first glance *Moonshine* does not appear to have attained the same success as Bridford in actual number of voyages completed, it must be remembered that we more than fulfilled our Danish commitments in that we exceeded the original required tonnage by 18½ tons. All this material was infiltrated into Denmark without loss. Part of the report is devoted to the extremely unfavourable weather conditions with which we had to contend.

From the inception of the operation to its conclusion Mr. H.N. Sporborg, C.M.G., of M.E.W., was always available to give his judgment and sound advice on all matters and was of immense help to me personally, as was also Mr. C.R. Wheeler, Deputy Steel Controller. They guided me over the many pitfalls connected with the organisation, and whenever I found myself at a dead end, I felt that I had only to consult either of them to find the solution.

Original Plan

1. During the first week in August 1944 an informal meeting was held at 17 Porchester Terrace, the home of Sir George Binney, at which were present:

Commander Sir George Binney, D.S.O., R.N.V.R.

Commander (S) R.C. Hollingworth

Mr. Ebbe Munck

Captain S.B.J. Reynolds, M.B.E., D.S.C.

Mr. Peter Coleridge

At this meeting we discussed the possibility of re-employing the Bridford vessels for the purpose of running arms, ammunition etc. to the Swedish coast and there transferring them to a Danish schooner or schooners for shipment to Denmark. Commander Hollingworth explained that this material as in very short supply and sufficiently large amounts could not be dropped from the air without putting his men in the field to considerable risk. An extremely successful operation would be capable only of delivering about four tons.

Mr. Ebbe Munck, who was over from Sweden, was most anxious to obtain larger amounts and said that about twelve tons at a time could probably be dealt with by transferring at sea, or alternatively it could be dumped in the sea at a given spot on the Swedish coast and marked with buoys, later to be picked up by schooners.

Owing to the then rapid advance of the war, this should take place in the September no-moon period at the latest. We were agreed that the plan seemed feasible, but would require further discussion as to ways and means. In the meantime, to put the necessary machinery into motion, Sir George Binney said he would approach the Ministry of War Transport, who would have to supply the crews for the vessels, and the Ministry of Supply, who would be extremely interested in getting steel products from Sweden. It would be up to S.O.E. who were primarily interested in the operation, to co-ordinate the various departments concerned.

2. Sir George Binney unfortunately had been seriously ill since the end of Operation Bridford and was only convalescing, and had been advised by his doctor that he must not take part in operations for some time. The doctor only won after a very fierce battle.

It was therefore suggested that I should take his place as far as the operation was concerned, but that he would always be available to give his advice on all matters, especially those connected with the political or inter-departmental sides, on which he had vastly more experience than myself. It must be remembered also that this was only a continuation of the "Binney" series of operations, which had kept the Skagerrak open since the fall of Norway, and we were merely trying to follow in his footsteps in a minor degree, without the full benefit of his leadership and after he had borne the entire brunt of organising these series of operations on his shoulders.

Revision of Plans

1. After going into the operation more fully, it seemed to me that we should find great difficulty in transferring up to 12 tons of supplies at sea in the Skagerrak during the very limited hours of a September night, even given perfect weather conditions, apart from the navigational difficulties of two vessels meeting at a given time without landmarks. This could not take place in territorial waters without almost certain interference of

Swedish patrol vessels, or in a spot outside them and within sight of the Swedish coastal lights, which would not lie in the direct German convoy route between the Oslo Fjord and Frederikshavn in Denmark.

Previous Dogger Bank operations had taken up to as much as six hours to transfer three or four tons of cargo. Some other solution to the problem therefore had to be evolved, buoying of the stores in Swedish territorial waters as an alternative presenting an even more difficult operation.

2. A brief outline of the position as it stood at the time was that the Danish Refugee Organisation had a fishing vessel, the *Mariana*, lying in Gothenburg harbour and flying the Swedish flag. This vessel was ostensibly plying between Sweden and Denmark for the purpose of bringing Danish refugees to Sweden. She was allowed to do this with the full knowledge and active co-operation of the Swedish Government, but was in actual fact engaged in smuggling Swedish sub-machine guns to Denmark, with the consent of certain high personages in Sweden.

This, coupled with the fact that the Bridford vessels were perfectly at liberty to trade freely with Sweden, provided they were able to break the German blockade, gave the Operation a much simpler aspect, if the cargo could be transported to Sweden packed as some perfectly harmless material for the Danes and there transferred to the *Mariana* for shipment to Denmark.

The difficulty was to find some material easily disguised which was urgently needed by the Danes, and which could not be provided by Sweden. Nor could it be of very large dimensions owing to the size of our holds and the smallness of our hatches. It could only be something likely to be used for saving Danish lives, and thus appeal to the Swedes on humanitarian grounds, who would be willing and even anxious at this stage of the war to make a big gesture on behalf of their blood brothers the Danes.

The British Iron and Steel Corporation would be both the consignor and consignee of the material, as they had been trading with Sweden all the war and would give the transaction a perfectly natural façade. It would be packed in the appropriate cases to correspond with the varying types of machinery for the mythical vessel envisaged, and would have the usual authentic markings.

3. After further discussion with Mr. Peter Coleridge we evolved the following story, with an alternative if it failed. This was subsequently agreed to by Mr. Ebbe Munck and Commander Hollingworth, to whom we had frequently referred. All our plans came under the attention of Colonel J.S. Wilson, O.B.E., head of the Scandinavian Region. The story would be unfolded to the Swedes by Mr. Ebbe Munck on his return to that country, where he was in close touch and on excellent terms with certain influential people.

Plan A

On his approach to his Swedish friends, Mr. Munck was to say that "He had learned with great distress from his connections in the Danish underground movement that when the Germans finally evacuated Denmark, they intended to massacre a large number of Danish patriots, which would include many Jews. If he tried to smuggle them out at that time they would only be replaced by further hostages. Although for security reasons he could not mention his name, he knew of a prominent Dane who had at his disposal an old British steamer of 1200 to 1400 tons, made in 1902 or thereabouts, lying in Jutland, who could arrange for it to be used to transport these refugees to England when the right time came, thereby saving the Swedish Government the difficulties entailed by possibly having to take them into Sweden.

Unfortunately, the engines of this vessel were in an extremely bad state of repair, and the parts, owing to their age, could be obtained only in England. But in a recent visit to that country, he was lucky enough to co-opt certain very good friends in shipping circles, who would be extremely willing to supply the necessary parts for such a worthy cause. He had also learnt that the British merchant ships which ran the blockade of the Skagerrak during the previous winter, intended to resume their trading during the winter months and would be available to transport the machinery.

If his Swedish friends would help him in the transfer of this vital cargo to the fishing vessel *Mariana* by smoothing out any difficulties with the harbour authorities, customs, etc., it could be transported to Denmark in quantities of about 12 tons at a time."

Plan B

Mr. Munck thought he would not have any difficulty in "putting this across" to his Swedish friends, but if they did not swallow it, he would then approach the Social Minister, Mr. Gustav Moeller, a member of the Swedish Government concerned with the export of Swedish sub-machine guns for the use of the Danish Resistance, and who had "fixed" this particular transaction sub rosa with the police officials and customs in Helsingborg.

When mentioning this to Mr. Moeller, Mr. Munck would say that "The Swedes had supplied the sub-machine guns, but that they were of very little use without the requisite ammunition, and if Mr. Moeller could 'square' the necessary authorities in Gothenburg, as he had done before in Helsingborg, he was in a position to obtain the ammunition from England, which could be shipped in the guise of some perfectly harmless material."

Organisation & Preparations

1. General.

(i) At the conclusion of Operation Bridford the four motor coasters, *Nonsuch*, *Hopewell*, *Gay Viking* and *Gay Corsair*, were taken over by the Admiralty at a meeting called by A.C.N.S.(H), Rear Admiral Brind, on the 5th April 1944.

At this meeting it was decided that the vessels should undergo trials to try to discover the cause of their main faults, and that the crankshafts should be modified. During the summer they would be operated by the Navy for use in "Overlord" or for Air-Sea Rescue work, if such repairs and modifications could be carried out in time.

Alternative methods for employing the vessels had been under consideration, which included running cargoes for the U.S.S.R. from Stockholm through the Gulf of Finland, and in the Adriatic or Aegean running special supplies.

If it proved necessary to continue the Bridford operations in the autumn the vessels would be handed back to the Ministry of War Transport in good running order and in good time. A suggestion by Mr. W.G. Weston, M.W.T., to keep the Merchant Navy crews on board to maintain the unit as a team and to give them additional training was turned down. It seems a reasonable assumption that the running of these vessels as fast transports in "Overlord" for carrying required stores or personnel could have been carried out equally well by Merchant Navy crews who knew them thoroughly as by naval personnel who would have required some considerable training in the maintenance of this type of diesel engine. The interchange of crews could have been only for a matter of three months if the Merchant Navy crews were to undergo further intensive training, as insisted on by C-in-C. Nore, if Bridford was to be resumed in the autumn. The point on training was stressed by A.C.N.S.(H) at the meeting.

The changing over from the Red to the White Ensign might well have compromised the Merchant Navy facade of the vessels, which we had gone to great trouble to build up for the purpose of the Skagerrak operations. It must be remembered that these vessels were originally gunboats, and even after adding the superstructure they could not be called exactly typical motor coasters, and the swapping from one ensign to another and then back again would not be likely to improve their "respectability".

(ii) The Ministry of War Transport, with the unfailing co-operation of Mr. J.W. Bayley of the Ellerman's Wilson Line, Hull, combined to find some scheme for keeping the crews together during the summer, with possible winter operations in view, otherwise the greater proportion would have been returned to the Merchant Navy Pool and scattered all over the globe.

A satisfactory arrangement was devised eventually through the good offices of Sir John Fisher, Director of Coastal Shipping, who agreed to place them on board certain small tankers designed for Overlord. This had the great advantage that each Captain had his own ship and his own crew in practically the same state as in the Bridford operations; also, the Captains did not have to revert to the rank of mate, as they would have done if returning to ordinary Merchant Navy duties. As these tankers were not equipped with wireless, the Marconi Company, in conjunction with Ellerman's Wilson Line, agreed to keep as many of our Radio Officers as they could on as close call as possible.

(iii) As this was to be chiefly an S.O.E. venture and not primarily a commercial enterprise as in the Bridford Operation, that organisation would have to put up a case to the Admiralty to secure the necessary ships. The Ministry of Supply would support the case in that although the supply position did not warrant the mounting of an hazardous operation for itself, it would be extremely valuable to get steel products from Sweden if run in conjunction with some other project such as this.

The position as regards ball bearings had deteriorated since the summer owing to a 25% drop in production caused by the V.1., and the fear that the as yet untried V.2. might cause even greater damage; one of these landing on any of the bearings factories might cause a serious shortage of certain types. In the opinion of the Ministry of Supply the cargo of two Bridford vessels would bridge over any crisis likely to arise.

(iv) The Admiralty were approached by S.O.E. through Mr. C.H.M. Waldock, the head of M.I., who in turn raised the matter with A.C.N.S.(H), Rear Admiral Brind. At a meeting held by him on 23rd August 1944 it was agreed that the operation should take place on the same basis as Bridford, with the only two boats available at the time, the others not yet having completed their overhaul.

The first boat in full trial had given 16 knots at 1150 r.p.m. with a displacement of 145 tons. Both had undergone modifications and it appeared that some at least of their faults had been rectified. A bad vibration period had been discovered between 1150 and 1400 r.p.m. which meant that we would be restricted to revolutions up to 1150 owing to our displacement with a heavy cargo, but that we could increase to 1400 r.p.m. in case of emergency.

Owing to the rapid progress of the war at the time the two vessels would remain in Sweden and await events, as Mr. C.R. Wheeler, Ministry of Supply, did not consider it necessary to put them and their crews to the undue risk of making the homeward voyage unless the necessity arose owing to a sudden shortage of bearings caused by enemy action. If the war did not progress as anticipated the ships would probably return in the October or November no-moon period.

Gothenburg was to be made our port of discharge, as we then considered that the Free Harbour would be the best place to transfer the Danish supplies in preference to Lysekil, as the sight of a Danish schooner arriving there and taking over cargo from our vessels might cause suspicion to arise amongst inhabitants and officials who were not in the picture.

D.D.C.F.M., Captain Cowland, agreed that we should have the services of Lieut. Commander (E) E.C. Thomas and his naval maintenance staff as before. Any repairs in Sweden would be carried out by the Gotaverk yard in Gothenburg, but if the necessity arose Lieut. Commander Thomas or his Chief E.R.A. would be flown out to supervise.

The operation would be in the charge of C-in-C. Nore, and F.O.I.C. Humber would be responsible for the training and working up of the crews.

The two other vessels, M/Vs *Gay Viking* and *Gay Corsair*, would remain under the White Ensign and were handed over to D.D.O.D(I).

2. S.O.E.

(i) Once the Admiralty had agreed to the use of vessels for the operation all possible speed had to be made with our preparations to get ready in time, as it was then 19th August and our first possible sailing date was to be 15th September.

Lieutenant Colonel H.E. Temple, with the assistance of Mr. Menzies, produced a very ingenious list of machinery and spare parts for the mythical Danish steamer, with the exact weights and dimensions of the cases required to take them.

Lieutenant A. Blanner, R.N.V.R., in conjunction with Station XV, arranged all the packing of the ammunition and the building of the required cases. These had to be exceptionally strong and specially reinforced, as it would have been unfortunate in the extreme if some unsuspecting labourer working the crane in Gothenburg had dumped them too heavily on the dock and they had broken open and revealed the contents.

We are most grateful to Mr. G.H. Riches, Ministry of Supply, for his part in supplying all the necessary "authentic" documents in connection with the cargo.

Major Jack O'Reilly acted in all dealings with the Customs Authorities, and it was due to his excellent liaison work that everything went without a hitch. Amongst other things, it was essential that we should be able to leave the United Kingdom without clearing customs, so as to keep our destination secret.

Twenty-six tons of cargo were loaded on the M/Vs *Nonsuch* and *Hopewell* in Hull by 11th September, which speaks for the efficiency with which the work was done.

(ii) The scuttling charges in the ships which we had installed last year had been removed when they had been handed back to the Navy. After the capture intact of *Master Standfast* by the Germans during the previous autumn, we felt that some infinitely quicker and simpler method must be devised than that installed when we took over the ships.

Major J.C. Adamson initiated a system of Cordtex wiring to the existing charges in the mess deck and engine room, with additional charges in the W/T cabin to make certain of destroying the Radar and other most secret equipment. This wiring led to a primer on the bridge with a watertight screw cap. All that was required to blow the charges was to plug in two detonators attached to a Bickford fuse with a five-minute delay, and pull a pin in the same manner as a Mills bomb to ignite them. This unit was carried on the bridge and, when in enemy waters, was always at the hand of the Chief Officer, whose duty it was to scuttle the ship if need be. This could be done with the minimum delay and did not involve searching round with a torch on a dark night trying to find the initiation point. Both vessels were rewired and fitted in a matter of two days and nights continuous work by Station XII.

(iii) Emergency rations and self-heating soups for use in the Skagerrak, where all fires were extinguished, were supplied, together with a sufficient supply of Benzedrine to keep the crews alert in case of need. A case of medical supplies, which had been specially selected by Major H.W. Ireland, was also issued to each vessel. .45 Colt automatics and the necessary ammunition were supplied for the use of the officers on the bridge in case of a surprise boarding party.

(iv) A "scrambler" was installed in the Ellerman's Wilson offices in Hull, where we had been lent the board-room for our sole use by the courtesy of Mr. Bayley. The "green line" and the room proved absolutely invaluable, as I was enabled to hold conferences with the Captains and Chief Officers, and consult with C-in-C's staff at the Nore, and with London, which took place almost daily during the operational no-moon period. It also made it simple for our meteorologist to get weather reports from the Admiralty Forecast Section up to the very last minute before sailing. These final reports often made all the difference to our decision as to whether we should sail or not.

(v) The same series of telegrams as in Bridford would be used for communications with Sweden, worked on the one time pad system, as was the special code used by Mr. Waring between Gothenburg and our departure port or fjord.

All communications relating to our sailing or probable sailing were transmitted from the Humber to C-in-C. Nore and S.O.E., who in turn transmitted them to Sweden via the above system. On receipt of our time of departure from the Swedish coast, relayed through Gothenburg and Stockholm, S.O.E. immediately informed C-in-C. Nore on the "scrambler" so that they should have the maximum notice to lay on air cover. The average time taken to relay these messages was about two hours, including coding and de-coding.

Organisation
A. United Kingdom
(i) It had finally been agreed at A.C.N.S(H)'s meeting that I should be in charge of the expedition both for S.O.E. and M.W.T. I was nominally a civilian, late Captain Reynolds, late Chief Officer Bingham, M.N.

There was considerable difficulty as to the guise I should assume as leader of the expedition. It would have been peculiar to say the least of it if I had remained a Chief Officer for this purpose, both in the eyes of the crews and the Swedish authorities, to say nothing of the Germans if I had happened to fall into their hands. It must be realised that when the *Master Standfast* was lost the enemy obtained all her documents, which disclosed the rather unusual duties and position of Chief Officers and my part as Vice Commodore to Sir George Binney.

It was eventually decided that I should receive a temporary commission as Lieut. Commander, R.N.R. R.N.R. seemed to me to be the right solution, rather than R.N.V.R. as it was the natural follow-on from the Merchant Navy, and would considerably ease any difficulties if I was plied with awkward questions in the event of capture.

I still could not return to Sweden in the name of Reynolds, owing to my past activities in connection with Operation Performance. For the purpose of disguise in Operation Bridford I had grown a beard and had gone unrecognised amongst people I had frequently come into contact with two years previously in Sweden. I returned this winter with no beard and dressed as a Naval officer, and strange as it may seem, with one or two exceptions which did not matter, remained unrecognised as Chief Officer Bingham, M.N. of the winter before. In fact, several members of the Swedish customs and Marine Police asked me personally, "Where is the man with the beard who used to come here last year?"

(ii) Owing to S.O.E's much closer connection with the operation, it was considered advisable that the two chief officers who were supplied by them should be paid by S.O.E. and not by M.W.T. as before. That they should still appear as "genuine" merchant seamen by remaining on the ship's articles, they would be paid by the Ellerman's Wilson Line and their pay refunded by S.O.E. They would act as liaison officers between the various departments concerned and naval authorities, as before, apart from their duties as gunnery officers, and could act for me in my absence, or in the event of one ship being in Sweden and one over here.

Captain Lord Fitzwilliam, D.S.C., (Chief Officer Lawrence) and Mr. E.B. Ruffman, D.S.C. (late Captain R.A.) both of whom were with us during Bridford, volunteered their services for the expedition. Lord Fitzwilliam having the greater experience would act for me as Vice Commodore.

When the third vessel, the M/V *Gay Viking*, was acquired from the Admiralty, we secured the services of Mr. J.B. Woodeson, late Captain R.A., who had been wounded in the leg in North Africa and captured by the Germans, and subsequently spent a year as a prisoner of war in the hands of the Italians before being repatriated.

(iii) Mr. Peter Coleridge was again responsible for all the details of the operation and for our general welfare. At the mere "waving of a wand" anything "from a flea to an elephant" appeared in the shortest possible time. He was in fact as always invaluable.

B. Stockholm
Mr. R.B. Turnbull and Mr. H.W.A. Waring were responsible for handling our cargo in Sweden. Our responsibility ended as soon as we had delivered it safely at the port of destination. Mr. Ebbe Munck was solely responsible for the negotiations with the various Swedish officials concerned and had completed these by 14th September 1944, the day before our first possible D-day, and only a week after his return from this country. This cannot have been easy, and the speed with which they were carried out speaks for his ability as a negotiator.

C. Gothenburg

Mr. Waring made the arrangements in Gothenburg for the landing of our cargo through the hands of our agents, the Wilson Co., who had acted for us in all previous operations and who made the transaction outwardly appear perfectly normal. They were of course in complete ignorance of the contents of the cargo.

Lysekil and not Gothenburg was eventually decided upon as our port of destination. There would be no necessity for the Danish schooner to go there at all as the cargo would be discharged direct into a lighter, which would then be towed down the coast to some secluded fjord and there trans-shipped. It was further felt that far fewer customs and harbour officials would have to be "in the know" in Lysekil, and we were also on excellent terms with them from our operations there last year. It would be difficult in the extreme to prevent someone smelling a rat in a port as large as Gothenburg, where memories still lingered of our misdemeanours in the Performance Operation.

In spite of this Gothenburg would be used for loading the steel cargo, as we did not wish to give warning locally of our impending operation by having cargo sent up to Lysekil and then stored. We also had all our fuel oil and stores transferred to Gothenburg to give the impression that a resumption of the operation was unlikely.

In addition, as we no longer had the *Dicto* and *Lionel* anchored in Brofjord to use as base ships, the use of Gothenburg would make things far easier for the crews if they were to be kept hanging about during the moon period. Lysekil, or in fact any small port on the west coast, was in a prohibited area, and the facilities for the crews being allowed ashore at all were very limited. Living aboard in extremely cramped quarters in a very cold climate in ships not built or equipped for those temperatures was not exactly conducive to morale.

Mr. Waring was undoubtedly the mainstay of our organisation in Sweden, as he was in all past operations. Apart from the handling of our inward cargo, which necessitated very close liaison with the Danish contacts, (not an easy matter in itself owing to their extreme lack of security and inability to realise that at all costs our Merchant Navy crews must not be compromised) he was also in charge of the welfare of our crews on arrival, the handling of our outward cargo, and liaison between H.M. Legation in Stockholm and the Swedish Naval Staff in Gothenburg.

All this was only a side-line to his other duties, most important of which at the time was as negotiator for the ball bearing deal between the S.K.F. Company and H.M. Government.

Owing to the fact that the Germans had four destroyers and a cruiser in the Oslo Fjord apart from other naval craft, for minelayer duties and as escorts to the convoys plying between Frederikshavn, Denmark, and the Oslo Fjord, the danger of interception was greater than the previous year when their heavier concentrations were at Kristiansand South. If by chance they got news of our impending arrival they would need very little notice to lay on a strong intercepting force just outside territorial waters, and would not be chasing us from Kristiansand but coming out to meet us. Nor would the patrol have had to cover a very wide area, as they knew as well as we did the Swedes had mined both inner and outer territorial waters since the previous winter, up to a point about ten miles north of the Hallo Light.

It would be the natural assumption that we would not enter them south of this point. It was only a matter of thirty miles from the northern edge of these minefields to Stromstad, marking the Norwegian-Swedish frontier: previously we had always refrained from approaching anywhere near this boundary.

Owing to this mining we were also deprived of more than thirty miles of the coastline to the southward which we had used before for slipping into Swedish waters. Although we intended risking the Swedish minefields if we found ourselves being chased by the Germans, we were disinclined to do so without very good reason, as we had been strictly warned by the Swedish Foreign Office that they were highly dangerous even for shallow draft vessels. There had been several instances of Swedish fishing vessels ignoring them and being blown sky-high.

Apart from any leakage through the Swedish Secretary General, which we hoped was unlikely as he had been informed of the impending operation for his "personal and most secret" information, there remained the "bugbear" of having to inform the Swedish Navy so that they in turn could warn their patrols, for as we had learnt from past experience their Navy could not be termed exactly "friendly". I insisted, therefore, that the maximum notice they should receive of our arrival must be as from 2200 hours on the night of our entry into the Skagerrak. It is not a very far cry from Gothenburg to the Oslo Fjord for anyone desiring to pass on the news.

Mr. Waring personally informed the Swedish Naval Staff on times transmitted from London. The need for this security was impressed on H.M. Minister, Stockholm, in a telegram from the Foreign Office. Mr. Waring very wisely appeared rather vague as to the exact time they were to be informed: on one of our many abortive attempts when we had to turn back when actually in the Skagerrak, he did not tell them until 0030; on our eventual successful voyage his memory was even worse and they were not informed until 0100. There were no repercussions because of this from the Admiral, West Coast, perhaps because the war had swung so much in the Allies' favour since the previous winter. It is after all always best to end up on the right side.

Lanshovding Malte Jakobsen, Governor of the County of Gothenburg, who had always been a good friend to England, and was also anxious to help the Danes, was made aware of the impending operation and greatly helped in the smoothing over of customs etc. at Lysekil. He was also responsible, after we had discharged and gone to Gothenburg to load, for warning us not to use Lysekil as a port in the future, owing to there having been a possible leakage of information through one of the officials.

Ministry of War Transport
Immediately the two vessels were made available I had meetings with Mr. Hole and Mr. Craig, Foreign Shipping Relations M.W.T., who at once procured two of our last year's crews: they were then serving on the Chant tankers operating from the Hamble river, and had made frequent voyages to France carrying supplies for the invasion.

It was somewhat difficult to make a choice from the four Captains and their crews then available: Captain H. Whitfield, O.B.E., who was aboard M/V *Gay Viking* last year and with whom I sailed, and Captain D. Stokes, O.B.E., late M/V *Hopewell*, were finally selected. Lord Fitzwilliam had sailed as Chief Officer with Captain Stokes during the Bridford operations.

When the third vessel was finally taken over, Captain H.W. Jackson, O.B.E., was appointed as Master at the request of M.W.T.

M/Vs *Nonsuch* and *Hopewell* were handed over by F.O.I.C. Humber to M.W.T.'s representatives in Hull on 28th August 1944, and the Merchant Navy crews signed on, Captain Whitfield being appointed to the M/V *Nonsuch* and Captain Stokes to his old ship the M/V *Hopewell*.

M.W.T. were most anxious that the crews should be told of the nature of the undertaking before asking them to volunteer, as they would be exposing themselves to extra risk in the event of capture and possible discovery by the Germans of the type of material they were carrying. I pointed out that from a security point of view this might well ruin the whole project and compromise a number of people unnecessarily, first of whom might easily be members of the Danish Underground movement. They must further realise that immediately the Merchant Navy crews were recalled they would guess that it was for a renewal of the Bridford operation, and if they were told the full facts there would almost certainly be a leakage. We had learnt from experience the complete inability of certain members of the crews to refrain from talking when under the influence of drink, and after the then recent publicity in the press they would be even more inclined to talk. Still more dangerous would be the aspect in Sweden: we were likely to be there for some considerable time, and if any of the sailors revealed, in the bars or cafes of Gothenburg, what we had really been carrying, it needs little imagination to realise what the result would be.

I further emphasised that in the event of capture or questioning by curious Swedes or Nazi agents in Sweden, they would all be in a far safer position if they knew absolutely nothing. A clear conscience is very difficult to shake under cross-examination, and they could quite truthfully say they had no idea they were carrying anything other than ships' stores and engine parts for Sweden.

It was finally agreed that neither Masters nor crew should be told anything at all, nor would the Ellerman's Wilson Line realise the nature of our cargo, apart from the innocent details inscribed on the ships' manifest.

Mr. J.N.S. Craig, on whose shoulders fell the greater part of the work for M.W.T. in connection with the operation, was extremely helpful and was always willing to do everything in his power to bring it to a successful conclusion.

The Nore Command

The control of the operation was placed in the hands of C-in-C. Nore, who took the greatest possible interest. Both he and the members of his staff were invariably anxious to help with all the means at their disposal, and

I personally shall always greatly value the experience of having worked under his command.

Remembering our experiences of last year with our engines, C-in-C. made a signal to the Admiralty on 29th August 1944 requesting that a third vessel should be allocated to us as a stand-by. This request was not acceded to fully, but it was arranged that the M/V *Gay Viking*, then carrying out trials, could be used if the necessity arose. She would in addition be fully equipped and the necessary calibration of the W/T carried out so that she would be ready with the least possible delay. This wise precaution proved correct, as the M/V *Hopewell* broke a crankshaft on our first attempt to reach Sweden, and the *Gay Viking* was allotted to us as a third ship.

C-in-C. further tried to secure for us the later type of Radar as he had always maintained that it would be our most valuable piece of equipment. This was undoubtedly the case both in Bridford and Moonshine, and many times saved us from running into enemy patrols or unknown surface craft. Unfortunately, the type of generators needed were in short supply and we were unable to obtain them.

Communications between the motor coasters and the Nore Command were worked on the one time pad system in conjunction with Admiralty cypher No. 5. With very few exceptions this system worked admirably with signals both to and from the vessels. These were greatly facilitated by the use of broadcast NN, the Nore Command Port Wave, and additional ship-shore calling waves to which we did not have access in Operation Bridford. We were fortunate on our side in securing Mr. E. Hodgson, M.B.E., our best radio officer from the previous year. In addition to their having further training in Admiralty signals procedure and Radar, he went to great pains and trouble in tutoring the junior officers in their tasks. This took place almost daily during our long spells of inactivity when we were held up because of weather conditions.

Admiralty
(i) Operations Division (H)
I had further consultations with Captain Pizey, D.O.D.(H) and Commander Walker after A.C.N.S.(H)'s meeting on 23rd August 1944, concerning the details of the operation, before it was handed over to the control of C-in-C. Nore. He was also responsible for putting through my commission as speedily as possible through A.C.N.S.(H) and Mr. Waldock, Head of M.I.

(ii) Intelligence

Reports on enemy dispositions in the Skagerrak, their air patrols, and number and types of aircraft stationed in Norway and Denmark, in so far as they affected the operations, were furnished by Commander (S) N.E. Denning, O.I.C., Admiralty.

I paid him numerous visits to talk over intelligence reports, and the times of sailing of the German convoys from Fredrikstad, Norway, and Frederikshavn, Denmark, as these intimately affected the time of our arrival in the convoy route, which was just outside Swedish territorial water. He went out of his way to keep us accurately informed, and whether we were in the middle of the North Sea or waiting to sail from the U.K. or the Swedish coast we always felt certain that we should receive the latest information with the minimum delay, and that he would not let us run into trouble unnecessarily, in so far as it was in his power to prevent it.

When we were in Sweden any relevant information was passed through Commander A.E. de B. Jennings, N.I.D.(Q), and transmitted to us in cypher direct to Gothenburg.

When we were at sea Commander Denning informed C-in-C. Nore, who would signal us to return if the occasion warranted it.

(iii) Naval Meteorological Branch & Admiralty Forecast Section

Captain L.G. Garbett, C.B.E., and his staff gave us invaluable assistance and placed one of their officers at our disposal for the duration of the operation. We were fortunate in again having the services of Sub. Lieut. M.A. Choyce, R.N.V.R. who had been with us for the whole of the Bridford Operation, and who knew the conditions under which we could operate better than anyone else.

At a later stage of the operation when Sub. Lieut. Choyce was in Sweden, we were lent Lieut. A.F. Coles for a short period to take his place over here. This came at a time when meteorological officers were in very short supply, and we are extremely grateful to Captain Garbett and Captain Beatty for going to great trouble to obtain someone for us. Owing to the vagaries of the air service to Sweden and the limited time we then had left in which we could operate, we could not afford to miss a spell of fine weather by flying Choyce backwards and forwards from there to the U.K.

One cannot emphasise sufficiently the part which the weather played in the operation, and that we had to have a man on the spot to draw the weather charts, so that we had a complete picture of what was happening. It was impossible to rely on short written forecasts as we had learnt from the early part of Operation Bridford. Not only had the meteorological officer to know his job thoroughly but he also had to know the ships and what they could do.

It must be realised that these ships were not built to cross the North Sea in bad weather and at high speeds carrying heavy loads of freight. They did stand up to reasonably bad weather as we proved this year, but not bad weather as judged by the standard of big ships, and then only when we were reduced to our slowest speed, sometimes to the extent of cutting out our centre engine.

For the purpose of running through the Skagerrak in the night we had to be able to proceed at 16 knots, and this was only possible in a head wind of maximum Force 5. Above this we would have to reduce because of heavy pounding. If the sea was on the beam, it was just possible to keep up our speed in a Force 6, and with a following or quartering sea we could compete with even worse weather, but only at the expense of bad steering, as we would yaw 40 degrees and more either side of our course.

Sub. Lieutenant Choyce himself did not fully realise the effect of the sea on our vessels until he had been out with us in a heavy swell, and that on a day which he had judged to be ideal for us: he was substantially correct, but had forgotten the aftermath of several days' successive gales. Swell was something we were continually misjudging or apt to forget, in our eagerness to be off. It was only after bitter experience that we realised we must allow anything from 24 to 48 hours for a heavy swell to subside, as it only needed moderate winds to kick up a very nasty sea on top of one of these: at least a nasty sea from our standpoint. Often after weeks of hanging about and waiting, it was almost impossible to resist going out in the first fine spell, knowing full well in the back of our minds there was bound to be too much swell.

It was our habit, knowing the shortcomings of our engines, to nurse them at moderate speeds for the first 24 hours of the voyage, preparatory to the final dash of 10 to 12 hours through the Skagerrak, when we wanted all they could give us, and in the hope they would not break down. We therefore had to have almost guaranteed fine weather for a minimum period of 30 hours. It is almost unbelievable, but it is a fact, that from our first attempt in the middle of September, when the weather was perfect but we were recalled by the Admiralty, until Christmas, these conditions did not prevail. In a short period of fine weather at the end of December fog was so thick in the Humber that we were unable to leave our berth. Again, from January until the end of March only the shortest spells prevailed, enabling us to get to Sweden and return: the outward voyage was by no means a pleasure trip.

The question remains as to whether we were very lucky last winter during Bridford, when one or more voyages was made during every no-moon period from October to March, or exceptionally unlucky with Moonshine.

A succession of depressions chased each other across the Atlantic causing successive gales in the North Sea, which hardly ceased the whole winter. There were admittedly intervals when the winds would drop, but they never lasted long enough to allow the sea to subside as well.

Sub. Lieut. Choyce's judgment was invariably sound, and often proved correct in the face of adverse opinion from the Forecast Section: he was unshakeable in his decisions once they were made, and nothing would induce him to see things into the weather chart which did not exist. As can be imagined, in a desire to get the operation done, we were always inclined to try to make the forecast better than it really was. On more than one occasion he saved us from being too impetuous, and rarely did we find him at fault. There were times, however, during this almost unbelievable winter, when the devil himself could not forecast what the elements would produce next. Sub. Lieut. Choyce unquestionably gave us of his best, and did an excellent job for us.

In addition, we owe our thanks to the Forecast Section of the Admiralty, who, on the numerous occasions on which we consulted them over very tricky decisions, gave us all the information at their disposal. It is not their fault that the "seaweed" sometimes let them down.

General Survey of the Operation
1. From the start of this winter's operation we seemed to be dogged by bad luck – if it was not the weather it was the engines, when these would fail us and cause us to miss one of the golden opportunities of a fine spell which came to us so infrequently. We had learnt to expect engine trouble,

but not the almost continuous series of gale warnings which arrived from the Admiralty on one's breakfast plate with the regularity of *The Times*.

It started on our first voyage in September, when everything was going almost too well. The weather was perfect, the engines were running at their best, and intelligence reports were good, for it was before the heavy convoy traffic between Norway and Denmark had begun, but we were recalled in a signal from C-in-C. Nore, when we were nearly at our dusk position at the approaches to the Skagerrak.

While returning the M/V *Hopewell* broke a crankshaft, which more than dampened our spirits, for it seemed that in spite of the modifications, we were to suffer again from our old engine troubles, which had hampered us so consistently a year ago.

C-in-C's decision to recall us was unquestionably correct, for a heavy concentration of enemy surface craft was engaged in laying mines in our path in the Skagerrak.

From then on, our hoodoo seemed to pursue us, to culminate in the collision between the M/V *Hopewell* and the M/V *Gay Viking* in the Skagerrak in very poor visibility, when the *Gay Viking* was lost.

A superstition seemed to exist amongst some of the sailors that it was because I had shaved off my beard, and on many mornings, when the clouds were scudding across the sky at what seemed to be a hundred miles per hour, I was greeted with the familiar request: "Please grow your beard again, Sir!"

In the light of some of the decisions taken on our unsuccessful attempts to reach the Swedish coast, it must be borne in mind that these were the only vessels in the United Kingdom capable of doing this particular operation.

They had to be fast, the faster the better. (N.B. Operation Bridford was planned on a minimum speed of 20 knots, and ended up at about 17½: Moonshine was reduced to a bare 16.) To ensure our running through the Skagerrak during the hours of darkness, they had to be of shallow draft to go over the minefields, which restricted their size, and they had to have the range, therefore they must have diesel engines. The round trip was over 1,000 miles; during Bridford we had to carry enough fuel for the return voyage.

It is unbelievable that this is the only fast Diesel we have tried to produce in six years of war, and that, to put it mildly, a very bad one, against an enemy who were adept in their production. Our M.T.Bs and M.G.B.s, equipped with Packard engines, to add to the risks of their already hazardous tasks, were forced to do battle loaded with high octane.

In Operation Cabaret, using Class "D" M.G.B.s, we had to carry tins of this fuel on the deck, otherwise we would not have had enough to get home.

Fast diesel craft capable of 25 knots or more would have ensured a continuous Skagerrak service entailing little risk. We would have been able to outdistance any of the usual patrol craft, and been many miles outside the danger area by dawn, to say nothing of what our M.T.B.'s and M.G.B.'s could have accomplished in the way of offensive operations against the enemy. To the best of my knowledge no offensive surface patrols actually entered the Skagerrak after the fall of Norway.

In the future, when we may have to rely on our "little ships" for safeguarding the Channel, cannot they be equipped with modern high-speed engines? It surely cannot be said there are not the brains in this country to compete with the Germans and even the Swedes over this type of engine. If there are not, then we must emulate the Japanese and copy someone else's.

During the course of the winter, although we achieved, and more than achieved, our primary object, a number of abortive voyages took place: a brief summary of these is given below:

	Mileage covered. outward.	Successful voyage homeward.	Successful voyage	Unsuccessful attempts.
M/V *Nonsuch* (Flagship)	10,640	1	1	8
M/V *Hopewell*	9,800	1	1	6
M/V *Gay Viking*	9,660	1	Lost on voyage.	6

To give a true picture of the operation, it is necessary to record the effect of these abortive attempts on the morale of the crews. There is no question in my own mind that these took far more out of everyone concerned than a successful voyage, even if the latter involved a greater mental strain.

The crews would return dispirited after long hours at sea, nearly always wet and suffering from the effects of severe sea-sickness. Even fishermen who had been to sea for fifteen years and more seemed unable to stand up to the violent movement of their vessels. It is no exaggeration to say that if it was at all rough 90% of officers and men would be sea-sick, and to the extent of being physically knocked out. A tribute to their spirit, however, which was significant of the enthusiasm they displayed in everything connected with the operation, was that they never lost their keenness to see the job through, come what may. We had only one instance of a man wishing to leave during the whole winter out of a company of some sixty officers and men.

For days and weeks on end we were held up waiting for the right weather, unable to move. We dare not put to sea for training purposes in the fear that our engines would breakdown and cause us to miss a chance of doing the operation. Owing to the excessively muddy water in the Humber Estuary our water pumps wore out very rapidly, which necessitated frequent changes, and this all took time. We always had to be ready to leave at six hours' notice, and in addition were controlled by the tides, so it can be seen that all we could do was to possess ourselves in patience, and await the psychological moment. And it needed the patience of Job.

This had to be accomplished without any regular discipline: discipline as understood in any of the Services does not prevail in the Merchant Navy. It could only work on the basis of good relationship and respect, and an unfailing determination on the part of everyone to stick together until we could write "Finis" to the operation.

It is probably needless to point out to anyone who has experienced the difficulties that arise from this endless waiting about before any hazardous enterprise, even with a disciplined body of men, what we had to contend with without this same discipline.

I am deeply grateful to all the officers and men for the way in which they backed me up unquestioningly in all my decisions. It must be recalled that only the Chief Officers knew of the significance of the operation; the ships' companies only looked upon it as another Bridford, and therefore it was the actual number of voyages that worried them – of primary importance in their minds was the homeward cargo, when in point of fact it was vice versa.

At times it appeared that I should never be the bearer of good tidings, and the number of occasions on which I had to give the signal to return for one cause or another might well have caused greater hearts to lose faith in their leader. I myself wondered whether I had become too weather conscious, and should have carried on. Looking back on the operation I hope I can safely say that on only one occasion was I doubtful as to whether I made the right decision. In making these decisions I always tried to keep before my mind the one and only rule I think one must try to stick to in any operation – "Is the operation vital?"

If it is, then all and every risk must be taken to carry it out. Moonshine was not vital, only very important, therefore one had to try to stick to the limits laid down for the operation. Men's lives and ships were at stake, and their loss would not have justified the results. One could have relied on luck to pull it off, but there are many dead men who have relied too much on their luck. In the category of vital operations, I would put "Rubble" and Performance". In these I think a policy of stake all was more than justified.

It was in view of this continuous inaction, and our missing several opportunities by being held up in the Humber owing to fog – which always seemed to arrive with the fine periods – that I asked C-in-C. Nore if we might move to Aberdeen, for use as a departure port. It had the additional advantages of shortening the voyage to Sweden by 80 miles or more, we were not controlled by tides, and could get out at any time to do sea training for a few hours. More important than anything else was that we could slip out in thick fog, not having the more than 16 miles of dangerous estuary to navigate, as in the Humber.

We moved there early in the New Year during a lull in the gales, and finally made our successful voyage on 13 January 1945 from that port. During our stay there we received every facility from Rear-Admiral Sir Lionel Wells, F.O.I.C., and his staff. He very kindly lent his own cabin, which was equipped with a "scrambler" for conferences.

The change of environment undoubtedly put new heart into the men, and gave them the impression that this move might dispel the hoodoo. It is very unlikely that we should have been able to make the voyage from Hull, as adverse weather conditions during the first night out would have prevented our making the required speed.

2. My report on one of our more trying unsuccessful attempts is given below, together with our successful voyage to Sweden and the return.

Unsuccessful Voyage, 21st October 1944.

On 21.10.44, after nearly a month of bad weather, the forecast showed a possible chance of sailing. Wind would not be more than a Force 4, from the N.E., with a good chance of it veering to S.W. in the Skagerrak on the day we would be due to go in.

My opinion was the sea would not have calmed down sufficiently for our vessels after a week of high winds in the North Sea and south easterly gale the day before. On the other hand, the future seemed to hold no brighter prospects and we were fast approaching the end of the no-moon period, and the forecast showed nothing to be gained by waiting another day: but in the event of our having to turn back it did not appear that we should meet any really bad weather. After weighing all arguments in consultation with the Masters and Chief Officers I decided that we should make the attempt, fully realising it to be a gamble on the weather.

Permission to sail having been received from C-in-C. Nore, M/Vs *Nonsuch*, *Gay Viking* and *Hopewell* left Albert Dock, Hull, at 1740 hours on 21.10.44. and passed through the Humber Boom at 1923 hours.

During the night there was a heavy swell from the S.E. causing us to roll heavily, and wind was Force 3 to 4. On 22.10.44. conditions remained much the same but with the wind increasing to Force 4 and freshening in the squalls. Visibility was good with seven tenths cloud. We were proceeding at 1150 revolutions, which are our maximum safety revolutions. Owing to the state of the sea however we were only making just over 15 knots instead of our usual 16½ knots. At 1420 hours a plane passed over at a great height, flying in a north easterly direction and leaving a vapour trail. It was too high to distinguish what it was.

At 1600 hours M/V *Hopewell* reported seeing another plane through a gap in the clouds, flying at about 1000 feet.

At 1700 hours, after checking our position with the other two vessels, it appeared that we should not reach our dusk position until 1930 hours, more than two hours later than we had intended. This, however, still left us time to reach the Swedish coast by dawn provided there was no increase in wind and sea. In fact, we were hoping we would be in the lee when we got well into the Skagerrak, and that the sea would have died down sufficiently for us to increase to an emergency speed of 20 knots at 1400 revolutions at midnight. We had calculated that we could safely do this for about six hours without breaking anything.

At dusk however the wind increased to Force 5, but did not cause us to reduce speed.

At 1930 hours we altered course from 053° to 061°: the wind was still increasing and we were then meeting the sea head on and beginning to pound heavily. I decided however to carry on for another two hours as the glass was high and steady and there still seemed a chance that the increase in wind was only temporary as it had been in the squalls all day.

At 1945 hours our Gyro compass broke down owing to the violent movement of the ship. This was repaired by 2000 hours, although it would be of no use for three hours until it settled down. Our surroundings did not appear to fit in correctly and we suspected a fault in the echo sounder.

At 2100 we obtained several echoes on the Radar, and planes were heard flying very low overhead: they continued to circle us for some time.

By 2130 the wind had increased to Force 6 from the E.S.E. with a short heavy swell from the E.N.E., and we were pounding so badly we were forced to reduce to 1000 revolutions.

At this juncture the odds seemed to be definitely against us, and if we carried on with conditions appearing to get worse there was every chance of our being still two hours or more from the Swedish coast by daylight. This would mean passing across the main Oslo-Frederikshavn traffic route after dawn. In addition, we were unable to man our forward Oerlikons owing to breaking seas, and a great proportion of the crews were greatly handicapped owing to severe sea-sickness, both of which facts would greatly reduce the fighting efficiency of the ships if we became involved in any kind of action.

A decision could no longer be delayed owing to our fuel position, and taking everything into consideration, including the breakdown of our navigational aids, I considered circumstances did not warrant our carrying on and thereby putting the three vessels and their crews to a very considerable risk.

If one vessel alone had been making the voyage the risk would probably have been worth taking.

At 2130 hours I gave the order to return, our position then being approximately 57′ 40 North 7′ 47 East, and about 125 miles from the Swedish coast. With a following sea we increased to 1150 revolutions, intending to keep this up for several hours in order to be as far as possible from the Norwegian and Danish coasts by daylight and to enable us to send a wireless message giving information of our return at the first safe opportunity. It was fully realised that this would not be in time to prevent the Swedish navy being informed, i.e. midnight on 22.10.44. I did not feel justified in breaking wireless silence before 0500 on 23.10.44. At 0515 hours the following was passed to C-in-C. Nore:

"All three vessels returning owing to strong head winds. Further message giving E.T.A. follows."

At 0530 hours M/Vs *Gay Viking* and *Hopewell* lost contact with us in a heavy rainstorm, and although we reduced to 850 revolutions for an hour, we were unable to pick them up.

From 0800 hours on 23.10.44 we were reduced to 850 revolutions owing to shortage of fuel. Wind and sea were moderate but increasing during heavy rainstorms. During daylight a number of Danish fishing vessels were seen off the N.E. corner of the Dogger Bank.

At 2000 hours the following message was passed to C-in-C. Nore from M/V *Nonsuch*:

"Lost contact with other two. E.T.A. Boom 0400 24.10.44."

At this time we knew that the other two were in the vicinity as we had picked up a message from *Gay Viking* being passed to the Nore.

At dusk the wind increased and by midnight was blowing Force 7 from the north west with very heavy rainstorms. It was fortunate that we did not meet this a few hours earlier in the North Sea.

We passed through the Humber Boom at 0200 hours on 24.10.44, and anchored off the Middle Light Vessel at 0240 hours. M/Vs *Hopewell* and *Gay Viking* anchored at approximately 0220 hours, having sent the following message to C-in-C., Nore at 1902 hours on 23.10.44:

"E.T.A. Flamborough midnight 23.10.44."

On arrival all three vessels had sufficient fuel left for two to three hours steaming.

The vessels had been at sea for 57 hours and covered a distance of 834 miles. Although our object was not achieved valuable experience was gained.

M/V *Gay Viking* was leaking badly into the mess decks, due to broken spray strakes, but this was rectified in six or seven hours after our return. All the vessels were ready to go to sea by the following day.

I cannot stress too strongly the keenness of all crews, who in spite of a very unpleasant trip were most anxious to make the attempt again as soon as possible.

Engines.
Only minor failures occurred on M/Vs *Nonsuch* and *Hopewell*, nothing of consequence. Average engine revolutions for the trip were: M/V *Nonsuch* 1037 revs., M/V *Gay Viking* 1025 revs., M/V *Hopewell* 1035 revs. It is therefore obvious that the engines were never put to any stress and any major breakdown would have been unwarrantable.

Communications.
These were very satisfactory, although reception on M/V *Nonsuch* faded out at 1900 hours on 22.10.44. This has since been rectified by renewing the valves.

Navigational aids.
These were badly affected by the motion of the ships in heavy weather. Gyros on M/Vs *Nonsuch* and *Gay Viking* both failed and the Echo sounder on M/V *Nonsuch* gave false soundings owing to stripped gearing.

In addition, all electrical equipment on the bridge was affected by heavy spray, and also owing to heavy rolling D/F bearings were unreliable.

Successful Voyage to Sweden, 13th January 1945.
During the December moon period it was decided to move the motor coasters to Aberdeen for use as a departure port. It had the advantage over the Humber in that we were less likely to be held up by fog and were not controlled by tides, and could also undergo sea training. In addition, it shortened the voyage to Sweden by about five hours. With the permission of C-in-C., Nore and C-in-C. Rosyth the date fixed for moving to Aberdeen was 3rd January 1945, three days before the first possible D-Day. Owing to gales we were unable to make a move before 6th January, arriving at Aberdeen on the 7th, after meeting strong head winds and just in time to avoid a further gale. Additional gales prevented the operation taking place until 13th January.

Conditions then appeared favourable, with light variable winds all the way across and no likelihood of any change for 48 hours or more. Intelligence reports were against us, there being every possibility of a mine laying operation taking place in the Skagerrak. It also appeared extremely likely that this would be in the deep water in the centre of the Skagerrak, which was our usual course. After consultation with London, it was decided that we should sail, owing to the lateness of the season and the urgency of the material. Naval Intelligence would keep in close touch with us on W/T, giving us any further available information.

The three motor coasters left Aberdeen at 1935 hours on 13th January 1945, after waiting for a final weather report which indicated no change.

At midnight there was a light westerly wind, slight sea and moderate swell from the N.E. During the following day wind increased from the west, and at midday was blowing Force 5 to 6. Visibility was 1 to 2 miles, with low cloud and drizzle which made it almost impossible for us to be spotted by hostile aircraft. Wind increased during the afternoon and there was a short steep sea which made any chance of returning impossible even if we had received any W/T message. W/T reception was also very bad on all ships, so I decided to increase speed. When we reached our dusk position at 1850 hours at the approach to the Skagerrak the wind had increased to Force 7, the sea was very rough and we were yawing anything up to 40° either side of our course.

At 2200 hours the wind began to veer to north and we lost the *Gay Viking*, the last ship in the line, when doing a sharp Radar turn. By 2300 hours the wind had veered to N.N.E. and was blowing Force 6, gusting to Force 7 with a rough beam sea. It appeared at this juncture that we would be lucky if we reached the Swedish coast by daylight. Fortunately, at 0230 hours wind and sea decreased and we were able to increase speed.

We made an excellent landfall and at 0430 sighted the Vaderobod light at full distance, and by 1600 had picked up a pilot off Vaderobod inside territorial waters. *Gay Viking* had arrived twenty minutes before us. We lay off Vaderobod until daylight, when we proceeded to Lysekil in inner territorial waters, arriving at 0929.

The voyage was without incident and nothing was seen except flak and searchlights off the Danish coast in the vicinity of Hantsholm.

Owing to the probability of any minelaying operation taking place in the centre of the Skagerrak, which then appeared unlikely owing to the bad weather, we had changed our course line to take us along the edge of the shallow water on the Danish coast with the intention of going into their minefields if intercepted.

Owing to a full gale and blinding snowstorms on the following day, we were unable to proceed to Gothenburg to load.

On 17th January 1945 the ships proceeded to Gothenburg on the inside route, although the wind was Force 7 and the sea rough, we were in the lee most of the way. The Swedish navy provided us with a Fleet Sweeper as escort.

The ships arrived at Gothenburg at 1245 on 17th January. There were only minor engine defects, but average engine revolutions for the voyage were only in the region of 1040.

W/T reception on M/Vs *Nonsuch* and *Hopewell* was only about 40% efficient, but *Gay Viking* was up to 90%.

It is interesting to note the change in the Swedish attitude since last year, every facility being given to us at Lysekil and Gothenburg, and also on the voyage round the coast, during which certain incidents occurred before.

Return Voyage, 5th February 1945.

During the time spent in Gothenburg waiting for the no-moon period, I made a visit up the west cost with Mr. H.W.A. Waring, Ministry of Supply representative in Sweden, to find some small out of the way spot to use as a departure port, it being hopeless to leave direct from Gothenburg owing to the fact that the Germans would almost certainly get immediate news of our departure.

The first place we visited was a fishing village called Fjallebacka, on the same latitude as Vaderobod. It had the advantage of having a very small population, which would ensure that any stranger arriving who might be placed there by the Germans would immediately be noticed. Unfortunately, there were signs of a certain amount of ice in the harbour, and in addition it would have been difficult to obtain a sufficient supply of shore lighting on which we were dependent: given time the latter difficulty could be overcome, and it is an ideal place to remember for future operations.

It was eventually decided that we should move to Hunnebostrand, Lat. 58° 26' north, Long. 11° 18' 0" east: it is slightly larger than Fjallebacka but has an excellent small harbour which at that time was ice-free. In addition, the entrance from outer territorial waters was a good deal simpler.

From 22.1.45. the weather turned extremely cold, and by 29.1.45. Gothenburg harbour was full of ice, and at one time even the ferries were having difficulty in crossing the river. Also reports showed that ice breakers were being used in inner territorial waters up the coast.

The motor coasters, lying alongside M/V *Dicto* in Lindholmen, which was being used as a base ship, were frozen in and it appeared that if conditions continued, we should have the greatest difficulty in leaving without damage to our propellers and also to the hulls of our ships, which would not stand up to really heavy ice. Luckily, on 31.1.45. there was a slight increase in temperature, and by 2.2.45. the day of our departure, the ice situation improved. The vessels had to be broken out of the harbour by ice breakers and towed into the river. By only using the centre engine and proceeding at minimum speed we avoided doing any damage.

We were met outside by a Swedish minesweeper which was to act as escort and would also serve as ice breaker if we ran into heavy ice. Owing to the fact that the inner route was frozen we had to proceed in outer territorial waters and even here encountered patches of ice all up the coast until we reached Hunnebostrand which was still ice free. The three vessels were safely berthed at Hunnebostrand by 1400 on 2.2.45. and owing to extremely poor visibility up the coast it is very unlikely that they were seen moving up by anyone from the coast who might be interested in their movements.

On 3.2.45. the weather was fairly favourable but we received a message not to start from the Admiralty, and during the night it was evident that an air attack was taking place in the Skagerrak, flak being seen out to sea.

On 4.2.45. the weather had deteriorated and looked most unlikely for the following two days, and a telegram was sent to London to that effect.

Although strong winds were predicted in the Skagerrak all the time according to the weather chart, we were surprised that at Hunnebostrand there was no wind at all, and by observations from some high ground could see no sign of sea or swell in the Skagerrak up to twenty miles out, where we expected it to be very rough. It appears that the depressions were being broken up by the very cold weather off the Norwegian, Danish and Swedish coasts, and the strong winds predicted were not materialising.

On 5.2.45. when studying the weather chart, which did not look very favourable, it seemed to me worth assuming that the cold was still taking effect and we could take it that the winds in the Skagerrak would not be as strong as appeared on the chart. We would, however, have to expect a heavy swell in the North Sea with head winds of up to Force 6, and also in the approaches to Skagerrak. Against this was the fact that we would get 10/10 cloud and very poor visibility in the early part of the night, and it seemed worth risking bad weather in the North Sea to get these conditions, especially in view of the state of the moon, which rose at 0100 hours. I eventually decided that we should take the chance and sail at 1730 hours: but during the afternoon fog appeared to be forming very quickly so I altered the time of departure to 1630.

In order to avoid having to ring Vaderobod for pilots and thus giving away our intention to leave, and with also the very possible chance of leakage over the telephone, I managed to get the chief of the customs to agree to go ahead of us in the customs launch and show us the channel, and in addition he only asked for half an hour's notice to do this.

After some talk and a bottle of "Moonshine" the Landsfiskal (sheriff) promised that he would have all the long-distance telephoning stopped for three hours after our departure.

The Swedish navy had asked to be warned of our departure through the Captain of the guard ship which was lying in the harbour: when I went to see him with Mr. Waring he was ashore, and I could see no good reason for chasing him all over the village, so the Navy were not informed, thus cutting out another source of leakage.

The three vessels left Hunnebostrand at 1630 hours, by which time visibility was reduced to half a cable owing to fog. The customs launch turned back in outer territorial waters and we left territorial waters at 1700 hours, thus gaining a full hour on the night owing to fog. Before leaving I had impressed on all Captains the necessity for keeping close station owing to the conditions. About 14 miles off the coast, we had two echoes on the Radar, one to port and one to starboard: these may or may not have been German patrol ships, as it would be about the position in which they generally put them. On the other hand, there appears to be no report of them putting out regular patrols for us.

At 2300 we got two large and one small echoes on the Radar, and did a 90° turn to port: this would be about 14 miles short of a line between Kristiansand and Hantsholm, and on the edge of the 100 fathom line. One vessel was seen to put its lights on and was probably a fisherman, but nothing was seen of the other two. The echoes appeared to be too large for ordinary trawlers. At this point we lost contact with the other two ships, who missed us as we made the turn. Visibility was very poor indeed and made station keeping very difficult. Up to this, excellent station had been kept, and it is surprising that we kept contact for so long.

At 0030 the fog cleared and there was a bright moon, but by this time we were past Kristiansand. The wind had increased to Force 4 from the S.W. and there was a heavy swell. We reached our dawn position an hour before sunrise, owing to making an early departure. At 0930 we were picked up by two Beaufighters, which were relieved later by a further two which remained with us until 1630.

During the day and the following night, the wind increased to Force 6 and the sea was rough with a heavy swell which caused us to reduce speed, and by the time we were off Flamborough Head at 0200 on 7.2.45 the wind had reached gale force from the S.W. We reached Hull at 0900, to learn that M/Vs *Hopewell* and *Gay Viking* had collided in the Skagerrak, with the result the M/V *Gay Viking* was so badly damaged that she had to be blown up, and M/V *Hopewell* had returned to the Swedish coast.

The following is an account of the collision given at a Captains' meeting held at the British Consulate General, Gothenburg, when a formal note of protest was registered:

"After leaving the coast the motor coasters kept station until 2300 hours when *Hopewell* lost contact with *Nonsuch*.

"As *Hopewell*'s gyro compass, log and echo sounder were out of action, at 2310 she signalled to *Gay Viking* to pass, as she was carrying steel cargo and was uncertain how her ordinary compass would be affected.

"Visibility was at this time extremely poor with some fog and drizzle and sufficient swell to cause difficulty in steering. In view of weather conditions particularly close station was being kept in order to avoid losing contact. The ships were invisible and station could only be kept on bow wave or wake.

"When *Gay Viking* was passing *Hopewell*, *Hopewell* yawed to port and *Gay Viking* to starboard, with the result that *Hopewell* rammed *Gay Viking* at an angle of approximately 45 degrees, holing her in the after part of the engine room. At the time of the impact *Hopewell*'s Captain had telegraphed to reduce speed and *Hopewell's* helm was hard astarboard and *Gay Viking's* helm was hard aport.

"After the collision *Gay Viking*'s engine room flooded immediately. Pumps were started but without effect. After inspection *Gay Viking*'s Captain recognised the situation as hopeless and the crew was called to boat stations. Quarter of an hour after the collision the order was given to abandon ship.

"The ship was still floating and the demolition charges were exploded by the Chief Officer, time being given for all rafts and dinghies to be well clear of the ship. All crew had been picked up by *Hopewell* by approximately 0030 hours.

"When last seen *Gay Viking* had split in two, the after part being still above water at a sharp angle. It was probably kept afloat by air in the after fuel tanks and hold.

"As a result of the collision *Hopewell*'s bow was stove in on the port side. *Hopewell* attempted to proceed but, against the sea, was taking in too much water through the collision bulkhead, and at 0100 hours it was decided to return.

"With gyro compass, log and echo sounder still out of action, *Hopewell* made a good landfall just south of Vaderobod, where a pilot was picked up. She reached Hunnebostrand at 1115 hours on 6th February 1945.

"All officers and men behaved extremely well.

"Mr. Waring stated that as regards the repairs to the damage sustained by *Hopewell*, we were arranging in conjunction with Gotaverk, whose yard was on strike, that repairs should be made at a small yacht building yard in Gothenburg. *Hopewell* was already at the yard and repairs, which must be classed as temporary, although adequate for the return voyage, should be completed by Monday, 12th February, after working full overtime. A Lloyds' certificate of seaworthiness would be obtained.

"It appears that the damage is confined to about twelve to fifteen planks, in all cases above the water line, twisted steel frames in the forepeak, a new spray strake, and repairs to the forward collision bulkhead, which is leaking slightly."

M/V *Hopewell* has since returned to this country after a successful voyage.

M/V *Nonsuch* carried a steel cargo of 35½ tons and M/V *Hopewell* 30 tons. A large proportion of this was conveyor band strip steel, which is a most important requirement and only obtainable in Sweden. In fact, it is the only country in the world where it is manufactured.

All members of the crew of *Gay Viking* have been repatriated, and it is significant of the spirit of the enterprise that every man has volunteered to serve in any capacity in the M/Vs *Nonsuch* and *Hopewell* in order to complete the operation.

3. Collision

The primary cause of the collision between the M/V *Gay Viking* and the M/V *Hopewell* was the complete failure of all navigational aids: gyro compass, log and echo sounder all going out of action at the same time. Failure of electrics always seems to be taking place on these vessels, as I believe is the case with all coastal craft, presumably caused in the case of wireless and Radar by spray on the aerials, and by general sweating of the ships and their violent movement on the other equipment. I do not know whether these faults can be cured, but the efficiency of the ships would be improved a hundredfold if they could.

The collision, apart from this, was due to trying to keep close station in very poor visibility. The responsibility for this was entirely mine as I had always insisted on it and particularly impressed it upon the Captains before leaving the Swedish coast. If the Master of the *Master Standfast* had kept close station as ordered she would not have been captured by the Germans last winter.

It is very unfortunate that the collision took place, as it marred an otherwise successful operation, but we were lucky that no lives were lost.

I should like to stress the exemplary behaviour of all officers and men when the accident took place, which was reported to me from all sources, and also the gallant effort of the M/V *Hopewell* in trying to proceed with the survivors on her course to England. It is an achievement that she managed to make a good landfall on the Swedish coast in thick fog and with no navigational aids except a very erratic magnetic compass: she was over ninety miles from Sweden when the collision took place.

The scuttling charges appear to have done their work well, as the M/V *Gay Viking* split in two just aft of the superstructure, and all the forward end of the ship sank immediately. When last seen only the after oerlikons were sticking out of the water. All secret papers were thrown over-board in the weighted confidential box.

After all dinghies and rafts were well clear of the ship, the Chief Officer, Mr. E.B. Ruffman, who had been left aboard for the purpose, pulled the pin. He had the unfortunate experience of getting hung up by his life jacket in his hurry to scramble down the ladder to the lower deck: after struggling to free himself with no success, he decided to jump as time was getting short, and he left his life jacket behind him. He finally had to swim for about 200 yards or more in water only just above freezing point with nothing to keep him up.

Several others suffered immersion owing to a rubber dinghy collapsing alongside M/V *Hopewell* when it was punctured by a broken spray strake.

After one of the dinghies had pushed away from the sinking ship, the sailors discovered they had lost the paddles, so had to return: the second engineer, Mr. Frobisher, seeing nothing else available, picked up the first things he could find, which were two frying pans from the galley and a large Swedish sausage which he thought might be useful if they were stranded. Finally all three were used as paddles. I quote this to show that in spite of their predicament they did not lose their sense of humour, as it caused a good deal of amusement at the time.

4. Attitude of the Swedes

The fact that the war had almost turned full circle on our arrival was reflected in the attitude of the Swedes. As opposed to previous years when they appeared to place every obstacle in our path to try to sabotage our efforts, they went out of their way to be helpful.

The naval authorities in Lysekil prevailed upon the naval staff in Gothenburg to allow us to proceed direct to that port without taking off all our guns and ammunition before going in. Their conduct over this last year appears in Commander Sir George Binney's report on Operation Bridford.

On our arrival in Gothenburg there were cheers and greetings by workmen all through the docks, and waiting on board M/S *Dicto* was an unexpected deputation composed of the Governor of the County, the Head of the Customs and the Head of the Secret Police – the latter incidentally did not recognise me – and throughout our stay there constant enquiries were made as to our welfare, ending with a message sent via Captain Henry Denham, R.N., Naval Attaché to H.M. Legation in Stockholm, from the Chief of the Swedish Naval Staff, who asked whether we had any complaints and was everything possible being done to help us, otherwise he would attend to the matter personally. This was an unheard-of honour when one reflects upon their previous attitude.

To cap everything, I was summoned with Mr. Waring to the presence of Admiral Bjorklund, Admiral West Coast, to arrange the details of our departure as he said that "so secret a matter should not be passed through the hands of a third party in case of leakage, but be arranged between us personally." A code was drawn up by which we could signify the date and time of our departure over the telephone, and he further gave orders that on no account were the guardship or any other naval vessels to follow us into outer territorial waters, and thus help to draw the attention of the Germans. During Bridford he had insisted they should follow us out.

Throughout our conversation he expressed the greatest concern for our safety. Our earlier dealings with him and this amazing volte-face need no comment from me.

The harbour officials and customs at Gothenburg, Lysekil and Hunnebostrand, gave us every assistance, and the inhabitants of the West Coast were genuinely glad to see us, and when we set sail there were many expressions of "Good luck and come back soon."

Final Voyage Report & Reasons for Abandonment of The Operation
1. On 7th March 1945 the weather appeared more or less favourable and with the permission of C-in-C., Nore, we decided to sail. Although at the time an anti-cyclone was almost stationary over the British Isles and giving very favourable conditions over the western half of the North Sea, fairly strong winds still prevailed over the eastern half of the Skagerrak. Owing to the lateness of the season it seemed advisable to make the attempt. M/Vs *Nonsuch* and *Hopewell* left Hull at 1655. On the passage down the river the starboard gearbox on M/V *Nonsuch* showed signs of overheating, but I decided to carry on, hoping that the temperature would not increase to danger point. At 1848 the gyro compass on M/V *Nonsuch* broke down, and after inspection proved repairs could not be carried out until reaching port owing to the fact the rotor had burnt. I therefore signalled to M/V *Hopewell* to take the lead. At 2044 M/V *Hopewell* signalled to us that she had severe overheating in the starboard gearbox, and had stopped the engine. As our most important navigational aids had broken down and we also had gearbox trouble I ordered both vessels to return to port, where they were alongside at 0145.

2. By 10th March 1945 repairs had been carried out on the gearboxes of both vessels, owing to the tireless efforts of Lieut. Commander (E) Thomas and his staff, who had worked day and night.

The weather again presented a somewhat difficult problem, as in spite of the anti-cyclone high north west winds had prevailed for two days in the eastern half of the North Sea, which from our experience would almost certainly have left a heavy swell. The anti-cyclone showed signs of shifting slowly in an easterly direction, and the meteorological officer assured us that we should not get worse than N.W. Force 4 to 5 in the Skagerrak on Day 2. I did not feel altogether satisfied as there were some signs of a depression over the Baltic which, if it moved westwards, would tighten the isobars on meeting the anti-cyclone and cause very strong winds in the Skagerrak itself. I therefore arranged with him that if such a situation developed, he should send us a signal by W/T saying "Weather unsuitable".

Intelligence reports were also somewhat adverse as there appeared to be a strong possibility of enemy mine-laying operations taking place in the Skagerrak. After consultation with C-in-C., Nore, both vessels left Hull at 1720 in perfect weather conditions.

Throughout the major part of the night conditions remained good with a light N.N.W. breeze and smooth seas. By 0500 however we had encountered a heavy N.W. swell and were rolling heavily with wind Force 4.

At 0300 the wind was blowing N.W. Force 6 and increasing with a rough sea and heavy swell, and by 0900 conditions were steadily worsening and the movement of the ship becoming extremely violent. It appeared to me therefore that the unexpected had happened and the depression over the Baltic was moving west, and if we continued, we might find ourselves in a position where we would be unable to proceed and have great difficulty in returning to the U.K. The order was therefore given to put back.

A W/T message was later received saying "Weather unsuitable".

After a somewhat turbulent voyage both vessels reached Hull at 0225 on 12.3.45. our position on turning round being approximately half way to Sweden.

On our return our meteorologist told us if we had continued, we should have run into a Force 8 gale, owing to the very rapid deepening of the depression over the Baltic and its rather unexpected movement in a westerly direction.

3. On 12.3.45. owing to the lateness of the season a decision had to be reached as to whether the operation should continue or not.

At a meeting held on 8.2.45. I had given it as my opinion that the vessels had a reasonable chance of making the homeward voyage as late as the April no-moon period provided they carried only a token cargo, thereby enabling them to do sufficient engine revolutions to give them 20 knots without breaking down due to overloading.

Since then, M/V *Hopewell* returned to this country with a broken crankshaft, the second this year, and M/V *Nonsuch* had to have a starboard gearbox renewed. In addition, there have been the two instances of gearbox trouble recorded above.

It therefore had to be assumed that the engines were no more reliable than last year, as the same troubles were taking place, although at incomparably lower engine revolutions than were used during the Bridford operation. A rough estimate of these is as follows: Bridford average 1275 revs., Moonshine average 1025. Owing to this, April could no longer be considered as an operational period without considerably increasing the risks, owing to the shortness of the night and the unreliability of the engines, which could not now be assumed capable of doing 20 knots for a period of ten hours (the period needed for making the voyage through the Skagerrak) without the almost certain risk of a breakdown.

It therefore appeared likely that the vessels would have to remain in Sweden for the duration of the war against Germany unless they could make the return voyage in the March no-moon period.

Owing to the urgent requirement of the vessels by D.D.O.D.(I) for the Far East it was decided that, unless on Monday 12th March 1945 the weather showed signs of remaining favourable for a period of not less than five days, thus allowing the vessels time to reach Sweden, load and return to this country before the end of the no-moon period, the operation would have to be abandoned.

On this date the weather appeared extremely favourable for making the outward voyage, but in the opinion of Lieut. Coles, R.N.V.R., our meteorological officer, and the Naval Meteorological Branch who were also consulted, the chances of a rapid return were heavily against us. The anti-cyclone then situated over this country was gradually breaking up and drifting over the North Sea, and in a further 48 hours a series of depressions would probably succeed it, and as we know from bitter experience these may well last for an indefinite period. The operation was therefore abandoned.

A contributing factor to the cancellation of the operation was the fact that there was a universal strike amongst all metal workers in Sweden, which would mean no chance of any engine repairs being done over there if we had a breakdown on the voyage to Sweden.

Summary of Supplies for Denmark:

1046	Carbines
936	Sten guns, all complete with four magazines each
4	Bren guns
4	Bazookas
120	Bazooka rockets
1,802,410	rounds 9 mm. ammunition
410,400	rounds .30 ammunition
4,992	rounds .303 ammunition

All necessary slings, magazines, Sten loaders, oil bottles and pull-throughs were included in this consignment.

Summary of Homeward Cargo for Ministry of Supply:

Material	Weight (kilos)	Value (Kronor)
Conveyor band steel	24,901	98,659
LMV centreless grinders type SLEE IK	7,504	37,000
37 complete railway axle boxes	7,400	16,160
9 complete axle boxes	4,779	12,079
22 bearings, I 26307/C003	965	2,409
Sandvik needle wire	6,192	19,479
2520 bearings type 32308	2,746	14,590
S.K.F. material, List Z.6.	3,962	25,965
S.K.F. material, List Z.5.	5,205	86,579
Totals	63,654 kgs.	312,920 kronor.

General Weather Conditions Affecting Operation Moonshine, from September 1944 to March 1945:
(*By Sub. Lieutenant M.A. Choyce R.N.V.R.*)
The weather conditions mainly influencing the operation of the small ships have been those of wind and sea. Unfortunately, during the above period, strong winds have been the rule rather than the exception over the

North Sea and Skagerrak. Gales have been frequent, especially during the months before Christmas. Numerous depressions have moved from west to east across the route, giving strong winds from all directions, with a corresponding disturbance of the sea. Lulls have occurred when high pressure ridges developed over the area, but frequently these were of such short duration that the sea remained rough from the preceding strong winds.

In general, conditions proved more favourable after December than before, as was the case last year.

Notes on individual months:

September	Fairly settled weather. During the first attempt variable light winds obtained as a weak anti-cyclone moved N.E. over the route. Later the weather deteriorated, and strong winds persisted.
October	Most unsettled. Only one period gave a 50-50 chance of good conditions for 30-40 hours, but the sea proved too rough as the winds increased again.
November	During the whole period stray winds persisted except for short lulls of from 15 to 25 hours, which were insufficient for the complete journey. Gales in the North Sea were frequent.
December	Unsettled weather in the early part of the month over the British Isles and North Sea. During the latter part weak ridge conditions developed and conditions looked favourable on 19th December. A weak trough moving eastwards caused a temporary increase in wind which was too much for the little ships, as the sea was still rough from a strong southerly gale which had persisted during the previous weekend. The winds for the next few days remained light south-westerly, but the moist air stream over England produced extensive fog, especially along the eastern coasts as far north as the Tyne. This fog persisting for several days prevented any ship leaving harbour, even though favourable conditions of wind and sea prevailed along the route beyond the coastal fog belt.

January

Winds strong and up to gale force up to the 12th, with only temporary lulls. A thin ridge developed on the 13th, extending from Scotland to South Sweden, with light westerly winds and fairly cloudy conditions. On this day the three ships left and arrived safely, though on the 14th a small depression developed between northern Scotland and South Norway, giving a temporary spell of strong winds along the eastern half of the route. The weather remained unfavourable with strong winds for the rest of the month.

February

The weather became more settled. A weak ridge extending across the British Isles early in the month was moving slowly eastwards over the North Sea. In these circumstances of light west-north-westerly winds and poor visibility in the Skagerrak, the ships left to return to England. Behind the ridge, depressions to the north of the British Isles produced strong winds over the North Sea, until mid-February, when an anti-cyclone over central Europe again gave a period of light winds in the Skagerrak. A weak trough moving over the British Isles gave worsening conditions of wind and sea in the North Sea, but the remaining ship was able to complete the journey.

March

During this month an extensive anti-cyclone developed over and to the west of the British Isles, giving a north-westerly air stream over the route area. The resulting periods of lulls proved of too short duration to be of use for the complete journey as small troughs forming on the edges of the anti-cyclone gave freshening winds over the route.

Engineering Report on M/Vs *Nonsuch*, *Hopewell* and *Gay Viking*:
(By Lieutenant Commander (E) E.C. Thomas R.N.V.R.)
During the winter of 1944/45 less engine trouble of a serious nature was experienced in these craft than during the preceding year.

In September 1944 the crankshaft in the starboard engine of M/V *Hopewell* fractured at No. 5 crank pin after approximately 100 hours; the engine was removed from the boat, the broken shaft was replaced by my staff, working in Messrs. Amos Smith's shop, and the same engine No. 50121, replaced in starboard position of M/V *Hopewell* without a bench test.

During the time the engine was out, the input shaft of the starboard M.R.5. gearbox was examined and found to be fit for service. In February 1945 the starboard gearbox of M/V *Nonsuch* showed signs of excessive heat (by manual test over 140° F.) and eccentricity at the Bibby coupling, the input shaft was suspected and the gearbox was removed and returned to Messrs. Self-Changing Gear Co., where it was found that the input shaft was split longitudinally, opening up under load, but practically imperceptible when not under load. The shaft was replaced, together with parts of the forward running gear and the same gearbox replaced in the ship.

About the same time starboard engine No. 50121 in M/V *Hopewell* again sustained a fractured crankshaft in practically the same place as previously, i.e. No. 5 crank pin extending across the free end web. The engine was returned to Messrs. Davey Paxman, as it was thought advisable to brake test after a new crankshaft had been fitted and no brake was available in Hull. The input shaft was examined when the engine was out, and no damage was apparent. On trial, however, a certain amount of heat was felt at the outboard bearing forward end of box. As there was no increase in the temperature of the oil in the box (48° C) and no sign of eccentricity in the Bibby coupling, it was decided to sail the ship. After approximately 30 hours' running, the Chief Engineer of the *Hopewell* decided that the bearing was running too hot and advised that the ship should return to the U.K. The gearbox was removed and returned to Messrs. Self-Changing Gear Co. who, after examination, reported that the ball race supporting the input shaft had been turning in its housing, causing the heat. The input shaft was not broken but had signs of a certain amount of fretting at the splines, so was replaced.

To sum up, in 700 hours' running M/V *Hopewell* broke two crankshafts, and in 760 hours' running M/V *Nonsuch* broke a gearbox input shaft. In 690 hours' running *Gay Viking* had no major mechanical trouble.

Other comparatively minor troubles consisted of a worn cutless rubber bearing, starboard propeller shaft M/V *Nonsuch*, found to be caused by an improperly fitted muff coupling, and a series of burned-out voltage regulators in every ship. D.E.E. was consulted regarding this, and was of the opinion that the trouble was probably due to faulty adjustment of the contact points in the coils. Hammond Rubery water pumps have been changed as a routine maintenance at approximately 10 hours' running in Humber water, and no instance of failure at sea has been reported. A certain amount of trouble was experienced in the early stages with the Dowty step up drive spindles, but since fitting modified parts supplied by Messrs. Dowty the trouble seems to have disappeared.

REPORT ON THE DANISH MILITARY AND NAVAL INTELLIGENCE SERVICES IN DENMARK

By Major S.A. Truelsen

Before 29 August 1943

Since the beginning of the war the Danish Military and Naval Intelligence Department was, as is known, in contact with the Intelligence Organisations of the Western Powers. This contact became especially effective during the period following 9 Apr 40, and received recognition from the highest Danish Military and Naval authorities.

Disruption of the System

As a result of the events of 29 Aug 43 and subsequent German measures including the arrest of Ritmester Lunding, the regular line-officers of the Section had, for the most part, to leave the country and continue their work from Sweden; and the old intelligence system was compromised and disrupted.

The New Intelligence System

Immediately after the release from internment of the Danish officers, representations were made by courier from the leaders of the Military and Naval Intelligence Sections in Sweden to General Gørtz requesting that the former Intelligence Department in Denmark be reorganised in the name of the Army. A leader, chosen from the old Intelligence department, was suggested and approved by the General.

The General gave his authorisation for the work to begin, but he did not wish that line-officers should be used at first, since a possible exposure might entail a new internment of Army officers, who were particularly conspicuous after their release.

It was left to the leader of the new Intelligence System to choose his men himself, decide upon the system to be used and form the necessary plans for the work. In the beginning the Army did not wish to be involved in the project.

The New Office

In Copenhagen the leader himself selected his colleagues, who, at first, were reserve officers. An office in one of the Ministries was chosen as the headquarters and used for Intelligence purposes after normal working hours. Here incoming material was first sorted and then prepared for transmission.

Mail

a) Cover address. Material was sent to Copenhagen from all over Denmark, in envelopes of an agricultural organisation and written on the back of Ministry forms as a precaution against possible snap censorship. It was thought that the letters of such an organisation would run less risk of being opened in the course of a possible check-up, especially as the agricultural organisation in question received about 1,000 letters a day on similar forms, which were normally used in connection with export of goods to Germany. The letters were marked in a special way when sent in by the various informants, and the Intelligence service established in the postal department of the Danish Ministry of Agriculture a number of officers, whose job it was to take out these special letters.

This system worked well and was never compromised. It was, nevertheless, soon abandoned as it might easily, through a mishap in postal delivery, have disclosed the identity of the leader of the Intelligence service, and thereby endangered the entire organisation; in addition to which, it had only been envisaged as a preliminary measure. In its place a number of poste restante addresses were arranged by agreement with two Copenhagen postmasters, both of whom had previously been Intelligence men, and whose exact attitude was known.

b) Post Restante. Two addresses were set up for each informant who sent in written information, and a system of codes was agreed upon, for use by telephone or telegram, by means of which it was possible to instruct any of the informants immediately to change the address in use and to cease sending to the old one. In this way it was hoped that all the people using a certain address could be switched over to another with only a few hours delay. This was considered a necessary precaution since the exposure of a single address could mean that material sent to it might fall into German hands over a long period, unless it could be stopped at source. Also, if the Germans received material sent to a certain address over a period of time, it might be possible for them to trace its origins.

It was agreed with the two postmasters in question that letters sent to the pre-arranged addresses should be taken by the postmaster and kept in his box until collected, which was done every day immediately after the arrival of deliveries at the respective offices. A danger signal was also arranged with the postmasters whereby, if the Germans should demand the delivery of letters bearing these addresses or desire a general check of poste restante mail, the postmaster would warn the Intelligence service which could then take the necessary precautions.

All warnings were to be given by telephone using fixed code words or sentences. If epidemics were mentioned in the code, it indicated that the danger was imminent and that the arrangements were on the verge of exposure, with the consequent implication of several participants.

Post restante addresses were used for a long time and had the advantage that the Germans could not discover from the postal authorities anywhere who held the addresses, and the uncovering of them simply meant that it was discarded and a new one arranged. The addresses were not discovered, perhaps because the administration frequently changed all addresses to new names. The system, however, had the disadvantage that any German interest in the mails would first and foremost be directed towards poste restante letters. In fact, there had, on several occasions, been discussions concerning the censorship of these letters.

c) Postman System. In the same way postal addresses were arranged for the main sources of information throughout the country. In some cases, special systems were used, as, for instance, in South Jutland, where an arrangement was made with two country postmen, who delivered letters to the postal district in which the organisation was interested. They were instructed that all letters bearing certain fixed initials, irrespective of the surname, and a certain address, where, of course, no one of that name lived, should be removed and delivered to a pre-arranged destination. In this way it was possible to use any surname, and to change it as often as desired, so long as the initials remained the same.

This system obviated the necessity for poste restante addresses, which would probably have been of primary interest to the Germans, had censorship been imposed. It also avoided the risk, where a cover address was used, that a German censor might discover an address and, thus, be able to implicate its holder. By having these fixed addresses, the staff in Copenhagen could, when questions were put to them or doubts arose during the preparation of material, send the queries to the main sources for further elucidation.

d) Hotel Addresses. As risks had to be avoided, a new system was worked out, which, as far as is known, was not used by any other underground organisation in Denmark. Arrangements were made with a number of hotel porters, whose sympathies were exactly known. They were chosen, for preference, at hotels where there were many German guests, and a set of addresses was arranged with each porter, which could have been those of German business men. Letters were addressed to the hotel, and on arrival were taken by the porter in the same way as other letters for the hotel visitors.

Any letters for the agreed names were kept by the porter until collected by the Intelligence Service's courier. The courier himself knew nothing of the system or who was behind it; and the porter knew only that something illegal was taking place, but not what it was. He knew none of the staff. For example, one of the addresses could be "An Herrn Kauffman Adolf Metzke, Hotel Cecil, Aalborg".

In our opinion the system was very safe. The porter was innocent and, therefore, could not implicate anybody else if he were arrested; and the disadvantage of poste restante addresses was avoided. The system worked rapidly and it was most unlikely that a snap censorship would cover letters addresses to German people living at hotels which were known to cater especially for German guests. This system is now in use throughout the whole of Denmark, and is an extremely safe one since it is possible to make frequent changes in the names used.

Telephone Codes & Telephone Cover Addresses
A source of information was, of course, established covering each and every entrance and exit route between Germany and Denmark, and telephone codes and telephone cover addresses were provided for these sources. Cover addresses were instituted with firms, whose reputation was

absolutely above suspicion. Codes were worked out, phrased according to the trade customs and selling points of each firm.

This system was mainly intended to give warnings, for example by priority telephone call, when a division arrived in or left the country or when large-scale military movements took place over the border. In South Jutland there were also telephone codes for important political changes in Germany, e.g. strikes, mutinies, disputes between the Army and the Party; and, in short, any signs of collapse.

Telephone cover addresses were similarly used to maintain contact with travelling Intelligence Officers. These officers were also able to report events in their districts by normal trade channels through a number of selected firms which had contact with the cover address firm. In addition, they reported by telephone to their address every second or third day, so that it was known that no unreported arrests had taken place. This, of course, was of the utmost importance to the system.

Establishment of Network of Informants

The next step was to establish a new network of sources of information. The head of the Intelligence Service and his second-in-command took a trip through the country, and informants were found everywhere, including South of the Danish-German frontier. These informants who had formerly been connected with the General Staff were avoided, partly because Ritmester Lunding had been sent to Germany and was under constant examination, which might well mean that sooner or later he would be forced to give away details of his former sources. It was, therefore, obviously undesirable to run the risk that a confession from him would also implicate the new Intelligence system.

Special efforts were made in the choice of informants to find people who were naturally in a position to obtain information, either because of their work with the Germans, or because their employment necessitated travelling. Since it was possible that circumstances might arise leading to the introduction of a state of siege, during which, of course, it would be forbidden for anybody to go out except doctors and similar people, these were especially chosen as informants. Those who were not suitable for Intelligence work proper were intended for use as couriers if necessary. In addition to doctors, veterinary surgeons, railway workers, important officials of harbour and shipping organisations, engineers, workmen, priests, teachers and policemen were chosen by preference. Good contacts were also established with harbour-masters, pilots and lighthouse keepers. Workers on German fortifications were never contacted directly by Intelligence Officers but were attached directly to the main informants.

Informants were encouraged to a greater extent than before to make written reports. From them a number of chief informants were chosen, who were ordered to form their own Intelligence networks, within a certain Intelligence area. All informants were duplicated. There was no contact between individual informants.

Informants had two tasks: first of all, through their social connections to get the more detailed intelligence material such as Divisional numbers, Fieldpost numbers, Regimental numbers, tactical dispositions, names of higher officers etc., in fact, all that a travelling Intelligence officer could only learn at great risk. Their second task was to note the size of the enemy forces in the towns and any additions or departures since the Intelligence officer's last visit. He could thus merely confirm whether the situation was unchanged, and, if so, leave the town immediately, without having himself to investigate the dispositions of enemy troops, which would normally take a disproportionate time for him, but only a moment for a native of the district.

The chief informants were located in Skagen, Hjørring, Frederikshavn, Brønderslev, Aalborg, Fjerritslev, Thisted,   Skive, Struer, Lemvig, Holstebro, Viborg, Hobro, Hadsund, Rnders, Aarhus, Silkeborg, Herning, Rinckøbing, Brande, Give, Skanderborg, Odder, Horsens, Vejle, Grindsted, Varde, Esbjerg, Kolding, Ribe, Haderslev, Aabenraa, Tønder, Padborg, Krusaa, Sønderborg, Odense, Assens, Faaborg, Svendborg, Langeland, Copenhagen, Helsingør, Hillerød, Holbak, Nykøbing S, Kalundborg, Korsør, Slagelse, Ringsted, Nastved, Vordingborg, Nykøbing M, Gedser, Nakskov, Maribo, Flensborg, Kiel, Rensborg, Hamburg, Lübeck, Berlin, Stettin and Warnemünde.

A harbour intelligence service was set up, as mentioned above, through naval officers, harbour masters, lighthouse-keepers, pilots etc., and the chief informants of this shipping Intelligence service were situated in: Copenhagen Harbour, Helsingør, Hundested, Nykøbing S, Kalundborg, Korsør, Dragør, Stevns, Praestø, Moen, Gedser, Nakskov, Langeland, Nyborg, Odense, Skagen, Frederikshavn, Aalborg, Grenaa, Aarhus, Vejle, Fredericia, Kolding, Haderslev, Aabenraa, Sønderborg, Flensborg,

Kiel, Hamburg, Lübeck, Warnemünde, Stettin, Esbjerg, Bornholm, Læsø, Anholt, Samsø, Hesselø, and Sejrø.

Informants had to send in a report at least once every week, and also had to report when important material was to hand. In addition to the informants' regular contacts, who were Intelligence officers, they were given passwords which made it possible to allow them to transfer to another Intelligence man in the event of their original contact being, for some good reason, unable to maintain contact with them.

In the case of informants in the South very complicated passwords were allotted and frequently changed. All informants reported direct to Copenhagen.

Intelligence Service in Germany
It must be noted here that Intelligence in Germany is based on the collection of information in the frontier regions where the chief informants keep themselves up to date with the trend of German public opinion by conversations with reliable workmen, drivers of fish-lorries and similar people. As far as more detailed information is concerned, this is based on reports from a certain few influential people in organisations inside Germany, which have facilities for securing the required material.

In this way, of course, the potentialities for securing a large volume of information are reduced. Since, however, the chief task of an Intelligence organisation operating under very difficult conditions is judged to be the obtaining of enemy dispositions in its own territory, it was thought inadvisable to increase the amount of material gathered inside Germany at the risk of a complete exposure of the Intelligence Service. The collection of details from Germany was, therefore, centred on the chief informants, who had no knowledge of the extent of the Intelligence organisation or its personnel, and the material was brought in by courier.

Travelling Officers
A number of travelling Intelligence Officers were chosen for the collection of information throughout the country; at first there were five of these, all of whom were reserve officers. Each was given a fixed part of Denmark for his area and took over the informants in that territory, in this way making use of their secondary job which was to act as support for the Intelligence Officers in their work.

It is emphasised that the informants, as already mentioned, were pledged in addition to submit independent reports, and these were of special importance should any significant occurrences take place during the absence of the Intelligence officer. These officers worked their areas chiefly on bicycles, although cars were used where conditions allowed it. These young men covered about 110 km a day on an average, whatever the weather. Their territories were of a size which would normally enable them to visit all the places once a week, although in the early days only fortnightly visits were possible.

It can be assumed that every town was visited in which there were facilities for billeting. If nothing was reported from any area, then it could safely be said that there was nothing to report. The Intelligence Officers had orders to maintain daily contact with the previously mentioned addresses in Copenhagen. As it was always the same officer who visited a certain district, a continuous contact was maintained with individual informants, who were thus kept going and encouraged to greater and even greater efforts. In addition, on each occasion when they were visited by an Intelligence Officer, they were advised about methods and conditions which greatly increased the value of the material collected. A further attainment was that each officer came to know his territory with its enemy dispositions so well that even the slightest changes could not fail to attract his attention.

Training of Intelligence Officers

Before an Intelligence Officer was used in the Field, he was given a short training course in Copenhagen. This was essential as the leader was the only trained Intelligence Officer. This training embraced a survey of the principles of the Intelligence system, a warning about the dangers which might, of course, be encountered in the work and guidance in how these dangers might be reduced, instruction in the means of acquiring information and a survey of the German Military organisation together with the peculiarities which were to be found in the German army on account of the length of the war. Officers were also instructed in the German order of battle in Denmark, followed by special instruction on the German forces which were to be found in the respective territories where they were to work. The organisation and methods of the Abwehr and Gestapo in Denmark were also taught.

This course lasted about a fortnight after which the Intelligence Officer was sent to his area, where he had an opportunity to test his training. He was then recalled to Copenhagen for a critical examination of his reports, correction of mistakes which he may have made and further instruction. This was repeated systematically and never omitted up to the time of my departure. When two Intelligence Officers had been trained and had worked in the Field for a time, new officers, on completion of their theoretical training, were first sent into the Field with one of the trained officers. They were told to give informants the instruction necessary to effect an appreciation of Intelligence work, which would bring about an increased value of the material collected.

Cover Employment for Intelligence Officers
All Intelligence Officers were installed as representatives in various firms, and were given the necessary credentials of the firm, such as samples etc. They were paid on a commission basis, which, however, did not represent very much of an income for them. Before an officer was taken on, the firm in question would put an advertisement in the daily papers asking for young representatives to visit certain trades.

These advertisements had the humorous result of causing competitive firms, after much deliberation, to take oppositional measures, since they thought that the firm in question was trying to cultivate new markets, an assumption which was not completely untrue. The directors of the firms used were, of course, aware of the illegal nature of the measure. All the firms were of the type in which representatives were natural; and the firm's customers were visited as a cover, but only to a very limited extent on account of the more important work.

False Identities
Intelligence officers were provided with false identities and the necessary papers. The identities were arranged in different ways because it was not desired that a single system should be used throughout, since the exposure of one false identity might mean that all the identities used by the Intelligence Service had to be changed. The following systems were used: A peaceable man was chosen whose circumstances were well known and who never undertook anything illegal. His personal details were investigated and entered on a false identity card. The person in

question did not know that he was being used as a cover identity for somebody else.

It was realised that this method would not withstand a searching Gestapo investigation, but would presumably be good enough if an officer were, for example, arrested for suspicious behaviour in his territory and taken for examination. In most cases, it was known that the Gestapo only examined a man's documents and sent an application to the registry in the district where he lived to find out whether, in fact, there was a man with such a name and address, according to the details entered on his identity papers. If nothing suspicious was revealed, and if the matter was of an unimportant nature, the arrested man was released after a short examination.

It goes without saying that after such an occurrence the man involved was issued with a fresh identity. Of course, if a thorough investigation were carried out, the system would be of no use, but we never had a case in which the proceedings went so far. We were not content with false identity cards alone, but also provided the officers, so far as possible, with false driving and hunting licences and similar documents, while, in most cases, they also carried letters addressed to them in their false identity. The letters were sent through the postmasters mentioned above, and after the necessary franking they were removed and delivered to the officers.

In the case of the higher officers a completely false identity was arranged. It was agreed with the parish registrar in a given district (in small districts the registry clerk) that he should send a "removal card" from his registry office to another district. Since it is customary that on a person's removal his registry card is taken out and sent to the district to which he is going, this meant that the possibility of checking whether the person has really lived in the district is, to a certain extent, avoided. It can only be checked in the district where he lives and where all the cards from former districts are kept.

Where this system is used the tax authorities are also advised of the removal and, thereby, the person concerned has to pay the tax for his false identity. The arrangement necessitates the issue of a false certificate of baptism by the parish priest of the district, which, however, does not often occasion much difficulty. When this is in order everything else can be arranged legally. The man in question receives a genuine identity card and ration book, is able to complete a declaration of personal details and pay taxes etc. The system does, however, make special contacts necessary and involves many people, so that it is not used to any great extent.

Finally, a kind of "evacuation" identity may be used. An unmarried man who had not taken part in any illegal activities, and who had never aroused suspicion, is evacuated to Sweden. The person who takes over his identity receives all his personal documents and pays his taxes and undertakes similar economic obligations. This system demands a great sacrifice on the part of the man evacuated and is used only in special cases. There was a specific department of the Intelligence Service which dealt with false identities.

Joint Intelligence Service for Army and Navy

When the Intelligence Service had been functioning satisfactorily for some time there was a demand for an increase in Naval information. At a meeting with the Naval Staff, it was arranged that they should help to enlarge the network of naval informants. It was agreed that material from all informants should be sent to the Intelligence Service as established. The informants were to be visited by Intelligence Officers and information sent to the Military Intelligence Service. Any additional information which the Navy could obtain should also be passed on to the Army. In this way a joint Intelligence Service for the Army and Navy was established, and the system has worked excellently to date.

All material from informants and Intelligence Officers was forwarded to Copenhagen through the channels already described; and the increased work demanded of the staff made it necessary to rent a number of apartments in Copenhagen as offices and quarters for the staff officers, who, for security reasons, had all gone underground by this time. The names in which the apartments were rented were those of actual people, who were not, however, connected with illegal work and rented the apartments without any idea of the purpose for which they were used. The contracts were all signed by others than the lessees, to give the latter the opportunity of being able to say, if anything went wrong, that they had no knowledge of the affair.

All matters concerning the payment of rent etc., were dealt with by a private business man, who thus joined the staff as a kind of quartermaster, without taking part in the real Intelligence work, and did not, therefore, run the same risk of exposure as the other members of the staff. This quartermaster was informed of the nature of the transaction, and privately introduced to the people who had rented the apartments. These were instructed to forward all communications about the leases to the quartermaster, and in this way the possibility of any civil transaction of a nature likely to compromise the organisation was avoided, and it was possible to get warning of any interest shown by the Germans in the lessees.

The photographic section was set up in one of the apartments. It handled all photographic work and after a while a system was in operation whereby all mail received was photographed and sent to Sweden in the form of undeveloped films. This system also applied to mail from Sweden to Denmark.

Officers' Quarters

The addresses of apartments used by staff officers were known only to the leader, and his address was known only to his second-in-command. The leader had three apartments for his use, but his second-in-command knew the address of only the one he normally used. The other two were a reserve in case the second-in-command were compromised or circumstances demanded that the leader should change his apartment.

Location of Apartments

The five apartments which were used as offices for every day work and as residences for some of the staff officers were rented in a new block, in which it was possible to secure adjacent flats. They covered, therefore, all means of ascent in the building, were connected by cellars throughout, had adjacent balconies and common end-walls. In the adjoining apartments fixed cupboards were set up in pairs opposite each other on either side of the partition walls between the apartments. The back panels of the cupboards were loose and by cutting a hole in the wall between the cupboards, and thereby between the flats, it was possible to pass from one to the other. The cupboard doors were fitted with Yale locks so that they could be opened and shut from the inside and the loose backs of the cupboards had handles on the outside so that they could be pulled shut by anyone using this means of egress. A shelf concealed the loose back.

The apartment used as an office had a microphone fitted into the letter-box, connected with a loudspeaker in the office, which made it possible to hear what was happening on the staircase, and to know, for example, if a Gestapo raid were taking place. If the Gestapo arrived unexpectedly and the door was not opened when they rang, there would presumably be a conference in front of the door, and the people in the office could hear through the microphone what they intended to do, and whether, for example, they were going to knock down the door, if so, it would obviously be time to withdraw.

While work was in progress in the flat everyone had orders to take with him, in the event of withdrawal, a certain number of papers, namely those with which he was working plus a certain part of the records, so that after such a withdrawal only the photographic material would be left. The system made it possible to retreat through four apartments without showing oneself outside the building, and, if conditions were favourable, to leave the block well away from the point where the Gestapo were carrying out investigations.

Handling of Mail

All mail was brought to the office by messenger after the last delivery. Fair copies were typed at once, maps were inked in and the material dealt with, including the necessary record entries. The staff had records for all the towns in Denmark where German troops were quartered, or had been formerly. By making immediate entries under the names of towns it was possible to make a comparison of the new information with that already received and to judge its quality and authenticity. In addition, a good general view of German troop movements in Denmark could be formed.

The staff kept charts of the German order of battle in Denmark, on which even the smallest details were included. After new reports had been entered on the record cards details were marked on the charts the same day, with the result that they were always up to date. If any questions about battle order were put to the section by the Army, the Navy, the Freedom Council or the M. Committee, they could be answered immediately from the charts.

Clean copies of the charts were made once a month and sent out with comments in survey form, as it was the task of the staff to assess the coherence of the various forces and their tactical relationships, taking the divisions as units. For example, the Fieldpost numbers which were given in reports were entered in a special Fieldpost number card index, and by those means it was possible to follow the movements of single German units in Danish territory.

As soon as reports had been dealt with in this way they were photographed and the film developed to ensure that detail and lighting were correct. The film which had been developed was used for record purposes and immediately sent into the country where records were stored. When the first film had been developed and had not revealed any necessity for technical alterations, the reports were photographed again. The new film was the one which was sent out, undeveloped and packed in various ways. If the reports were to be sent out by courier, whether within the country or abroad, the films were carried in special containers placed in the rectum or vagina. The original reports were burnt immediately after use because of the handwriting on them.

Flat Security

All the apartments were fitted with telephones, and none of the members of the staff went up into a flat without first telephoning and receiving an all clear, as the Gestapo nearly always answered the telephone if it rang in a place which they were investigating, in the hope of getting additional clues. It is hardly necessary to say that a definite system of rings on the doorbell was in use.

Every morning the leader got a list of telephone numbers which the Germans had arranged to tap during the night, as a safety precaution for the telephones used. He also received a list of arrests carried out during the night so that he could immediately take the necessary precautions to circumvent any German attack on the organisation. Frequent reports were also received about activity in the various Gestapo offices, and together with the leader's contacts with two high Gestapo men, they gave an indication of whether any large-scale action was about to take place.

The Gestapo men had latterly become very corrupt and willing to give information about any measures in preparation against the Danish underground movement in return for payment or promises of safety after the war for themselves or their families. Their information was, as a rule, accurate and they showed a loyalty in their co-operation unusual in Germans, which was partly due to the fact that their families had been exposed to severe persecution in Germany. At no point, however, was any trust placed in them which they could abuse.

Routes to Sweden

A number of routes were used by the Intelligence Service for forwarding material across the Sound. At first there were those used by other illegal organisations, but later the Intelligence Service had its own route which was used for specially important mail. The boat used had secret spaces for mail in the water and petrol tanks, and a secret space for passengers. The route was used for passengers in exceptional cases only, such as the evacuation of military couriers and very important members of the underground movement.

The following occurrence, which took place at the beginning of 1944 is a good proof of the effectiveness of these secret spaces. A boat was captured after being used for four or five months and taken over by the Germans. The mail was not discovered, and as late as June of the same year the boat was still being used by the Germans without any likelihood of the mail being found. As the organisation progressed a number of routes were gradually established from the East coast of Zealand to several destinations on the Swedish coast.

The Intelligence Service in Stockholm did a good job in arranging through the Swedish Defence Staff that all post bearing the Intelligence Service's fixed addresses should be forwarded unexamined and reach the representative of the Intelligence Service in Sweden as quickly as possible. Intelligence Service mail therefore had priority over all other illegal mail.

The routes now in use, so far as Denmark is concerned, are chiefly the work of the Danish Naval Staff, and they are administered by it in accordance with the joint Intelligence Services' wishes. All mail, as described above, is in the form of undeveloped films and is packed in cigarette or tobacco packages, or delivered in rectum containers. A number of postal reception centres have been arranged in Copenhagen, run by people who are not connected with the Intelligence Service and have no knowledge of its organisation or personnel.

From the Intelligence Service in Sweden greatly reduced photostat copies of letters are sent occasionally, and in this case the film is cut into strips and pushed down into the lead channel of an ordinary pencil and shut in with a piece of lead. These strips can only be read by the use of a microscope. The arrangement has worked successfully even though it will always be a difficult problem for an intelligence service using this method to get mail forwarded with sufficient speed.

Telecommunication with Sweden
A telephone or telegraph connection is therefore desirable with Sweden, and it is possible that this may be established in the near future. A transmitting and receiving set has been obtained for the Danish side, which works on ultra-short waves, about 2m. and downwards. These sets receive on a beam and there is very little possibility of their being located, although, on the other hand, there must not be any obstructions in the form of buildings etc., between the sender and receiver.

The Danish transmitter and receiver have an effective radius of 12 to 15 km only. Attempts are being made from the Swedish side to secure similar sets, which do not, however, require such an unobstructed channel and which have a variable radius of 3 to 30 kms. Experiments are also being made at the moment with infra-red rays which should be almost impossible to locate.

Before I left Denmark, we were trying to arrange the use of one of the wires in a cable running from the Danish to the Swedish coast and belonging to the State. The intention is to make a connection with Sweden, which would be of inestimable value. Arrangements in Sweden are complete, and the Danish dispositions are already so far advanced that the scheme should be in operation almost immediately. Furthermore, it is intended to attempt to set up a parallel telephone connection by pulling a cable from the Swedish to the Danish coast by fishing boat. So far as is known, 8 km of cable, of the same thickness as the ordinary field engineer cable which should last about a year under water, have already been acquired with the assistance of another illegal organisation. Laying the cable will, of course, involve great difficulties and dangers, and it will remain to be seen whether it proves successful.

Mail from Sweden, except when sent by the method described above, always arrived as undeveloped films and was delivered to various postal collection centres, where it was sorted and from whence it was fetched by messenger.

Expansion of Intelligence Personnel
The establishment of the Intelligence Service was such that in the first weeks, while the system was being worked out, the personnel consisted of only two officers, namely the leader and his second-in-command, with a female secretary. During the next two months the number of officers

was increased to nine plus one woman secretary. Only the three officers, who formed the staff, and the secretary were normally in Copenhagen. The others travelled as Intelligence officers.

One of the officers in Copenhagen worked as photographer. Later the establishment was increased to fourteen officers, two civilians and two women secretaries, owing to the fact that contact had been made with two young naval lieutenants, a first lieutenant and a captain of the General Staff, all chosen by the leader of the Intelligence Service and released from the rest of their service through the assistance of the Army and the Navy.

After 1 May the personnel was again increased and then consisted of eighteen officers, two civilians and four female secretaries, and the informant network consisted of three or four hundred people; this number representing regular informants who were constantly engaged on Intelligence work. This last increase was connected with the undermentioned reconstruction and expansion of the Service. All the people in the Service were included in the various schemes, mentioned above, with regard to training, identity etc., which were established at a very early date in the history of the Service and never subsequently abandoned.

Ration Cards

All these people had, for security reasons, to live underground and were not able to get the necessary ration cards in the proper way. The Intelligence Service, therefore, procured two hundred ration books every quarter for their use. Any spare books were distributed among other illegal organisations, which, however, also had their own ways and means of getting them. The basis of the Intelligence Service's system was its contact with reliable doctors at large hospitals. Through them the section received reports of people who had died during the quarter at the respective hospitals. Whenever a patient died the doctors and nurses, making use of the deceased's papers, rushed to the Registration Office to draw his ration cards. In this way even the dead made their contribution to forwarding the work of Resistance.

Economic Situation of the Intelligence Service

Since in the beginning there were no funds available in the Army for illegal work, it was left to the leader to find the necessary financial support. Money was, therefore, obtained from private sources, chiefly from the landowner class of Zealand and Fyn. The two landowners who took over the collection of this money have carried out an important and arduous task which they continue to perform. During April and May 1944, however, the Army was able to secure an allotment of about 10,000 Kr a month.

Originally this sum would have covered the necessary expenses, but by this time they had more than doubled on account of the Service's expansion, and the Army has now promised that the necessary amount will be forthcoming. None of the members of the Intelligence Service received any extra renumeration. The salary received by the regular officers from the Army and Navy covers their expenses, and in addition they receive 20 Kr a day to cover board and lodging when they are travelling, which for travelling Intelligence Officers means almost every day, with the exception of the instructional courses which they attend every two or three weeks in Copenhagen. They are also recompensed for travelling and representative's expenses.

The largest items of expenditure are partly travelling expenses, including car travel; outlay on the purchase of meat and bacon used to bribe German informants in Germany, and the upkeep of the many apartments. Rent was paid for eight apartments in Copenhagen, three in Frederikshavn, three in Aarhus and three in Kolding, in addition to which furnishings had to be provided.

Private economic support of the Service continues. The leader decided from the start not to accept foreign capital for use by the Intelligence Service, as it was desired that this should be a purely Danish organisation, and thereby show that it was still an integral part of the Army and Navy. This principle was adhered to even during very difficult periods, and at one time there was even hardly enough money to send anyone out.

At this time the Intelligence Officers pooled their Army or Navy pay or civilians income in a common fund to make it possible for journeys to be undertaken. All these young officers have made great sacrifices and shown keen enthusiasm for the Service, which gives one great confidence for the future.

Immediately after a meeting which had taken place in Stockholm to discuss other matters, the leader of the Intelligence service was approached by a member of the Freedom Council, who had been in touch with the

British representatives in Sweden. He had arranged that about 20,000 Kr should be made available monthly for the Intelligence Service; but, with the concurrence of the Army, and in accordance with the principles mentioned above, the leader refused this offer and the arrangements.

Telegraph communications with London
During March, April and May 1944 there had been very close contact between the leader of the Table organisation and the leader of the Intelligence Service. This co-operation arose out of an offer to the Intelligence Service that it should have its own wireless, or to be more precise telegraph connection with Intelligence Departments in London, as the British were anxious to establish a direct contact with the Intelligence Service of the Danish Army and Navy.

The material which could be sent this way was not large in quantity, but it did make available a channel for the direct and speedy transmission to London of the most important naval and military information. As such information ceased to have any real value as soon as it was even a few days old, and since it was considered that the establishment of this link would not affect the position of the Intelligence Service in Stockholm, the offer was accepted on the condition that a private code should be given to the Intelligence Service. This was because it was obviously undesirable that Intelligence material should be given in clear, to the wireless operator or to anyone else outside the Service. The code also made it possible for the Intelligence Service to receive enquiries from London about matters which were specially urgent or of particular interest.

It was agreed with London that all Intelligence queries concerning Denmark should be sent to the Intelligence Service in the code, and to no one else. All intelligence was thus centralised in the Army and Navy Intelligence Service and the code name given to the Service covered "the Chief of Army and Naval Intelligence". This arrangement was approved by General Gørtz and worked excellently, which was to no small extent due to the good co-operation with the leader of the Table Organisation, who did everything in his power to facilitate the Intelligence Service's telegraphic communication system. A contact address was arranged where telegrams from both sides could be handed in, and where the leaders of the Table Organisation and the Intelligence Service met daily, partly to exchange telegrams and partly to plan any measures which might be necessitated by the illegal work.

Amendment of the System

In consideration of possible restrictions in Denmark in the event of invasion, or through German anticipation of one, the Intelligence Service was reorganised at the end of April and beginning of May 1944 on the basis of a possible closure of the Storebælt [a strait between the major islands of Zealand (Sjælland) and Funen (Fyn)]. The system was greatly decentralised, it now being possible to do this since a fully trained staff of Intelligence Officers was at our disposal.

Under the old system the closing of the Storebalt would have disrupted the Intelligence communications system and one could not have been certain that information would arrive punctually, especially as conditions would, presumably, change so rapidly that the old methods of communication between sections of the country would not be able to keep pace with them. There was also the risk that during such a closure of the Storebalt there would be a corresponding prohibition of mail, or at least a strict postal censorship of everything which crossed. The possibility of such restrictions was at least sufficient to occasion the following decentralisation of the system.

The Four Staffs

In addition to the original staff in Copenhagen, which continued to be the chief directorate, a staff was set up in Frederikshavn which covered the whole of Vendsyssel and Himmerland. The later division, however, was covered only so far as was possible in consideration of Limfjord Bridge; otherwise, it came under another staff which was set up in Jutland with Headquarters at Aarhus. This staff covered the whole of Central Jutland to a line North of Henne and Fredericia, including those two towns. South Jutland, Fyn and Germany came under the staff at Kolding.

The chief of the Southern section was Intelligence leader for the whole of Jutland, although the other two staffs had freedom of action in the normal daily routine: a ruling from higher up was necessary only on important matters. The three staffs were, as before, under the leadership of the Copenhagen staff, which had to be consulted when important decisions were to be taken. Such a consultation was, however, necessary only if the matter in hand would not suffer by the delay. The individual staff leaders have great freedom in their daily work, and naturally in this Service a wide margin must be left for the exercise of individual judgment.

Each staff had to arrange in its own territory exactly the same system as used in the early days, for instance, it had to set up cover addresses, postal addresses, including poste restante and hotel porter addresses. The leader of the staff had to rent office premises, an apartment for himself and his female secretary (they always live together for reasons of security) and an apartment for the wireless operator.

Every staff was allotted a wireless operator, as it was planned that each staff should have an independent transmitter and code to London. This arrangement was made in agreement with the leader of the Table Organisation. The travelling officers who are now under the various staffs never live in the same town as the staff, and the leader is responsible for security in his area.

As soon as the system was inaugurated the first task was to secure a number of postal addresses. Poste restante addresses were the first to be used, since they require least preparation and are quickly arranged, which means that the system becomes more quickly a close-knit organisation throughout the country as temporary addresses can be given immediately to the other staffs. Later hotel addresses were arranged in the manner already described. A telephone code name was established for each staff with a genuine firm, for the same purpose as mentioned above. A number of security rules relating to the use of apartments and offices were set up, but they are not given in full here; attention, however, is drawn to what has already been written about the staff in Copenhagen and the systems in use there, all of which have been retained.

Wireless Service

Each staff leader has to supervise and approve the work and methods of the wireless operator under his command. A number of transmitting points must be selected for the use of the operator in that area around the town where the staff is located. About fifteen to twenty such points have to be fixed and the operator himself can choose which one he uses on each occasion, provided he ensures that the same point is not used twice. A guard, usually consisting of five men, also has to be provided to help the operator.

One member of the guard brings the transmitter to the point chosen immediately before the time for sending; and they arrange to watch all the streets adjacent to the transmitting point in such a way that contact between them is maintained the whole time. The man who brings the set keeps in contact with the other members of the guard, and it is arranged that one man can be seen the whole time from the windows of the apartment.

Just before the message is to be sent the operator arrives with his code telegram; and from the time transmitting begins the watcher in the window keeps his eyes on the guards outside. When the German radio location vans, which normally arrive in the district after about ten minutes, seem to be approaching one of the neighbouring streets, the guard who is watching that street warns the others who pass on the signal to the watcher in the apartment, who stops the transmission while the DF cars seem to be dangerously near. As soon as the transmission is finished the operator leaves the apartment immediately and the guards take care of the transmitter.

Messages from England are usually sent by the B.B.C. during night broadcasts. These are received on ordinary small receivers which can be found in every home and would not attract attention even during a search. The sets are provided with a special small fitting which increases the strength of the note.

The telegrams received in this way are delivered to the leader of the staff the next morning and deciphered by him and his secretary.

Co-ordination
When all arrangements have been made concerning addresses etc., they are reported to Copenhagen in the first place, and also to the leaders of the other staffs. The system is then co-ordinated as the leaders of the various staffs know how to get in touch with the other leaders by telephone, post and courier. It is intended that, so long as conditions allow, the leader of the Intelligence Service should meet the other staff leaders about once a fortnight in Jutland to advise them and settle the principal problems.

Codes
A code was issued to be used in sending the most important messages between the various staffs. Messages between staffs are carried by messenger and female secretaries are used for this work, since women stand less chance of being searched. All important messages are carried in rectum or vaginal containers.

Field Photography

Sometimes the message is photographed in miniature and a Leica set has been issued to each staff for use in the Field. The arrangements for photographing documents are as follows: A screw bolt with a wide thread, which fits the bush on the camera's frame, is screwed into the back of a bookcase or other piece of furniture which can be quickly pulled out from a wall. This screw bolt is fixed exactly one metre from the floor, which is the height at which four folio-sheets can be photographed in one exposure.

When photographing is to be done, the piece of furniture is swung out from the wall, the camera is screwed onto the bolt (a spirit level is used to see if it is perfectly horizontal) and fixed in position with a nail. Two table lamps are used for lighting, each of 75 candle-power. Exposure tables are supplied to each staff, but they are not given any further photographic equipment on account of the possibility of raids. After the photograph has been taken the film is placed in a rectum container and sent off. All the leaders have been through a course in photography.

Reorganisation of Information

When the internal dispositions of the various staffs were completed, visits were made to the informants in the respective districts, and they were each given two addresses to which they could send reports. As before a code system was arranged for changing addresses or temporarily stopping reports. All informants are now divided up among the staffs, and report directly to their respective staff instead of to Copenhagen as formerly.

Intelligence Officers

The material gathered by Intelligence Officers of a certain staff is delivered to that staff, and in this way the leader receives directly all information from his territory.

Telegraph Material

He immediately decides what has to be sent on by telegraph, and in this connection, orders have been given that special attention is to be paid to troop movements to and from Norway. The staffs at Aarhus and Frederikshavn should be able through their informants, to give the time of a convoy's departure before it leaves.

Rules were laid down that the telegraph was only to be used for important naval information or unusual troop movements of an important character, such as arrivals or departures of divisions from the area. Details must not be given, but should be sent via Stockholm. When the material to be forwarded by telegraph has been taken out the leader notes any important information for his own use and sends the original reports to Copenhagen with a note of the source.

Registering
Under this new system all sources of information have a code number. Incoming reports must all be forwarded on the day of receipt since no material may be left in the office when it is empty. If the reports are micro-photographed which is not at the moment necessary and only causes delay, the originals must be burnt immediately. Copenhagen deals in the normal way with the material received and sends it out as quickly as possible to Stockholm.

Everything continues as before under the old system, except that Copenhagen receives material in collected form and there are no single letters from informants in Jutland and Fyn. Only letters from informants in Zealand, Lolland, Falster and Bornholm are sent direct to Copenhagen, which is also the sectional staff for these areas.

Envelope Check
Incoming envelopes are checked at intervals by sending those which appear most suspicious, from an examination of the backs, to a contact in the technical branch of the Police, who investigates them to see whether the letters have been opened by any unauthorised person.

The above-mentioned postal system to Copenhagen works only so long as Storebalt is not closed. If, however, it should be closed, mail collected by the staffs in Kolding and Aarhus would be sent up to Frederikshavn, whence it would be sent to Sweden, unrevised, by routes established for the purpose. The staff leaders would, however, still remove the normal telegraph material before the mail were sent to the Northern section.

In such a contingency the Copenhagen office would deal with Zealand, Lolland, Falster and Bornholm, as it would carry out the same functions as the staffs in Jutland in dealing with material and forwarding it to Sweden. The staff leaders in Jutland would make a survey of the most important material and send it to Copenhagen by the established courier routes, micro-photographed and carried in rectum containers. This material would be for the use of the Military and Naval authorities, the Freedom Council, the N. Committee and the HQ of the Intelligence Service in Copenhagen.

A number of courier routes for this purpose have been arranged to Zealand by fishing boat, with a view to the possibility of the Storebalt being closed. One route is from Kerteminde to Reersø and return, which has been tested several times. The other routes are from Svendborg to Skalskør, from Langeland to Skalskør, from Als to Faaborg and from Haderslev to Assens; the last two being intended for use if the Lillebalt Bridge is also closed. These four routes have not all been tested yet, but this was being done when I left the country. Passwords have been allotted to the various routes, and the material would be taken by courier in the way already described.

Personnel

Personnel is divided among the various Staffs as follows:

Frederikshavn Staff:	4 Officers, 1 W/T operator, 1 Secretary
Aarhus Staff:	4 Officers, 1 W/T operator, 1 Secretary
Kolding Staff:	5 Officers, 1 W/T operator, 1 Secretary
Copenhagen Staff:	4 Officers, 2 Civilians, 1 W/T operator and 2 Secretaries

When it says above that the officers belong to a staff, it does not mean that they are used for staff work, but only that they come under the orders of the staff. The real staff work is deemed to be within the capacities of the leader himself and his secretary. The rest of the personnel are always out travelling, and the most experienced of the Intelligence officers have been chosen as staff leaders. They have all been with the organisation from the beginning, done all the training and have all been travelling officers.

Remarks About the New System

It can be assumed that the new system, which must, if other conditions remain unaltered, bring with it a great increase in the amount of material, is being carried out now. When I left the country only a few details were left to be arranged in the various Staffs. Some members of the Copenhagen Staff had already left in the beginning of May to prepare the setting up of the Staffs in the new districts.

When the new system is completed, the future can be viewed with confidence.

Decentralisation means greater safety for the system, and it will entail better security for Copenhagen. There is much less chance of the whole organisation being rounded up simultaneously throughout the country, since if a single staff is compromised, the others can continue to function without disturbance. The extremely difficult conditions in which work is carried out in Denmark must, however, be taken into consideration when the possibilities are weighed of the continuance to the last day of the Intelligence Service. If a round-up by the Germans should be successful it must be judged to be due to a final failure of the good luck which is an essential to the success of illegal work in an occupied country: but unfortunately, this is a factor against which plans can hardly be made.

The new system should also be far more effective from the point of view of the wireless service, as material is not so long in transit, the distance from informant to staff being smaller. Information can, therefore, be sent to England much more quickly and its value will obviously be greater. In the same way it will be possible to send far more material by telegram when the situation makes this necessary, for instance, when events progress very rapidly, as there are now four transmitters instead of the one which was used in Copenhagen.

On account of the increased Staff, informants will be visited and instructed more frequently, and the Intelligence material dealt with better and more quickly. Just before my departure the network of informants had been widened considerably as contact had been made with many doctors and journalists throughout the country; and these new contacts should be working by now.

Co-operation With Other Resistance Organisations
In addition to the real intelligence work there was close contact between the leader of the Intelligence Service and the chiefs of the other illegal organisations, that is to say the most important of them.

There was also regular co-operation between the M. Committee and the Intelligence Service, which supplied the Committee with details which were of importance in the building up of armed Resistance groups. This included especially information about German forces stationed around the mobilisation areas, and the leader of the Resistance district had to get details through the M. Committee of what was in his district before taking any action. At appropriate intervals the M. Committee received a survey of the numbers of German troops by districts. No information of a secret nature was given, but only general surveys.

Of course, there was very close contact between the military and naval staffs and the directorate of the Intelligence Service, and these staffs received immediate notification of important events in the country and South of the Frontier.

In addition, during the last few months there was some contact between the leader of the Communist party and the leader of the Intelligence Service. The Communists promised to undertake the job of securing certain information about German fortifications in Jutland, including plans and other items of interest to the Service. This arrangement had first come into effect just before my departure, but it is quite probable that it will yield excellent results.

The leader of the Intelligence Service already had long-standing contacts with the principal politicians, including the "Nine-man" Committee, and received political information through them. A special department has now been set up in the Intelligence Service to deal exclusively with material concerning internal politics. Such a specialised solution had not formerly been possible owing to the shortage of personnel, especially since the military side of the work was obviously considered to take priority.

The leader of the Intelligence Service had, in addition, particularly valuable and productive co-operation from Fleming Juncker, a prominent landowner and the leader of the Resistance groups in Jutland. An agreement was reached between the two whereby the most suitable of the Resistance groups should be used as Intelligence groups, with the dual purpose of keeping them together and helping our Service as much as possible. It was essential, during the build-up of the Resistance groups that the two leaders were in constant contact over the choice of people for the groups because there were so few potential leaders in Jutland.

A man already in the Intelligence Service was often chosen as district leader for the Resistance group; and, although on security grounds, this was not particularly desirable, it was necessary owing to the scarcity of suitable people for work in Resistance groups. Juncker was a great help to the Intelligence Service in Jutland. He has assisted in the instruction of many informants, and has himself acted as an Intelligence man while travelling. It was through Juncker also that the very fortunate connection with the Table organisation was established.

Final Remarks
What I have set out in this report is a survey of conditions in Denmark on my departure on 15 May 1944. The systems discussed have all worked satisfactorily, and the new organisation is as good as completed. My successor is a highly qualified man, Line-Officer, and Captain of the General Staff. His relations with my former colleagues are excellent and he has their complete trust, which is an unqualified essential to an Intelligence Service which must be run effectively both in quality and speed. Furthermore, he is courageous, talented and able to make decisions. He is regarded as a fully trained Intelligence Officer, having been a member of the Staff in Copenhagen for four months before my departure.

According to my knowledge of conditions, and especially my knowledge of my colleagues who are carrying on the Intelligence Service in Denmark, in whose zeal, interest, self-sacrifice and courage I have the greatest faith, one can with confidence look forward to the continuance of the Danish Army and Naval Intelligence Service in Denmark.

Major S.A. Truelsen,
Stockholm, June 1944

APPENDED INFORMATION I

Cable Connection between Denmark and Sweden
Since July the Intelligence Service has had a cable connection from Denmark to Sweden. We were able to fish up the German multi-core cable and connect up the three unused "cores". In this way daily telephone contact over the Øresund has been established and operates to the great

advantage of rapid communication. The secret sending points at each end are manned continuously by Intelligence Officers.

A *Minestrone* connection between Zealand and Sweden is about to be set up at the moment.

Wireless contact between London and the four Intelligence Staffs in Denmark is now as excellent as could be wished.

Postal Connections

The routes to Sweden from Copenhagen are still working extremely well, despite serious losses of personnel and material. Mail from Jutland goes via Frederikshavn to Sweden. As soon as any difficulties are encountered in the forwarding of mail to Copenhagen, it is duplicated in Jutland, so that it goes from Frederikshavn to Sweden, and also via Copenhagen.

Connection between Jutland and Copenhagen is by means of courier the whole way. Two people collect material from the staffs and bring it over. When, however, conditions are very difficult, the courier goes no further than to Nyborg, where a railway man takes the material on board the ferry and delivers it in Korsør to another railway man. He, in turn, hands it over to the courier who is waiting and who takes it on to Copenhagen.

If the ferry is not running the mail is taken over the Storebalt by fishing boat.

Tapping of German Telephone Cables

During the last three months work has been carried out to secure an effective tapping of German cables, and is now on the point of success. For some time, the telephone connection between Shellhus in Copenhagen (Gestapo HQ) and the Gestapo in Helsingør has been tapped. The listening has been very successful, and on several occasions, it has been possible to warn people before they were arrested.

At the moment five German lines are being tapped:

Shellhus to Helsingør.

Gestapo HQ in Dagmarhus to the department in Shellhus.

General Hanneken (Army Command Staff in Silkeborg) to the German HQ in Nyboder School, Copenhagen.

The German G.O.C Denmark to his Staff in Copenhagen.

The HQ in Silkeborg to the Regiment on Fyn.

Co-operation with Sabotage Leaders
All information of interest from the sabotage point of view is passed on
to the leaders of this work, as for instance when German divisions leave
Denmark. Sabotage is then carried out on all railway lines which are to
be used by the division. In this way it has, on several occasions, been
possible to hold up a division for periods up to eight days.

Intelligence During Invasion etc.
The Intelligence Chiefs concerned have orders to attempt to keep on the
German side of the front with the whole of their staffs, and each with a
wireless operator, since it is calculated that work can be carried on under
cover of a crowd of refugees. Even if this crowd should be forced South
into Germany the Intelligence men will follow them and carry on their
work there.

APPENDED INFORMATION II

Report Explaining the Work and Organisation of the Dutch Military and
Naval Intelligence Department in Sweden after 29 August 1943

Establishment of Intelligence Offices in Sweden
Owing to the events of 29 August 1943, and the arrests which
followed, it seemed advisable for those officers of the Military and Naval
Intelligence Service, who had been connected with the British authorities
(S.O.E.). to go to Sweden. They were personally too compromised to be
able to continue their work in Denmark and there appeared to be good
possibilities for carrying on the task in Sweden in the form of a connecting
link between a reorganised Intelligence Service and the Military and
Political Directorate (Resistance Movement) on the one hand, and the
free allied world on the other.

These officers were, therefore, ordered to Sweden individually as their
circumstances made it desirable.

Immediately on their arrival in Sweden they contacted the Swedish
General Staff, with whom connections had been maintained throughout
the war, and contact was similarly re-established with the Allied
representatives.

A villa was then rented through the Danish Legation and their offices for collating intelligence material were set up, as well as photographic studios and a drawing office. In addition, the villa housed between six and eight of the officers employed on this work. A twenty-four hour watch was maintained so that flash reports could be sent on at once.

The Chiefs of the Military and the Naval Intelligence Services were then appointed as attachés to the Legation and given their own offices in Stockholm. These "official" offices became reception centres from Denmark for all Military and Naval Intelligence matter, which was sent on to the villa after perusal.

The office in Stockholm was soon expanded to include a counter-espionage section. In time this section grew so large that it was given separate offices under its own departmental chief. The villa was similarly organised as a separate section under its own chief, and both sections worked under the two Naval and Military leaders.

Treatment of Intelligence Material

1. By far the majority of the material came from the Military and Naval Intelligence Organisation in Denmark. After 29 Aug 43, General Gørtz and Admiral Wedel, Cs in C of the Danish Army and Navy respectively, appointed Major Truelsen as leader of this organisation, and he re-organised it until it covered the whole of Denmark and parts of Germany. Material was sent over to Sweden on undeveloped films by various postal routes or with the crews of freighters. At the Swedish coast, it was received by personnel who were appointed directly by the Intelligence department at Stockholm to whom it was immediately dispatched. The films were then forwarded straight from the Stockholm Office to the villa, where they were developed, so that on the next morning, they could be catalogued, distributed and forwarded to Britain.

In addition to undeveloped films (known as type "A" consignments), parcels containing special matter, original maps, letters, certificates etc. (known as "B" consignments) were sent from Denmark. After perusal, the latter were sent to the Intelligence Office and then distributed with the rest of the material or forwarded.

2. Further military information has been obtained from the interrogation of civilian and military refugees as soon as they arrive in Sweden. Bureaus have been set up at three places along the coast under the command of

Danish Military personnel, and all refugees are to pass through one of the bureaus where they impart such information as they may have. Material collected in this way is immediately sent to the Stockholm Office where it is treated in the same way as other information.

3. It happens occasionally that someone is sent back to Denmark to obtain a particular piece of information, but owing to the efficiency of the existing organisation, this only occurs very rarely.

4. Information about all persons travelling from Denmark to Sweden legally are to be found at the Stockholm Office. When any one of these is believed to be in possession of valuable information, contact is made with him so that he can supply the information in question.

Liaison with Swedish Authorities

The work of the intelligence organisation in Sweden is not illegal. The job is done discreetly, and, while the Swedish authorities are not involved and are, officially, ignorant of it, the chiefs of the Intelligence offices are in contact with the highest authorities who have given the organisation their sanction and have, at times, afforded it positive support.

Counter Espionage Section

Besides the Military Intelligence sections, there is, and has been mentioned above, a section for counter espionage. This has developed so far that it can form the foundation of the task in Denmark in every feasible situation from an invasion to SHAEF's period of winding up. This section has extensive card indexes of the various categories of suspicious persons.

The strength of the section has been considerably enhanced by reason of the fact that the Stockholm Office has attached to it a large number of very efficient Danish Police of the Criminal Investigation Department. These are usually reserve officers. The relationship with the Danish civil police organisation in Sweden has been arranged in an agreement with the chief of the Civil Police Organisation.

Relation with Danforce

The Stockholm office also co-operates with the Intelligence Branch of Danforce (the Danish Military Command in Sweden). When a considerable part of Danforce has gone to Denmark, this office will take up work as an integral part of Danforce. In addition, the Stockholm office deals with the investigation of controls and personnel in Danforce's camps as well as all Danforce's connections with Denmark whether in the spheres of political, military or resistance groups.

Political Intelligence Section
Besides these two main sections, a political intelligence section operates under the two chiefs. This section has three main functions:
1. To forward political material to the Allies.
2. To infiltrate political material to Denmark from outside.
3. By means of personal contacts with the Swedish authorities and individual important members of the Swedish Government, and by supplying these with information, to improve fighting Denmark's position by developing Swedish goodwill towards Denmark.

Lieutenant Colonel E.M. Nordentoft and Captain Mørch, R.D.N.,
London, January 1945

Index